Still So Excited!

MY LIFE AS A POINTER SISTER

Ruth Pointer

with

Marshall Terrill

TRIUMPH
BOOKS

Library of Congress Cataloging-in-Publication Data
Pointer, Ruth.
  Still so excited! : my life as a Pointer Sister / Ruth Pointer with Marshall Terrill.
    pages cm
  ISBN 978-1-62937-145-0
  1. Pointer, Ruth. 2. Singers—United States—Biography. 3. Christian biography. 4. Pointer Sisters. I. Terrill, Marshall. II. Title.
  ML420.P75A3 2016
  782.42164092—dc23
  [B]   2015022550

This book is available in quantity at special discounts for your group or organization. For further information, contact:
    Triumph Books LLC
    814 North Franklin Street
    Chicago, Illinois 60610
    (312) 337-0747
    www.triumphbooks.com

Printed in U.S.A.

ISBN: 978-1-62937-145-0

Design by Amy Carter

Page production by Sue Knopf

Photos courtesy of Ruth Pointer

I would like to dedicate this book to God, family and friends, and associates.

God—for his constant love, protection, and mercy.

Family—to my husband Mike Sayles, whose constant love and support was the driving force behind this book. My five children: Faun, Malik, Issa, Ali, and Conor. My grandchildren: Onika, Sadako, and Bailan. My great-grandson, Orland Kahnamae Coombs, who is on his way into this world. My first family: Mom, Dad, Aaron, Fritz, Anita, Bonnie, and June.

Friends—a woman needs her girlfriends, and my very first was Gloria, who was with me from kindergarten through first grade. After Gloria, I got lucky with a succession of close girlfriends. They include Marjorie, Edna, Pat, Mary, Betty, Shirley, Cledie, the entire Watson family, Helen, Carolyn, Laura, Natalie, Cecille, Mindy, Cynthia, Sue, Irma, Minnie, Andrea, Leslie, Jeanie, Barbara, Eve, Luci, Ria, Luisette, Paula, and Kathy.

A woman also needs her "unique" friends: Max, Christian, and Craig.

A woman also needs prayer and spiritual support. It started in the Church of God with my mother's friends, whom she called her Prayer Band: Imogene Lee, Willa Mae Tires, Ali Mae Reed, Lillian, and James Hirt. And special thanks to Pastor Charles E. Blake of the West Angeles Church of God in Christ in Los Angeles.

Associates—a woman in music needs her band. This is my "A-Team": Will Lee, Stacy Henry, Jervonny Collier, Steve Sullivan, Kevin Flournoy, Fred Clark, and my precious niece Roxie McCain Pointer.

A woman can use a little advice every now and then: to all our past and present managers and attorneys, good and not so good. There have been lessons in all our choices.

A woman also needs a support team: radio deejays, concert promoters, drivers, pilots, flight attendants, sky caps, airport ticket agents, and of course, fans around the world that make everything possible.

A woman also needs her music, the greatest gift in my life. I can't think of my life without it.

—Ruth Pointer

To my patient wife Zoe for putting up with my crazy hours and obsessive behavior —traits essential for writing a book; Pete Ehrmann, whose editorial touch and lightning-speed work enhances everything I do; Ruth Pointer, a true survivor and one of the hardest working individuals I have ever met; Mike Sayles, who championed this effort from the start and made it happen; Mindy Lymperis, for her brave recitation of her history with the Pointer Sisters—we bonded quickly, and I know I have made a friend for life; Jeremy Roberts, who introduced me to Ruth Pointer; Tom Bast of Triumph Books for his steadfast belief; and to Michelle Bruton, who took great care to put the final gloss on this work.

—Marshall Terrill

Contents

Introduction

THERE ARE JUST SOME THINGS YOU SHOULD NEVER have to tell your children.

I've always tried to shield my kids from my past. I knew from the beginning of this book project that I could be opening up a Pandora's box. But the kids are grown. I feel my husband and I have given them enough life tools to face any ridicule that may come from making the more private parts of my life public. Not only are they old enough to understand a few things, they are old enough to forgive. Still, opening myself up to the scrutiny of the world opens them up to having to deal with the onslaught of old—and some not so old—and painful wounds.

The world has known me as part of The Pointer Sisters for over half my life. And that's been a very public life for the most part. But when it comes down to brass tacks, there are certain truths we must all face about ourselves, and sometimes you don't always like what you see when looking into the mirror. In my case, there were a lot of things I didn't like in that reflection. I would like to say that I saw a stranger, but what I saw was the true reflection of who I was. An alcoholic, a drug-addicted woman who thought more about getting high than tending to her family's needs. I was a torn soul and I didn't like it. But I couldn't do anything to set things right. At least, that is what I allowed myself to believe. But the beautiful thing about being broken is that it allows you to pick up the pieces of your life, if that's the route you want to go. And I did so want to journey along the path of sobriety. I just didn't know how to fit the pieces of the puzzle that was me together. So I lived with the beautiful lies I told myself. They were so much more palatable than the ugly truth.

Self-deception binds you to a spiderweb of excuses; it chokes your humanity right out of your soul. I had children I had to raise, and here I was waiting for God to slap me in the face and chastise me for my failures. The truth was I didn't feel a real kinship with God. I was never going to be perfect, and I knew that from the time I was a child in my parents' church. I had no sense of God's mercy or his love. I had no clue that His grace would set me free. And God knows that I had been searching for that freedom since I could walk.

There was a certain slavery, a vicious poverty in my unrequited journey toward accepting the truth about myself. It's been a long path of muddy self-indulgence: cocaine, alcohol, food, and sex. God felt distant. I was lost, but angry. I was bound by the notion that my lifestyle wasn't hurting anyone, yet deep inside I knew that if I didn't straighten myself out soon that I would die, leaving my kids without a mom.

Sometimes you need silence in order to listen to God whisper to you…and he's been whispering to me a lot lately. I think he's been telling me it's time.

This year I celebrate my third decade of sobriety. It wasn't an easy adjustment, and it took a near-death experience to get my undivided attention. But I have been faithful. I have been diligent. And it has taken years for my life to settle down. I do not take my sobriety for granted. After all, it is a gift from God.

I have shared my story with my 12-step groups (you read that correctly—it is plural) and others who have needed guidance, but never with the public. God's timing is always perfect, and I had to wait for my cue.

So, let the music begin.

—*Ruth Pointer*
April 2015

CHAPTER ONE

The Devil You Say!

··

YOU ALWAYS LOOK BACK WONDERING HOW LIFE could have played out differently. Growing up, our household was totally straight-laced and strictly run according to religious values that allowed for little freedom or individuality. Maybe if my parents had embraced the notion that the quest for unattainable perfection was impossible and that my childhood didn't have to be so rigid, I would have coped better. Maybe I would not have ended up pregnant, drunk, high, and alone back in the day. But those are big, hypothetical maybes. Today's version of me gets that kids need rules. They need structure and support, but they also need freedom to define themselves by cause and effect. Sometimes that means falling short of expectations, making mistakes. Getting broken.

I wish someone had told me that being flawed was more than a rite of passage. It was okay. It was part of growing up and into yourself. It was part of learning. It wasn't an entirely unhappy upbringing, but it sure was filled with pressure, disappointments, and unrealistic expectations handed down to me from my mother and father—both of whom were ministers of fear and flawlessness. I'm not knocking the ministry.

All I'm saying is that it's hard to feel like a normal kid when the word "no" is the most constant word in your household.

No lipstick. No fingernail polish. No makeup. No skirts above the knees. No jewelry. No records. No movies. No dancing. No dating. No impure thoughts. No alcohol. And definitely no sex until marriage!

No, no, no!

Make that "hell no," though of course in our uptight house, the first word was implied.

When I was about 10 or so, my mother allowed me to pick out a pair of new shoes for Easter. I was constantly looking at clothes and activities to separate myself from my sisters. For some reason I just wanted to be different and stand out. I picked out the flashiest shoes I could find—black suede with five-inch heels. Mom was horrified. She scolded me and then marched me right back to the store to return the shoes. She was almost angrier at the sales clerk who sold them to me than she was at me.

"You can clearly see she's a child, why would you sell a pair of shoes like these to a child?" she demanded. In spite of her anger and my humiliation, they would not take the shoes back. So Mom took the shoes to a repair shop and had the heels cut down to where they were ugly little stubs. The shoes were permanently bent and looked like rocking chairs. My mother made me wear them to Easter Sunday and for several months afterward. My two brothers ragged on me mercilessly about those ugly shoes. It stung so bad that I didn't wear heels again for the longest time.

My parents were determined to protect us from what my dad called "the devil's work." I instinctually rebelled—a trait that had followed me for a good portion of my adult life. I had been force-fed so much fire and brimstone and fear of eternal damnation that I was afraid every time I left the church that I might go to hell before Sunday dinner.

Being forced to constantly strive for perfection through Christianity—that's just an unattainable goal. Only Jesus was perfect, and being held up to that standard meant automatic failure. The collateral damage to my youth was a negativity and insecurity that carried into my adulthood. Instead of learning righteousness and the beauty of God's mercy, love, and grace, I learned failure and inadequacy. I felt I could never measure up to my parents' expectations and that I was unworthy of God's unconditional love. I didn't realize that I didn't have to be a saint to merit that love. Lord knows, I was no saint; but neither were my folks—well, maybe my mother was.

They were both from the Deep South. They met in Arkansas. My father, Elton, was a sweet-natured man with an obscure criminal past he didn't talk much about to us. Daddy was charismatic and handsome, a snazzy dresser who easily caught the attention of his congregation—especially the women. He was very strong, yet like a teddy bear in some ways. He was passionate and sensitive. If he heard someone swearing it would bring him to tears, and he would say, "Why do people have to talk that way?" I kind of get it now.

When I was a kid we lived across the street from a community park in Oakland, California, so we heard a lot of harsh words. My dad kept a pair of binoculars near the window, and I remember from time to time seeing him use them to watch people at the park. If someone got into a fight, he'd grab his Bible and head out the door to smooth things out.

My mother would say, "Elton, somebody's gonna hit you in the head if you don't stay out of people's business!" Well, that didn't happen. Somehow Dad always managed to successfully calm things down. Dad insisted that our number always be listed in the public phone book. "We're gonna keep an open line in case someone is in trouble and needs prayer," he said. It didn't matter who or when, my dad was always available to help people at all times of the day and night.

I often wondered what led my father to become a minister. Daddy was born in 1901 in Little Rock, Arkansas. He once mentioned to me that he had done some drinking and smoking in his youth, and he made it clear he wasn't proud of it. Years later, my brothers Aaron and Fritz talked about the strong possibility that Daddy got into bootlegging, gambling, numbers running, and possibly a few other criminal activities when he moved to Chicago in the 1930s. I recently discovered a census report on an ancestry website showing that he lived with an older woman called "Susie Pointer" whom he listed as his spouse. Whether Daddy was actually married before he met my mother or he was just trying to protect Susie's reputation, I can't say with any degree of certainty. If a marriage certificate exists, we haven't found it. Frankly, it tickles me pink to think that the upright, righteous dad I knew might have lived "in sin."

I do know the following story is true: Daddy once lent a trendy overcoat to his brother-in-law so he'd look sharp for a special occasion. When his brother-in-law went to my father's apartment later that night to return the coat, he was gunned down in cold blood. The hit man had clearly mistaken the man in the coat for my dad.

Daddy had an epiphany after that incident and got right with God. He hightailed it back to his family in Arkansas, eventually became a minister, and dedicated the rest of his life to the Lord.

My mother, Sarah Elizabeth Silas, was born in Roseboro, Arkansas, in 1924 and later moved to Prescott, Arkansas. She grew up with five brothers and was the only girl. She became a minister at age 14 and never lived a secular life that involved dancing, partying, or wearing makeup. My mom was the polar opposite of my father; she was the disciplinarian of the household and at church and didn't pull any punches when it came to what she wanted you to do. I can still recall her sitting in the choir stand, or up at the pulpit if she was going to be speaking, and looking down at me. Her expression said it all: you'd better straighten up, young lady, and start listening! That look absolutely terrified me.

Mom was blunt and to the point, but she was also sweet. The congregation always looked forward to her taking the pulpit because they knew the service would end on time when that happened. I loved my mom, but she kept her distance in those days. As a teenager, I was much closer to my dad. Although he could be as unyielding and straight-laced as my mom, he was definitely more lenient. When Mom would go to missionary conventions with her church friends, Daddy would allow me to do things she would never agree to. Despite her no-nonsense attitude, she did have a big heart and worked very hard to provide for her family. As I grew older we became much closer. Eventually she loosened up and appreciated who I was instead of disapproving of me for being different from her. She enjoyed hearing about my exploits on the road with The Pointer Sisters, what I was doing socially, and even got a kick out of my crazy relationships. At the end of her life we were best friends. I miss her so much.

Daddy was working as a minister when he met my mom through her mother, Roxie Silas, who saw him preach the gospel at a traveling summer revival. The revivals back then were held inside a large white tent. A stage and pulpit would be constructed for the pastor, elders, and the choir, and rows of folding chairs set up for audience members. Smaller tents and burlap bags (filled with straw) were distributed to families to sleep in for the 10-day revivals, which concluded every night with a service. Before the end of each night, Daddy came into the tent and filled it with one of those vintage DDT bug sprayers filled with insecticide to keep away the bed bugs and mosquitoes. It did the trick, but our tents were foggy and we could barely see. It's no small wonder that we didn't develop a respiratory problem or die in our sleep from that stuff. I can still smell that distinct odor of the insecticide, which never fails to immediately take me back. The best part of those revivals was the food we devoured after each service. A small stand served ice cream, soda, and some of the best greasy hamburgers I've ever had in my life.

When Roxie got home from the revival where she first laid eyes on the handsome, imposing preacher man, she pulled my mother aside and declared, "I met your husband today." As the saying goes, "From her lips to God's ears." Whether she was actually obeying God or just her equally powerful mother, Mom went with the program, and she and Daddy were married on July 20, 1941.

To borrow another familiar expression, my 40-year-old daddy-to-be must've thought he'd died and gone to heaven. His bride was barely 17. Despite the big age difference, their marriage worked. They were together for 38 years until Daddy's death in 1979. Mom told me later she wasn't in love with my dad when they married, but she was an obedient daughter and did what her mother told her. Eventually, she said she grew to love my dad.

If it was God (with a helping hand from Grandma Roxie) who united my parents, it was their kids who kept them bonded. They wasted no time starting a family. My eldest brother, Aaron, was born on April 19, 1942, almost nine months to the day my parents consummated their marriage. Brother Fritz followed in 1943, the same year my parents pulled up stakes and moved to West Oakland, California.

The Deep South had limited possibilities for African Americans then, and my parents didn't want their children to endure the harsh realities and extreme prejudices they had faced their whole lives. I'm sure that and the lure of a new adventure on the West Coast was all that was needed for them to accept an offer by a group of ship migrants to come to California and build a place of worship from the ground up: the West Oakland Church of God.

My parents' move to California was the second wave of the Great Migration, when an estimated six million African Americans left their rural Southern homes for jobs and new lives in urban industrial areas in the Northeast, Midwest, and West. At the time, the United States was gearing up for World War II and the Bay Area ports offered plenty of industrial work on the docks, ships, and railroads where goods were constantly coming in or being sent overseas.

West Oakland was one of the first settlements in the area, and African Americans began pouring into it, mostly through the historic 16th Street depot. Even in the Golden State, blacks couldn't live wherever they felt like it due to racially restrictive housing covenants. But West Oakland welcomed all newcomers. At the time, it was the largest African American community in Northern California, loaded with restaurants and jazz and blues clubs on what was known as the Chitlin' Circuit. Aretha Franklin, Ella Fitzgerald, Etta James, Ray Charles, John Lee Hooker, Sammy Davis Jr., Muddy Waters, James Brown, and Ike & Tina Turner (where I first saw them) were regular performers there. Black-owned businesses such as flower shops, barbershops, grocery stores, and garages flourished, and pretty much everyone knew each other.

The church-raising at the corner of Tenth and Myrtle was a community event with future congregants—mostly fellow emigrants from southern states—contributing sweat equity and labor to build a place for folks to gather and worship the same heavenly father. Once finished, it became a focal point for the neighborhood.

For many, the church became an integral part of their everyday lives. It's no exaggeration to say that there was something going on there every single day that drew people in. And being the preacher's kid meant that the Pointer children were volunteered for every single activity the church sponsored: the choir, holiday plays, Bible studies, Sunday School, Vacation Bible School, revivals, picnics. It never let up.

Once my parents got settled into their new house at 1176 18th Street, they started having kids again. I was born on March 19, 1946, in Oakland, as were my three sisters—Anita in 1948, Bonnie in 1950, and June three years after that. Anita was the only one of us born at home.

Today the West Oakland I grew up in looks a lot different than it did back then. New condominiums have sprung up, old Victorians are undergoing restorations, and once shuttered factories are now artists' studios. Non-profits and community gardens are on just about every corner, and the old tract homes are now fetching north of half a million dollars. Gone is the look and feel of what was once dubbed the "Harlem of the West."

Our abode was quite humble given the amount of people who lived there. It was a two-story duplex located in a working-class neighborhood that was borderline ghetto. It couldn't have been any more than 1,000 square feet of living space. The Pointers occupied the upstairs, and the Silases—my mom's brother's family of five—lived downstairs. My cousin, Paul Silas, who later became a star professional basketball player and coach, lived there as well.

My parents, my paternal grandfather Herman ("Papa"), and the six Pointer kids all made do with three bedrooms, a kitchen, and one bathroom. Bunk beds were a necessity (including a set for my brothers in the dining room), and quiet time simply didn't exist. My father used a small space in the garage as his study to prepare for Sunday sermons. Sometimes we kids would get so loud and rambunctious my father would cry out loud, "Oh, Lord, can't I get any peace?"

I had the same yearning myself during my growing-up years, which were an endless cycle of church-related meetings and services. The week would start on Saturday night getting ready for Sunday morning. Preparation ahead of time was a must: bath, hair, getting out the white Mary Janes and polishing them up with Shinola shoe polish, making sure that Sunday school lessons were learned. It was a long time before I learned that people took more than one bath a week. We used Tide when we wanted a bubble bath. My dad was always worried about water, electricity, heating, bills, etc. I remember he made a sign that he placed over a main light switch that read: "An ounce of prevention is worth a pound of cure." This was a not-so-subtle reminder for all of us kids to turn off the lights when not in use.

Sundays were dedicated to the Lord from sunup to sundown. Aaron, Fritz, Anita, and I would walk the mile or so to Sunday school, which started at 9:00 in the morning. There was an hour break at 10:00, followed by the regular Sunday service at 11:00. After the senior choir sang a few songs, announcements were made, collection plates were passed around, and acknowledgment of visitors, my father would take to the pulpit and preach…and preach…and preach. I'd look around and see kids snoozing, and sometimes their parents, too. The best part of church was when I heard the intro to the benediction, which signaled the end of the service:

Blessed be the ties that bind our hearts in Christian love
The fellowship of kindred minds is like to that above, Amen!

When the service was finally over, Daddy made it a point to stand at the door to greet and schmooze with every person filing out of church. That took up another hour. My mom used to scold Daddy about having ashy hands because he reached out to everybody. When we got home there was just enough time to eat and take a quick nap before we had to get ready for the evening services. Youth service commenced at 6:00 PM, followed two hours later by the general service, which was when the junior choir would sing. Daddy did that on purpose so that we girls would have a commitment to being there. That went for at least two more hours as Daddy expanded and improved on his theme from that morning.

Sunday nights after church are some of my fondest family memories. We'd all pile in my dad's Dynaflow Buick and go for a special treat. That big-ass boat had no safety belts, and the front and back seats were large as couches. We kids slid back and forth on them while noisily heckling each other until Mom warned us to stop...or else. Depending on the season, we'd buy hot tamales, ice cream, and watermelon. The melons were bought from a rotund woman who always wore a scarf around her head. We called her the "Watermelon Lady." The melons were piled on a big wagon in a garage, and my dad would pull up to the curb, hop out of the car, and commence thumping. When he found a likely prospect, the Watermelon Lady used a sickle-shaped instrument to cut off a chunk for a taste test. Sometimes we kids would argue over who got the piece, but mostly Dad ate it himself to avoid the drama.

When we wanted ice cream there was a Carnation Creamery factory not far from our house where we'd swing by after Sunday night service. Those went down well in the hot summer months. Nothing was hotter than the tamales we ate. They were so super-spicy that after downing a few I'd dip my tongue into a glass of ice water for a few minutes. We drove deep into the Oakland ghetto to hunt for the "Tamale Man." He wasn't too hard to find for he had an old-fashioned square wagon that he pushed from street to street. He made his own tamales and wrapped them in newspaper. My Lord, were they ever greasy and hot!

Churchly matters filled up my entire life back then. While I hardly ever studied my Sunday school lessons and usually showed up unprepared, I otherwise tried to do as I was told, dutifully participating in all church activities and contributing to my folks' ministry with as much enthusiasm as I could muster. Which wasn't much, because we never seemed to get a break from it. Even when we weren't in church, religion was jammed down our throats. I can cite no better example than the "Heaven and Hell" parties we attended (involuntarily) at the home of Willie Mae Tires, one of my mother's best friends. Willie Mae had an old-style home with furnaces built into the floor. In the hallway she closed the doors and turned up the heat so high you started to sweat right away. That room represented Hell. A bigger, lighter, more comfortable room where there were windows represented Heaven. If you chose Hell, you were served a bowl of spicy chili. If you chose Heaven, you were rewarded with ice cream and cake. I sure wasn't nuts about Hell, but I loved me some chili and never hesitated to go there first. When I was full I repented and went to Heaven to wash down the chili with that cool and tasty ice cream and cake.

The problem was that I had a strong appetite and a desire to be adventurous and do a lot of the things I saw my friends doing who didn't attend our church. There comes a huge responsibility with being the oldest girl in the family. I was expected to set a good example for my younger siblings and other young girls in the church. I wanted no part of that and actively resented the idea that something as random as birth order imposed higher expectations and greater responsibility on me than the ones who came after. The only thing I ever wanted to follow in my footsteps was my own shadow.

I consider myself a Christian today, but not the way my parents were. As I get older, I understand the issues and circumstances they had to deal with in raising six children. They did the best that they could with the knowledge they had. I suspect they also tried to keep us out of trouble. But the strict constraints they put on us were detrimental to us culturally and socially. We were so out of the mainstream that most of us went wild once we got out of our parents' grasp, and that wasn't good, either.

While all the fire and brimstone I heard in church and at the dinner table put the fear of God in me, the truth was that organized religion at the time didn't really click for me. It seemed mostly distant and contrived. Lord knows I wanted to please my parents to become the shining moral exemplar they wanted out of me, but nothing jelled. The predominantly black church membership was small, fewer than 100 congregants; ours was an offshoot of a larger church run by whites in another state. We didn't even sing gospel songs; the songs we sang came from a book of dry, boring hymns in the back of all the pews. It wasn't until we visited other churches that we got our real first taste of authentic gospel music. Some of our members wanted to project a middle-class image even though a majority of the congregation was dirt poor. For all the time we spent there, the most exciting times were the holidays because that's when the choir would sing special songs, my uncle Jack would perform a solo or my mother or sisters and I would sing gospel songs not in the usual hymnbook. And we always looked forward to the appearance of an occasional visitor known as "Sister Rosemond." Whenever she turned up, church became more fun than not being at church. When touched by God's presence, Sister Rosemond would jump up, scream, shout, dance, and run all over the place. After about 10 minutes she'd start to wind down, only to be suddenly seized by the spirit again for more frenzied laps around the church. Sometimes this went on for half an hour, by which time other members of the congregation—including my mom—would be shouting and whooping right alongside her. God help me, I may have even joined the parade once myself. I loved Sister Rosemond. When she walked through the church doors I'd nod and say to myself, *Oh yeah…we gonna have some church today!*

Mostly we had the Golden Rule and turn-the-other-cheek tirelessly drummed into us, and apocalyptical visions of heaven and hell so alarming that I suffered from frequent nightmares in which avenging angels and horses and chariots thundered out of the clouds on Judgment Day as the earth was consumed by a punishing fire. I was sure I was going to hell, because I just couldn't seem to get things right.

I sat through many a sermon by my mother and father vowing to abide by their lessons, only to mess up the next day by getting into a fight with one of my sisters or someone else. I'd feel instant remorse and tell myself, *I've blown it! I'm done and hell bound right now. There is no hope for me....*

Great way to spend your childhood, huh? There was so much perfection demanded of me, and so little room for error. Every time I said a bad word or thought something was wrong about another person, I punched my own one-way ticket to hell. I never had a sense of God's kindness and unconditional love.

My resentment of authority and those who wielded it manifested itself in different ways. I remember the first time was when I was in third grade at Cole Elementary School. My teacher was Mrs. Bolin, an elderly white woman who didn't bother checking her obvious distaste for people of color at the schoolhouse door. One day she was conducting a reading group in the front of the class. I was sitting in the back row reading a book and eating an apple when all of a sudden Mrs. Bolin charged up and yelled, "I said no talking!" Then she slapped me hard in the face.

Turning the other cheek never even occurred to me. Instead, I stood up, yelled "I wasn't talking!" and slapped her back.

I got sent to the principal's office and was detained there for a few days until they decided what to do. When I returned to class, Mrs. Bolin wasn't there. She'd been canned. The Lord definitely works in mysterious ways.

Around the same time I remember a boy my age following me home from school one day, and he didn't do anything for me other than get under my skin. When he got close, I snatched the tin lunch pail in his hand and whacked him upside the head a few times. He went crying and bloody. I fought with my brother Fritz plenty of times, and I wasn't afraid to take on anyone—boys or girls. While it may have appeared on the outside that I was quiet and obedient, inside I was raging.

A few years later my parents made me accompany another family to a national Church of God convention in Houston.

I wasn't much for going to begin with, and then on the eve of our departure I received news that my close friend Carol Donahue had just died. I was very distraught and begged my parents to let me stay home, but they wouldn't hear of it. Back then, no one in our neck of the woods had money for a plane ticket; so we made the 1,900-mile trek by car. I cannot begin to tell you how miserable that seemingly endless drive was. When we arrived at the Rice Hotel in Houston, racism reared its ugly face and we were told that while we could attend the daily convention sessions in the ballroom, we were not welcome to stay at the hotel. So we had to stay in the Texas Southern University dorms all the way across town. What galled me as much as anything was that none of the white members of our congregation stuck up for us. That bothered me for the longest time.

Daddy made $85 a week and Mom added a few more bucks to the till after she was ordained and became assistant pastor. We were poor ghetto kids and did all our shopping at the Salvation Army, Father Divine's thrift store, and at church pastor's aide contributions. I remember when Bonnie wanted a $4 gown but was unable to come up with the full asking price. She had to put it on layaway for 25 cents a week. One memorable holiday season the Pointers were designated as an "underprivileged family" by some Toys for Tots–like program sponsored by the University of California–Berkeley.

They took us to the campus, spent the day with us, and gave us lots of new toys. We went bananas! When we got back home, my parents made us turn over the presents to them so they could be given to kids who were more underprivileged than the Pointers. That just about killed us. I was obsessed with dolls and drew the line at giving up the one they gave me at UC-B. It had a ponytail, for God's sake! I'd sooner have given up one of my sisters to those poor kids. Whatever heartfelt pleas my parents made to me that day, I did not give up that doll.

Looking back, my mother sacrificed the most. I know she struggled and never really asked for much. I remember one holiday season when the suggestion was made that the congregation purchase a new outfit for my mother to wear. They literally had to vote on whether to provide her with a new dress. The vote ended up in favor of the idea, but it still sticks in my gut that it wasn't unanimous. I carried that particular memory into my adult life when I became a so-called singing sensation and started to make a substantial amount of money. Taking care of our mother and making sure she had beautiful clothes was a top priority for The Pointer Sisters. Mom loved receiving boxes of new clothes and other gifts in the mail over the years. As far as I'm concerned, it was never enough. I remember her working in other people's kitchens, in cafeterias, and at a cannery during canning season, just to bring enough food home for us to eat. You could actually do that back then. She never once complained and did whatever she could to contribute to our well-being.

Despite the family's tight finances, on my 13th birthday Daddy wheeled in an upright piano. I started taking piano lessons and kept it up several years. The excitement eventually wore off, though, as my intensely wandering mind prevented me from getting into practice mode (a problem that followed me into adulthood). Plus, I suspected my dad had plans for me to become the next church pianist. No thank you! But my sisters and I sang in the church choir from the time we could walk. The first choir we participated in was called "Little Soldiers." We wore big red bows and handmade ponchos with red edging and marched around the church singing, "We are little soldiers, marching off to war." I couldn't have been any older than six or seven.

The Pointer sisters weren't always musically marching off to war. We weren't averse to shakin' it out of the old folks' earshot. When my parents would leave the house, we'd tuck our dresses up into our panties and make little bustles out of them, then grab some of my brother's trophies and pretend they were microphones. We'd climb up on the piano stool and beat on pie pans with spoons, making that rhythm and jamming together. For the longest time we couldn't afford a television, so we did whatever we could think of to entertain each other.

Trouble was, Papa wasn't much entertained by our shenanigans, and as soon as our parents came home he'd run up and tattle on us.

"Better whip their butts—they were in there popping their fingers and shaking their behinds, singing the blues," he'd cry. "Terrible! Terrible!" And we'd get a BIG butt whippin', too. Lord have mercy!

We did like some of the church tunes that weren't all mournful and funeral-like. Three immediately spring to mind: "I Surrender All," "Once Again We Come," and "The Blood," which became one of our favorite songs to perform. The latter was a song we learned from the Watson Sisters, whom we met in church a few years later. The Watsons were a large family who lived up the street from us when we moved in 1961 from West Oakland to a larger home in Lake Merritt, thanks to an urban renewal relocation payout from the city. There were 11 Watson kids in all—nine of them girls—and all of them sang in their father's church. They called themselves the Watson Sisters. We got friendly with one another, and I'd often turn up at their house while they were singing. One day I went back home and said, "They're calling themselves the Watson Sisters. We could be the Pointer Sisters! We need to be singing, too!" It took a while for the idea to ferment, but a seed was definitely planted then.

Before long, our interest in music expanded and proved too strong for our parents to tamp down. There were only a handful of albums in the house. My mother owned and played just one record—a Mahalia Jackson 78—while my father was the proud owner of a couple of John Philip Sousa records. One day I brought home my first vinyl record purchase: "All Shook Up," by Elvis Presley. The only reason it made it through the front door was that the flip side, "Crying in the Chapel," was a gospel song Mom liked. It was the first piece of secular music that was ever played in the Pointer household.

My attention and interests increasingly shifted from home and church to mainstream culture and social life when I became a teenager. I got introduced to other kinds of music while visiting my girlfriend, Marjorie Dangerfield, expanding my tastes beyond Elvis. Marjorie and I met in church when we were in our teens. She visited one Easter Sunday and smiled at me as if she already knew me. That smile lit up a room. Once we struck up a friendship, I wanted more friends. I became notorious for inviting myself to other people's homes after church and would walk right up to an interesting prospect and ask, "Can I go home with you today?" or

"What are you having for dinner tonight?" Surprisingly, I was rarely turned away. Looking back, I was curious how others lived and wanted to taste it for myself.

My other friend, Paulette Holloway, helped me in my discovery of the sonic joys of The Temptations, The Supremes, Martha Reeves and the Vandellas, Junior Walker & the All Stars, The Chantels, James Brown, Ray Charles, and Little Richard. Even Redd Foxx comedy records, which might still be considered taboo today. While surprisingly tolerant of these new longings in me, perhaps due to his own past, my father remained overly vigilant and protective of me. When I was invited to my first party at a friend's house, he said nothing doing unless he came along as my personal chaperone. To avoid that humiliation, on the day of the party I snuck out of the house wearing the low-cut red dress I'd bought at the secondhand store and got on a city bus to go to the party. I had to get off that bus to transfer to another one, and when I did Daddy was standing there waiting for me. I was stunned and at a loss for words, so he spoke first. I was probably all of 13 years old.

"I'm just trying to make sure you're not lost and that you're okay," he said reasonably. "You want to go to this party? I'll take you the rest of the way."

I got in the car and Daddy drove me to the party. But of course he didn't just drop me off. He was my official date for the night, sitting there the whole time with my friend's parents and making it clear without saying a single word that any boy thinking about asking me to dance had better think again or suffer the wrath of God's personal assistant.

Daddy became a fixture at almost every party I attended. At these get-togethers, music was played, and young people slow danced and kissed, with the lights dimmed. That is, until Daddy would do a walk-through with his police-sized flashlight, shining it in people's faces, looking for me. It wasn't long before someone would turn to me and say, "Your dad's here again." Daddy became such a fixture that when on that rare occasion he didn't show up, people asked why he wasn't there. His manner wasn't offensive or brusque, and everybody loved him and accepted the situation for what it was—a daddy who was protecting his daughter.

When a male suitor called on me at home, the door had to be left wide open in whatever room we occupied. Needless to say, the bedroom was strictly off-limits.

My father loved me, and I him. But, man, he was pure hell on a girl's burgeoning social life.

It must've been one of those few times he wasn't my shadow that I met Larry Woods. He was a neighbor of Paulette Holloway, who hosted a lot of the parties I attended. Larry was the one all the girls fantasized about: 6'3", 160 nicely sculpted pounds, and medium-brown complexion, with slightly tinted red hair cropped tight. Always dressed in flamboyant Beatle-style and colorful silk mohair suits, skinny neckties, and San Remo shoes, Larry also happened to be the best dancer on the floor and never failed to turn female heads and hearts. Especially mine.

Larry looked so divine. Daddy would have said right off that he was really the devil in disguise.

This time, the Reverend Pointer would have hit it square on the head.

The Church of God in West Oakland, a place of worship that my parents helped found and build and where I spent a majority of my youth, circa 1950s.

Easter Sunday at the Church of God in Oakland. In this photo June (in the middle), Anita (sporting the horn-rimmed glasses), and I pose at the altar after the service. We received new clothes on Christmas and Easter and we had to capture the moment.

Hanging out with my sister Anita in Oakland, sometime in the early 1950s, most likely after church service. As this picture shows, Oakland was not as densely populated. We considered it "the country" compared to nearby San Francisco, which we called "the city."

Below: Weddings are wonderful for family pictures and showing off your best clothes. The Pointer family was very happy the day my oldest brother, Aaron, married Leona Dones, circa 1961. My parents, Sarah and Elton, are to the right of Aaron, the groom, while the bride's parents, Ray and Inez, are to her left. Sitting down on the left-hand side is my paternal grandfather Herman. I was a bridesmaid and my father presided over the nuptials at the Church of God.

Contact sheet of the first official Pointer Sisters photo session taken by Bruce Steinberg shortly after I joined the group. These pictures capture the essence of our personalities all before fame mucked things up.

Publicity photo session for The Pointer Sisters LP, snapped by talented portrait artist Herb Greene, in 1973. Herb instantly locked into The Pointer Sisters' retro-chic look, which helped us breakout and caused a fashion sensation.

On one of our first trips to Europe and during our "Superfly" phase. This was taken on the streets of Amsterdam and in front of a Rolls-Royce that chauffeured us to various spots around the city.

Comedian Carol Burnett had invited The Pointer Sisters to appear on her iconic television show several times in the early-to-mid 1970s, giving us exposure to millions of fans. Carol has remained a friend over the years and is one of the giant talents of our time.

In September 1974 we co-hosted The Mike Douglas Show *for an entire week. We invited a wide variety of guests, including boxer Muhammad Ali; activist Angela Davis; our cousin, NBA star Paul Silas; and our parents, who made their national television debut.*

Life was definitely a "Fairytale" at this point in our career. With my sisters collecting a Grammy Award for Best Country Vocal by a Duo or Group, New York City, March 1, 1975.

This rare photo was taken on March 8, 1976, when The Pointer Sisters performed a concert for inmates at the Cook County Jail in Illinois. They were appreciative that someone on the outside cared for them.

Metaphorically, The Pointer Sisters were smokin' in the 1970s and we had it all: looks, talent, flashy clothes, and plenty of attitude to match.

We made our feature film debut in the 1976 comedy Car Wash, *starring comedic legend Richard Pryor as "Daddy Rich," a money-hungry evangelist with a silver tongue. Richard was a good friend and crazier than a road lizard.*

Publicity photo for Super Night at the Super Bowl *in January 1976. We presented ourselves as the "girls next door," but behind the scenes I tore it up with drugs and alcohol.*

Music producer Richard Perry brought the Pointer Sisters back from the brink and helped re-imagine us as a trio in 1978 with his newly formed company, Planet Records. We teamed up on nine albums and produced more than a dozen Top 40 singles.

We're all smiles in this late 1970s-era photo, and for good reason: the Pointer Sisters were back and on "Fire."

Publicity photo for Special Things, *a 1980 album that went gold thanks to "He's So Shy," with June on lead vocals.*

CHAPTER TWO

A Man Took My Heart and Robbed Me Blind

· ·

I DON'T LIKE TALKING ABOUT MY FIRST MARRIAGE. More than taking my sexual innocence, it took my vulnerability and kicked it around like a ragdoll. Its repercussions reverberated throughout my life and my children's lives and left my father's ministry in shambles. My marriage to Larry Woods was no laughing matter.

I can't blame him entirely. He excited me, and I fed on that excitement like a vampire sucking the lifeblood out of its victim. He moved sensually, he looked good. Like most enticements, what you see isn't necessarily what you get. He was taboo and I was ripe for rebellion in the guise of love. The warning signs were there long before we married. In fact, they stood out like neon-lit billboards on a dark highway. Like the time his own mother essentially told me what a no-good sonofabitch her son was.

"I don't know why you're with him, chile," she said early into our relationship. "That boy ain't gonna amount to nuthin'."

Mama knew best, but I was 18 years old, in love, and in proper lust for the very first time. I craved being held without fear of death by fire and brimstone. I craved unconditional acceptance for who I thought I knew I was. I craved that freedom that comes from your first moments shed of emotional bondage. I thought Larry would give me those "ahh" moments of release. He gave me "ahh moments" all right. Ahh hell! Ignorance came with a price.

My parents drummed into me that if you had sex you got married. Well, Larry and I had sex. That is all it was. No fireworks, no violins, no making love. It happened in his parents' basement, where he slept. It felt like a dungeon down there, dark, dirty, and smelly. His folks didn't know what to do with Larry after he dropped out of high school, so they simply stuck him there out of the way. The sex felt like an out-of-body experience. I was there physically, but mentally and emotionally I had checked out. It was quick, passionless, and over before I knew it.

Larry was a lousy lover, but biology is a strict, cold science that doesn't take such things into account. I soon learned that I was pregnant. Many a subject was taboo in our household, and anything having to do with sex was at the top of that long list. My mom would beat me if she caught me touching myself. Birth control? Honey, it would have been easier talking about that to the pope himself. And equally pointless. It just wasn't an option in those days.

The first person I told that I was "with child" was my sister, Anita, a person I could always count on when the chips were down. I asked her to break the news to our parents. I figured I was already doomed, so adding rank cowardice to my sins was no biggie. Daddy and Mom took it calmly, much to my amazement, saying they'd do whatever they could to help me get through it all.

But of course, the first thing Daddy wanted to know was when Larry would make an honest woman out of his little girl. And he didn't waste any time asking Larry just that the next time that he came over to the house. They sat right down for a man-to-man chat. I wouldn't be surprised at all if the conversation included mention of the gleaming shotgun Daddy kept around in case he ran into a sinner with a greater fear of buckshot than of the Lord.

I was world-class clueless about men and about relationships. I actually thought I could save Larry from himself. I'd heard the rumor around town that he was a womanizer who skipped from girl to girl. But I figured all he needed was a little loving from a good, smart, and strong woman to set him on the right path. But Larry was the one who had all the angles figured out, including how to run circles around my head and heart. He played me cringe-worthingly good, and I blindly enabled him to continue leading a life without apparent consequence.

My handsome fiancée did some modeling on the side and was often paid to escort young women to cotillion balls because he was such an exceptional dancer. Looking back, I knew what that could lead to, given his reputation, so I was glad to drive him around to pick up some work. I was both his chauffeur and his secretary, even to the point of filling out his job applications for him. One time I was tired and begged off, and when he insisted I come along I asked why he couldn't handle it himself. Up popped another neon billboard.

"I can't read," he said.

What I should've done was run for the hills or take a flying leap off the Oakland Bay Bridge, but I felt sorry for my poor, illiterate man who could only get by on his good looks. We were married on August 9, 1964, and our daughter, Faun, arrived in January of the next year.

We were so young and broke that we had no choice but to move into my parents' home. By then, Aaron and Fritz were out of the house and there was room. Not that it mattered much, because my new husband didn't waste any time making himself scarce. The first time he didn't come home, I pathetically stayed up all night worrying that he'd been in an accident and was lying in a ditch somewhere. He was lying somewhere, all right, but it wasn't in a ditch. Days went by, and I thought I was going to lose my mind. Finally, someone in the know clued me in that he was with another woman.

Remember that scene in the movie *Waiting to Exhale* where Angela Bassett's character torches her husband's clothes after she discovers he has been having an affair with another woman? I swear that author Terry McMillan ripped that out of the pages of my life, because that's exactly what I did. I took every damn shred of clothing Larry owned out of the closet, set it in a pile in the backyard, soaked it with lighter fluid, and then set that sucker on fire.

When the flames were good and high, my mother, peeking out of the kitchen window, started to bawl.

"What are you crying about?" I asked, a tad pissed. "They're his clothes."

"That boy is gonna kill you when he gets home," she cried.

He almost did. When Larry finally found his way home and discovered the charred remains of his wardrobe, he beat on me like a punching bag. God knows how bad it would've gotten if my dad hadn't finally broken it up. I should've left him for good then. My parents had never behaved like this, and I knew all marriages weren't perfect. I had seen a few fights in my day between some aunts and uncles, but I never thought my life would end up this pathetic. It was humiliating.

It was poor Mom who suggested, no doubt out of desperation, that I get back with my husband. I had already caused her and Daddy so much grief that I decided to do as she wanted and give my marriage another shot. I moved back with Larry at his parents' home across town. However, that didn't last long. Several of Larry's brothers were known players, and one night an angry woman showed up with a gun looking for the one who'd done her wrong. She blew up that house with the shotgun and everybody hit the floor. I beat it right back to my parents' house.

After a few months, Larry and I finally moved back in together and got a small apartment in Lake Merritt. Our domestic bliss didn't last very long. Larry was a natural-born tomcat and wasn't going to be tamed. He made the occasional rare appearance here and there, but like The Temptations song goes, "wherever he laid his hat was his home." Soon after we moved in, I found out I was pregnant again. My response to this news was to go to some older girlfriends for advice on how to force a miscarriage. They suggested purchasing a bottle of Old Crow whiskey and slugging it down with some over-the-counter generic pills. But all I got was drunk and loopy. I called my mother and told her what I had done, and she came over to my little apartment to watch my infant daughter Faun and me while I sobered up. I can't believe how naïve and stupid I was at the time, but now I thank God that he spared both my son and me.

Malik was born in December 1965, and Larry didn't even know about his birth until a few months later. It was around then that the Church of God started turning the screws on my father to resign his position. The problem wasn't his leadership in the church but rather that his out-of-control children were an embarrassment to the congregation.

Aaron was too involved with sports to get into much trouble, but my brother Fritz was an avowed atheist who ended up serving a term in what was then known as the California Youth Authority juvenile prison for some petty crimes. He has since told me that he wasn't exactly miserable there. It was the first time he ever had his own bedroom and dresser. Eventually he turned his life around and had a distinguished career in academia as an English professor at Contra Costa College in San Pablo, California. He is now retired, traveling the world and living the good life.

Tongues wagged most furiously about the Reverend Pointer's four wayward daughters, who laughed too much, enjoyed themselves way too much at parties, and had a couple of children out of wedlock. As much as it pains me to say this, me getting pregnant before I got married to Larry was a real blow to my family's ministry. Regardless of how it made my mom and dad look, they forgave me and told me it was all going to work out in the end. That was unacceptable to the sanctimonious church crowd, and when Daddy ignored hints that he should voluntarily step aside from the pulpit, they voted to remove him from the church. They didn't even give him a pension.

Decades later it still makes me cry how Daddy was deserted by the church he built. My parents uprooted themselves from Arkansas to start that church and dedicated more than 25 years of their lives to nurturing it. When Daddy got the boot he suffered an emotional breakdown. He never held a decent job after that because he was considered too old to do anything else. It broke his heart and his spirit. Broke mine, too.

It also smashed whatever faith I had left. If that pious, self-righteous lynch mob—and that's exactly what they were—was doing God's will, who wanted a God like that? Their treatment of my father was unkind, unloving, unfair, and cruel. If the congregants could do that to their pastor, an aging, kind man who had served them diligently for years, I wanted nothing more to do with them and their poisoned environment. There had to be a better world somewhere else, and I went looking for it. I didn't have to look far.

It was the height of the civil rights, black power, and black arts movements in the United States. The childhood rebellion that stirred during my strict church upbringing was tame compared to what was on tap for me. I dove into the infamous Haight-Ashbury hippie/drug/free-love scene, losing myself in a haze of alcohol and drugs, seamy relationships, and anything else I thought would blot out my unhappy youth, rigid upbringing, and bad-girl guilt.

It pains me more than I can convey to confess that I even considered putting my own children up for adoption. I had no clue how to raise them, nor any inclination to learn.

My mother ended up caring for Faun, and Malik went with Larry's family.

I should've stayed there, but as immature and filled with self-loathing as I was, I let myself to be sweet-talked into getting back with Larry even though he was beating me up regularly. One night he even put his cigarette out on my arm. That scar is still visible today as well as the scar on my head where I was beaten unconscious with the heel of a shoe and some kind of string instrument, hanging on the wall, that he snatched off the wall to continue his torture when the shoe flew out of his hand. I do remember having to get nine stitches in my head. I'm usually asked about it when someone does my hair. My response is always truthful: I was severely beaten and a victim of domestic violence.

To cope with the mounting physical and emotional pain I began to take Benzedrine (speed) and Red Devils (barbiturates) and wash them down with Christian Brothers brandy. Looking back, I suppose this was how the cycle of additive behaviors that mushroomed when The Pointer Sisters became famous got its start.

I tried leaving Larry several times, but he said he'd see me dead first and even threatened to kill my family when he was done with me. I believed him, having once seen Larry beat my sister Bonnie almost to death with an old-fashioned metal phone.

When he heard about Larry's behavior, Daddy gave me his trusty shotgun and told me not to hesitate to use it.

I honest-to-God walked around in public with that shotgun in my arms. I even carried it with me once when I went to a bar to meet a guy. When I got there I kissed him on the cheek and put the gun on the floor within easy reach. Nobody said a thing about it. Would you?

Thanks to my double-barreled equalizer I was no longer so scared of Larry. When I found out he was dating—and also abusing—a high school rival of mine named Hazel, that was the final straw. First I called Hazel's mother.

"I know that my husband is with your daughter," I said. "I'm about to call the police and have him arrested. So if you don't want your daughter involved, you need to go and get her now."

It happened that my sister Anita was friendly with a couple of Oakland vice cops. My next call was to them. I told them where Larry was holed up with Hazel and said that if they didn't get there first I intended to blow his rotten head off.

They beat it right over there. Larry was wanted on several outstanding warrants, and when the cops moved in he tried to get away by jumping off the third-story balcony of an apartment building. I wish I'd been there to see him hit the ground, though it would have been a huge letdown to see him wind up with just two broken legs.

The last time I laid eyes on him was in the Big House, when I brought the divorce papers for him to sign.

"Damn, you're a cold woman!" he said so glumly as he signed them that I almost busted out laughing. Did he think I'd come to renew our vows?

Ol' Larry may have been great on the dance floor, but I busted some fancy moves of my own dancing out of his life forever that day.

CHAPTER THREE

Welfare Queen

THERE WAS A STEREOTYPE THAT EVERY RIGHT-LEANING politician held up as a prime example of what was wrong in the United States of America during the 1970s. This stereotype was a staple of speeches given by future president Ronald Reagan, who was then governor of California.

He called them Welfare Queens.

I guess I was one of them, by virtue of the fact that I was black and a single mother of two children who accepted government assistance/food stamps, lived in subsidized low-cost housing, pawned her kids off on her parents whenever I wanted to party, and had had multiple boyfriends and male suitors.

But I sure didn't feel like royalty. It was definitely one of the low points of my life, and reflecting back on it the word that comes first to my mind is "shame." I felt shameful because I had let my parents down by getting pregnant before I was married; because my marriage didn't work; because my alcohol (brandy and cognac), cigarette, speed, and cocaine consumption were spiraling out of control. My life was going nowhere, and in the absence of any idea what to do about it

I kept numbing myself with booze, chemicals, drama, and whatever other distractions I could latch on to.

I was probably more of a Welfare Princess than Queen, because with all the aforesaid problems I managed to hold down a job—illegal when you're collecting welfare—working as a keypunch operator for Pacific Far East Lines between Oakland and San Francisco, working out of a building at the tip of the Oakland Bay Bridge. It only paid about $400 a month, and it was the best I could do. Later on, the state found out about my little hustle and made me pay back every dime of unemployment.

To supplement my meager income I sold a little weed on the side. One of my regular customers was a construction worker named Carl Abram. We got more involved. It wasn't until later that I discovered Carl and my sister June had been going out. He claimed it was just a couple dates, and I didn't bother to check with June. I had enough problems of my own without taking on somebody else's.

June was pretty broken up about the situation, but that didn't keep me from eventually marrying Carl. Not an especially brilliant decision on so many levels. Circumstance is happenstance, right? Not always. Sometimes your circumstances are a choice, not a chance. Back then I enjoyed throwing caution to the wind, and it ended up biting me big time.

My kids, Malik and Faun, and I lived with my sister, Anita, and her daughter, Jada, in a two-bedroom apartment in West Oakland before Carl and I got married. It was located about 10 minutes away from my parents' house. Anita was doing the single-parent thing, too. I told myself that we were in a kindred situation, helping each other, supporting each other. I was in denial that I wanted family near so I could do what I wanted. I felt justified in that Faun and Malik were fed, bathed, and clothed by me. They had their basic needs covered. But what they needed the most—love and nurturing—they received from both sets of grandparents, not me. I often farmed out Malik to Larry's parents, while Faun usually went with mine.

I have felt guilt and shame about that ever since, but through counseling and 12-step work have learned to forgive myself. I pray my children have forgiven me, too. But that is something that they have to decide. I can't make that choice for them.

They have to sort out their own mistakes and regrets that have come out of their own sicknesses. I say sickness because that is all that I showed them for the longest time. They grew up with a sick mother who placed herself before their emotional needs—and what goes around, comes around. But I can't change any of that and neither can they.

Turning back the years of resentment isn't something that I can teach them. I pray that they don't see their lives as mistakes that can't be rectified. I freely admit that I neglected my kids. And I hope that forgiveness for that neglect is something that they have reconciled themselves to in their minds and in their hearts, whether they feel that they can tell me so or not.

The cruel, hard truth is that, at the time, I was most interested in getting high and hammered, having what I then considered fun. This meant sitting on a bar stool and drinking and snorting up a storm. I had no problem attracting members of the opposite sex. What man wouldn't want a woman who could party all night and drink him under the table?

I was wild as hell, and as long as there was someone buying the endless rounds of Hennessy, Remy Martin, Christian Brothers, and Cristal and providing that magical white powder, I didn't ask to see a resume.

Things weren't going a whole lot better for my sisters Bonnie and June, although they hadn't sunk quite as low as me. Bonnie in particular was driven, citing a desperate need to do something with her life. She was wild, fierce, and not to be denied. She hung out in Haight-Ashbury with the hippies, protested at Berkeley, wrote poetry with Angela Davis, and dated Huey Newton, co-founder of the Black Panther Party.

In 1969, Bonnie and June started singing together as the Pointers Au Pair, shortly joined by Anita. They were so eager and willing to make a living singing they'd hitchhike from San Francisco to as far as New York for a paying gig. Often they'd pretend to have a bad case of the crabs in case the men who picked them up had any funny ideas. Lacking inhibition, they were fierce, and sometimes they'd crash the stage of well-known veterans playing the Bay Area, including B.B. King and Herbie Hancock.

They even tried folk songs with San Francisco–based singer Michael Takamatsu and sang rhythm and blues in the clubs because that's pretty much all the house bands knew at the time. They played a couple of sleazy old bars on East 14th Street, earning a whopping $15 per engagement. Once they landed a gig at a private cocktail party for San Francisco television reporter Belva Davis, but even those rare swanky jobs didn't pay much. Bonnie tried topless dancing at a place called Girls Galore on Telegraph Avenue in Oakland but quit after a week because the old geezers in that joint gave her the creeps.

I bumped into that type plenty in the watering holes where I'd wet my whistle: lots of jewelry, shirts opened to their flabby navels, flashing wads of cash that were mostly singles.

Anita was fired from her job with the law firm the day after Christmas for the crime of showing up a few minutes late, and she joined Bonnie and June as members of the Northern California State Youth Choir. A few years before, the choir backed Edwin Hawkins on a Grammy-winning gospel record called "Oh Happy Day" that became an international hit, selling seven million copies.

At the time Anita was dating a car salesman who must've been tops in his field because he convinced her, Bonnie, and June to up and move to Houston, where he said he had "connections." For a small management fee, he promised them plenty of recording sessions, a record deal, and club dates that would rocket the newly christened Pointer Sisters to the top.

The launching pad turned out to be a joint called the Greek Cat Nightclub & Lounge, and when the girls arrived there direct from Oakland the owner had never heard of them or their car salesman. Oh happy day! But when they sang Aretha Franklin's "Chain of Fools" for him, the owner shrugged and said he already had a house band but he'd make room for them on the bill.

In Houston, they stayed with the sister of Anita's boyfriend. Naturally, she was less than thrilled with the arrangement, but out of deference to her brother she allowed my sisters to stay as long as they obeyed some ground rules that included no rehearsing in the apartment and putting up with their host's frequently expressed opinion that as performers they sucked. A few weeks later, she kicked them to the curb.

Fortunately, one of the singers in the house band took pity on Bonnie, Anita, and June and gave them shelter in her apartment. The place came with no rules or stipulations, but she did have some pesky roommates my sisters grew to hate: cockroaches.

Those suckers overran the apartment and there was no escaping them. My sisters waged war on those roaches and scrubbed that filthy place from top to bottom, squashing them with their feet and rolled up magazines, and it absolutely did no good. The disgusting insects came back in even bigger droves.

The final straw came about two months after my sisters arrived in Houston. One night as their grudging roommate was preparing for a night on the town, she picked up the luxurious wig she frequently wore and gave it a firm shake before plopping it on her head. A battalion of roaches nesting in the fake curls went flying. The Pointer Sisters lost it on the spot, while their host didn't even bat an eye and smirked that they ought to go back where they came from because they sure as hell weren't cut out for show business.

Houston was a Texas-sized disaster, and my sisters were stranded and alone. Bonnie did the only thing she could think of. She called home. Mom told her there was only enough money to bring one of them back to Oakland and said it had to be June, since June was her baby. Bonnie then called all the friends and acquaintances she could think of for help getting herself and Anita home. But everybody had the shorts, and when songwriters Bruce Good and Jeff Cohen suggested she call David Rubinson, who was rock promoter Bill Graham's business partner at the Fillmore Corporation in

San Francisco, even though she'd never met the man, she was desperate enough to give it a try.

"Mr. Rubinson, my name is Bonnie Pointer and you may have never heard of me, but my sisters and I can sing," she told him. "If you can get us out of Texas, I'll show you."

David had gotten his start at Capitol Records in New York in the mid-'60s, and moved to San Francisco to get involved in the burgeoning music scene there. He had actually heard about my sisters' talent, and he ended up not only paying for their passage back to the Bay Area but then got The Pointer Sisters live gigs and studio work backing such Bay Area artists as Boz Scaggs, Grace Slick, Elvin Bishop, Dave Mason, Bobbie Lamb, and funk artist Betty Davis, the second wife of jazz great Miles Davis. As word got around about my sisters' unique abilities, Bill Graham signed them to a management contract.

The girls went out almost immediately on tour with Elvin Bishop, Dave Mason, and Esther Phillips. The gig with Esther, a giant talent with a drug and alcohol addiction to match, didn't last long. She always went on stage draped in long, satiny gowns, ostrich feathers, and a big bouffant wig. My sisters put together simple red, white, and blue outfits, of which Esther disapproved because they weren't classy enough. She continually harped at the girls to invest in a better wardrobe, which was all but impossible since their salary for backing up Esther amounted to just $5 apiece per performance. Esther kept nagging them about it, and Bonnie finally told her, "Miss Phillips, we got to eat with this money! We got to pay the rent! Miss Phillips, please don't try to tell us what to do with our money." The girls' wardrobe instantly ceased to be an issue because they instantly ceased to be on Esther's laughable payroll.

In June 1971, Atlantic Records vice president Jerry Wexler, a legendary figure in the music industry, heard the girls sing backup for Elvin Bishop at the Whisky in Los Angeles and offered them a record deal.

As co-owner of Atlantic, Wexler had signed Ray Charles, Aretha Franklin, Bob Dylan, Dusty Springfield, Led Zeppelin, and Wilson Pickett. Wexler was an enormous booster of the Muscle Shoals sound and a well-respected producer in his own right. But he couldn't get a handle on how to market my sisters, who specialized in a unique blend of jazz, scat and bebop, and sometimes country—basically music of the 1930s and '40s. But now pop, folk and rock music were in the saddle.

Wexler sent them to Malaco Studios in Jackson, Mississippi, where they would cut a few songs under the then hot producer Wardell Quezergue, known to New Orleans musicians as the "Creole Beethoven." But the Black Beethoven must have been tone deaf during those sessions because there was no "5th Symphony" in the works. They sounded stilted and lifeless.

On my sisters' first two records they ended up sounding very similar to Honey Cone, a female trio that scored a million-selling Pop and R & B No. 1 single in the spring of 1971 with "Want Ads."

The first single was "Don't Try to Take the Fifth," with June on lead vocal, followed up by a single called "Send Him Back." As Anita would wryly note, the only place they were ever heard "was in our living rooms." They laid such a big egg with the record-buying public that Atlantic dropped The Pointer Sisters in 1972.

Thanks to David Rubinson, my sisters continued to get studio work backing others, and every now and then I'd get a phone call telling me to rush to the studio because June wasn't up to performing. June had major psychological issues stemming from an incident that occurred a few years earlier when she was gang-raped by a group of neighborhood thugs. It happened right in front of my daughter Faun, who was around five years old at the time. June begged the men not to hurt Faun, and they obliged, but what they did to June was brutal and sadistic. She actually knew her assailants but never ratted them out to the police out of fear of retaliation and that our older brothers Aaron and Fritz would take matters into their own hands. June bottled all the pain and trauma up inside her, which resulted in depression, addiction, and wild mood swings. Today it would be called a classic case of bipolar disorder. June stopped going to school. My parents sought help in the form of a therapist who would come to the house. June rarely got out of bed for the sessions.

When called to fill in for June I'd get paid up to $100 for a session, and let me tell you that made me the happiest bitch on the planet. It not only put food on the table and paid a few bills, but also gave me a sense of self-worth. And it sure beat the holy hell out of sitting in an office being a keypunch operator for eight hours a day.

I filled in for June on a Dr. Hook session (though I can't recall the song or album), *Recycling the Blues & Other Related Stuff* by Taj Mahal, and, most memorably, Sylvester and the Hot Band's "Why Was I Born?"

Sylvester James Jr. was the first openly gay man I ever met, and we clicked from the get-go. I loved his genderfunky gospel-falsetto voice, and besides, I was a born sucker for a finger-snapping man in drag. He was fun, campy, sometimes diva-ish, and totally glam and glitter way before David Bowie, T. Rex, or Roxy Music. When Bowie first came to town he didn't even sell out San Francisco's Winterland Ballroom. "They don't need me," he shrugged. "They have Sylvester." Damn straight!

The man who would be crowned "The Queen of Disco" wore sequined hotpants and a mess of wildly patterned scarves and bling. When Sylvester performed, anything went. One time my sisters backed him at a show in a Castro District warehouse where live chickens roamed the stage, a man jumped through a flaming hoop, and male and female streakers ran up and down the aisles. It was quite the spectacle.

It was through my friendship with Sylvester that I got to see and experience the gay community up close and meet a lot of sweet, tender human beings who'd been cut off from their families and society in general. One in particular went by the name of Pristine Condition, who was a member of the San Francisco psychedelic theatre troupe called The Cockettes. He loved us to death. Thank God it's better today, but I still see a lot of that, and it bothers me no end. It's no secret the gay community has always rallied around and supported The Pointer Sisters, and they are, by God, family to us. The Good Lord loves all His children and created us all equal. As a Christian I think it's flat-out wrong to condemn homosexuals, most of whom are just as moral and decent as you and me. It especially nauseates me when I hear that tired old raggedy-ass line, "Love the sinner, but hate the sin." It's hypocritical and an ugly part of organized religion that I don't like and can't abide at all. God is so much bigger than that.

He doesn't want any of our children to suffer, be condemned, or be separated from their families. Even though our society has evolved and moved forward in our acceptance of the gay community, we've not *fully* evolved. I'd like to see that happen in my lifetime. I wish Sylvester had. He died of AIDS in 1988. God rest his beautiful, untamed soul.

In early 1972, Bill Graham and David Rubinson parted ways, and The Pointer Sisters followed David to his new production company, David Rubinson & Friends. He signed them to Blue Thumb Records, a Beverly Hills–based record label founded by Bob Krasnow, Tommy LiPuma, and Don Graham. While they were an independent label, Blue Thumb had some street cred with a roster featuring acts such as Ike & Tina Turner, Captain Beefhart, Buddy Guy, Albert Collins, Dave Mason, T. Rex, and Dan Hicks & The Hot Licks.

I don't even recollect the circumstances of when I first sang for David, but he once told a reporter, "Ruth came in, sang a low A, and I just went out of my mind." He immediately proposed to make the Pointer trio a quartet, even though at the time most successful girl groups came in triplicate—The Supremes, The Ronettes, and Martha Reeves and the Vandellas. I was 26 years old, and really didn't have anything to lose. I had two kids to support and no husband and was living mostly on my meager income and whatever Uncle Sam decided to kick in. Singing was something I loved and that came naturally to me. So when my sisters asked me to join them permanently, it was a no-brainer. In December 1972, I tendered my resignation at Pacific Far East Lines and officially joined The Pointer Sisters.

Within six months the Welfare Queen would give up her throne for a new title: Pop Princess.

CHAPTER FOUR

Yes We Can Can (And Did Did)

You've heard that old cliché about how get-ting to the top in showbiz is actually much easier than the precipitous fall from the mountaintop? It happens to be true. In the case of the fabulous Pointer Sisters, it took only about six months for us to reach the summit. The man who took us there was our fearless manager, David Rubinson.

Some people made the big mistake of underestimating David when they saw his long ponytail, bushy beard, T-shirts, denim coveralls, and leather. But David's intelligence, unwavering faith, and uncanny vision made him truly special. Street-smart, well-educated (he had a college degree in literature), business-savvy, and cultured, David was the first man I ever met who made me think differently. I guess I'm a fine one to talk about judging a book by its cover, because before I met and got to know David, whenever I saw a white person I figured that was the sum and substance of him—you know, what you see is what you get. I had no notion of different nation-alities and knew virtually nothing about the world outside of the Bay Area. David taught me that white people could be Russian, German, Hebrew, Irish, Italian, Scandinavian, and so forth. I had always been an inward thinker. That's how I grew up. David opened my eyes to question my small thinking and how it limited my worldly view. Most of all, he taught me to open the scope of my ambitions and my dreams. He pushed each of us to transcend ourselves beyond the physical and intellectual borders we knew and subsequently confined ourselves to, and drove home that there was an entire universe out there waiting to hear what The Pointer Sisters had to offer. He gave us a worldly education that a university could never offer and money couldn't buy.

David stressed, first and foremost, longevity in the business. It would have been the easy move to push four black women from the ghetto into a rhythm and blues and funk/soul slot, but David instinctively sensed there was more to us. In the beginning we had no one to imitate or base our act on. We really weren't intimate with The Andrews Sisters, McGuire Sisters, or Billie Holiday, so we just started scatting stuff here and there. The rhythm and blues we were later exposed to became only one of the many musical styles we were influenced by; in addition to gospel, there was country, pop, jazz, and post-psychedelic rock. We listened to everything: Stevie Wonder, Marvin Gaye, Isley Brothers, Gladys Knight and the Pips, Laura Nyro, Jimi Hendrix, Crosby Stills, Aretha Franklin, Donny Hathaway, Roberta Flack, Sly and the Family Stone, Isaac Hayes, James Brown, Nash & Young, Ike & Tina Turner, The Supremes, Ashford & Simpson, Martha Reeves and the Vandellas, Bobby Womack, Wilson Pickett, James Taylor, Joe Cocker, The Temptations, Howlin' Wolf, and John Lee Hooker. We loved it if it was good. To David, we were musically a blank canvas, and that suited him just fine. He wanted us to sing as many styles as possible in order to reach the widest audience possible. Jazz happened to be a particular passion of his, and as a group, we were only too willing to delve into the catalogs of performers like Lambert, Hendricks & Ross, King Pleasure, Allen Toussaint, and The Swingle Singers.

Without a doubt, David was totally responsible for making The Pointer Sisters who we were. He was our savior, our flag bearer, and our protector. He pumped about $100,000 of his own money into the act and even bought my parents their first color television set. That sort of generosity went a long way with us.

We plain loved the man—but that doesn't mean that every now and then we didn't feel like slapping the taste out of his mouth. Like most producers, David possessed a Svengali-type of personality and practically defined the term "control freak." He had a mercurial, hair-trigger temper; a sharp tongue; and a brusque manner. And sometimes when things didn't go to his liking, he would rearrange the furniture in his office by picking it up and throwing it. He was under a lot of pressure, and I'm sure our casual attitude and bohemian lifestyle didn't sit well with him.

He put us on a $50 a week allowance, made us take tap dance lessons, and was constantly on our cases to rehearse—which consisted of endlessly singing our songs as we sat around the pool table in David's office, accompanied by a piano player, Norman Landsberg, in the corner. There was one time when Norman was trying to teach us the famous "Salt Peanuts" number by Dizzy Gillespie and demanding that we learn it note by crazy note. When we said that was ridiculous, he gave us grief about our "attitudes." Not long after that Dizzy Gillespie himself came to town, and David invited him to the office where we were rehearsing "Salt Peanuts" with Norman. We were ecstatic to meet this jazz giant and took the opportunity to ask Dizzy about the notes for "Salt Peanuts." His response was to burst out laughing. When he could talk again he said, "Have you lost your god-damn minds? That song is probably different every time I play it. It's the spirit, not the notes!" We all glared at Norman and said, "See!"

I remember singing "Yes We Can Can," "Cloudburst," and "Wang Dang Doodle" until we were all blue in the face. More often than not, by the time those endless sessions finally concluded we'd be swigging from a liquor bottle and passing around a reefer to break up the monotony. David did not join in. He was what I would call a "clean hippie." No drugs, no excess, no bullshit, all business.

"What the hell do you think is going on?!" he'd scream when he felt we weren't serious enough. "This ain't no game! We got to get down to business and do it right or not at all!"

I wasn't much of a fan of his yelling at us like we were children, but I can't say I blame him for getting upset. It was his wallet on the table (he fronted the money for our first recording sessions to the tune of about $35,000), and he needed us to deliver the goods to Blue Thumb. "Get hot or go home!" was a frequent phrase used in the music industry, and more often than not you get only one shot at it, if you're lucky. David knew we all needed to be in top form vocally, mentally, and physically.

David did enjoy having a fine wine with his meals, but I never saw him get bent out of shape or loaded. Lord knows we sure gave him a good excuse to get that way. No matter how loudly he screamed and tried to control our behavior, it was hopeless. One strait-laced white dude versus four rebellious, high-spirited, hard-partying black women was a flaming mismatch from the get-go. But God love him, he was a glutton for punishment and always came back for more.

About the only thing David didn't try to control was how we dressed, which was just as well because we were so broke we picked up most of our wardrobe at secondhand shops and thrift stores. David actually loved our look and encouraged us to wear our vintage 1940s threads on the upcoming album cover. The results were stunning thanks to the superb photography of Herb Greene, who was a major player in the '60s San Francisco art scene. His exceptional portraits of The Grateful Dead, Led Zeppelin, Janis Joplin, Carlos Santana, Sly Stone, Jeff Beck, and many others created an astonishing family album for an entire generation.

We spent an entire day with Herb in his Haight Street studio, taking the now iconic cover photo of us in our retro-chic garb and hats. Getting the four of us to sit still for the shoot must have been like herding cats for Herb, but he was a terrific sport during the entire photo session and made it fun.

The girls and I pooled our money to rent a condominium in an Oakland suburb close to a prison facility. Our transportation to and from San Francisco was a red Audi, but it should have been bright yellow because that sucker was a lemon through and through. It never ran smoothly and stopped and started whenever it felt like it. It shook, rattled, and rolled throughout the Bay Area, and our trips became even more touch-and-go after Anita and I, the only licensed drivers, took the wheel. We both started wearing contact lenses at the same time and couldn't see worth a damn. Until we adjusted to the lenses, it was like the blind leading the blind.

But you know what? Those were damned good times for The Pointer Sisters. No matter what happened, we were all together, in it together, and we lived and sang as one. Everything that happened, good and bad, brought us closer and made us stronger.

Vocally, I knew my place. I might've been the oldest sister, but I was the newest member of the group. It wasn't lost on me that I hadn't paid a fraction of the dues my siblings had in the years before I joined the group. The last thing I wanted was for it to look and sound like I had come aboard to commandeer the ship. More than once in those early days I opted out of an opportunity to sing lead and deferred to one of my vocally talented and charismatic sisters. I felt my time would come if I hung in there long enough. The others had been doing it for a long time and deserved to be up front. I was just happy to have a seat at the table and a spot at the microphone.

To their credit, the executives at Blue Thumb did not repeat the mistake Atlantic made of trying to model The Pointer Sisters after other contemporary acts like Honey Cone or The Jackson 5. David was involved in every aspect of our debut album (he had been a gifted engineer before he became a producer) and meticulously planned it to the utmost detail. He booked us to record at Pacific Recording Studio in San Francisco in the autumn of 1972. One of the first songs we cut was the basic track for the Allen Toussaint–penned "Yes We Can Can." The socially conscious song was a musical vow to make the world a better place and had been originally recorded in 1970 as "Yes We Can" by Lee Dorsey. I had always enjoyed Lee's version, which had a New Orleans style tinge. We sped it up and gave it an R & B/funk flavor with a drum- and bass-driven sound. Anita took lead vocal while Bonnie, June, and I provided the tight harmonies and showcased our tongue twisting talents to the fullest. I knew the song was good but had no idea it would turn out to be our first big hit in the summer of 1973. (When Barack Obama used the slogan "Yes We Can" for his 2008 presidential campaign, we half expected and hoped to get a call requesting permission to adopt "Yes We Can Can" as his official campaign song. What would have been more natural? But it didn't happen, and messages we sent to the Obama folks went nowhere. Too bad.)

Years later I heard that David had shopped our demo of this song to several labels and Blue Thumb was the first to bite. I may well have known it at the time, but to be pain- fully honest, my memories of those days are hazy on account of all the drinking and drugging with which I celebrated our quick success. Writing this memoir has actually forced me to research and rediscover The Pointer Sisters' history all over again. I've had to rekindle and reacquaint myself with some unpleasant memories and situations, as well as the other kind, but I want to set the record straight now before some stranger does it for me.

For reasons still murky to me, after we cut that first track David switched recording locales to Wally Heider Studios at

245 Hyde Street, between Turk and Eddy Streets. The build-ing had been occupied by 20ᵗʰ Century Fox for film offices, screening rooms, and storage until Heider transformed it in 1969 into one of the hippest recording studios in the country. It quickly attracted attention in the rock world, and Jefferson Airplane, Harry Nilsson, Crosby, Stills, Nash & Young, Creedence Clearwater Revival, and the Steve Miller Band were among the top acts that recorded there. It was at the Grateful Dead's request that the studio doors were covered in the airbrush paintings that announced the building's hipness. The biggest thrill for me was seeing band equipment stacked in the hallways that belonged to Sly and the Family Stone, Santana, and Herbie Hancock. It signaled to me that The Pointer Sisters were being taken seriously.

I don't know if it was the new studio, the vibes, or, frankly, the weed, but those were some of the most magical days of our lives. The songs, the arrangements, the trademark har-monies, the complex vocal moves, and interactions with the musicians on the sessions—it all seemed to come together and naturally fall into place. My low register laid the foundation; Bonnie added the brassy tone, Anita taking the alto-soprano role, and June, the soprano falsetto. Together our wide range and nicely stacked harmony blended naturally. Many times we only needed to rehearse a song for about an hour before we put it on tape, and often achieved a master vocal in just three to four takes. But some of the songs, like "Cloudburst," were difficult, requiring hours of study in order to be done in four-part harmony and always with the understanding that it would have to be duplicated live.

We were singing a variety of highly complex material that was polished to near perfection, mixing R & B ("Wang Dang Doodle") with bebop ("Cloudburst"), boogie-blues ("Jada"), and mid-tempo light rock ("River Boulevard") to form an eclectic, energetic, and joyous style that would come to define our sound. No tricks, just carefully arranged, excitingly performed, damned good singing.

Back then, the musicians and artists were uniquely woven together most of the time. We would usually all come in together and lay down a track because they wanted the energy we provided and vice versa. After a take, we would emerge from the vocal booth and the musicians from the separate studio where they'd play, as sweaty and exhausted as if we'd just come off a handball court. Sometimes the spirit got so high the musicians would play something completely out of context or just improvise a note or a riff, or we would sing something not on the page, and the results were awesome. Those days were more inspired and less mechanical than today. I so miss that.

With *The Pointer Sisters* album in the can and set for a May 1973 release, it was time to pay some attention to how we looked. On our tight budget, designer costumes were not an option. We had always shopped at secondhand stores, not only because it was cheap, but also because all of us had that sort of old jitterbug, Chicago-nightclub spirit running through our veins and enjoyed dressing that way as well. We bought vintage gowns, waist-cinching jackets, wigs, teardrop wool hats, boa feathers, cocktail jewels, high heels, and chic hankies, which was and still is our trademark. We camped it up big-time and were more than a little surprised when our style soon set the trend.

It was not a reflection on our look that we made our first public appearance at a swanky San Francisco landmark called Bimbo's on Columbus Avenue. Decked out in art deco, red velvet, and chandeliers, Bimbo's was a former speakeasy and after-hours gambling club built in the 1930s. Owner Agostino "Bimbo" Giuntoli was an Italian immigrant who arrived in America in 1922 with just $2 in his pocket. He labored as a janitor and cook at the Palace Hotel and started to build his American Dream. Bimbo made his club a first-class entertainment venue with jugglers, dance troupes, stand-up comedians, and chorus lines. Film star Rita Hayworth got her start there.

Rita probably did a hell of a lot better than we did in her first performance at Bimbo's. We were flat-out awful that night. We all had the jitters so bad I'm surprised we got through a single song. But Bimbo either liked us anyway or just felt sorry enough for us that he gave us a second try, and we were much better.

On May 5, 1973, we played at a small theatre-dance hall in San Francisco called The Village. It was another dress rehearsal, unpublicized and largely unnoticed. In other words, there was a noticeable absence of asses in the seats. But that turned out to actually be a good thing because our live act had a lot of kinks to be worked out. For one thing, we didn't pay enough attention to how our backup band was dressed. One of the members took to the stage wearing a hooded white robe that made him look like he'd just come from a Ku

Klux Klan meeting. We half expected him to set a cross on fire during intermission.

I actually blew my voice out that night by singing too hard. Though I'd been singing my whole life, I really wasn't aware of how to use my voice and breathe properly. So I cut loose for all I was worth, and as a result I could hardly even talk, much less sing, for the next few days.

Ten days later I needed my voice at its best because that's when The Pointer Sisters got the biggest break of our career—singing as a fill-in at the famous Troubadour in Los Angeles on May 15.

How it happened was that David Rubinson, who also managed Herbie Hancock at the time, found out that Herbie's opening act, pop-soul singer Ronnie Dyson, was canceling his scheduled performance that night at the last minute. I never did find out why Ronnie had to cancel that night, but he's in my daily prayers for it to this very day.

"I'm putting my girls in there," David told Troubadour owner Doug Weston, who took it more calmly than we did at first. But it was a huge break, and we decided not to let our lack of experience or anything else daunt us. June, Bonnie, Anita, and I would go out there, strut our stuff, sing our butts off and see what happened.

Like ol' Colonel Sanders used to say, we were flat-out finger lickin' good. Our own special recipe of hot scat, rock, jazz, and bebop had the packed house jumping and hollering for a solid hour and demanding multiple encores. I'd go so far as to say that L.A. had never seen or heard anything quite like us before.

Diana Ross and Helen Reddy were in the house that night with their husbands, Bob Ellis Silberstein and entertainment manager Jeff Wald. They came backstage to tell us how blown away they were by our performance, and Wald promptly booked us for four performances on Helen's network TV summer replacement variety show. A critic gave us a fantastic review in the next issue of *Newsweek* magazine, and we were truly off to the races.

We not only did *The Helen Reddy Show* a handful of times but also performed on *The Flip Wilson Show*, *The Carol Burnett Show*, and the *Cher* show. We performed an epic dance medley of songs from the big band/swing era with Cher, actress Teri Garr, and comedian Freddie Prinze, which was later nominated for an Emmy. The bookings came so fast that when Johnny Carson's people called to get us for *The Tonight Show*, we couldn't fit it in our schedule and David had to politely decline.

When *The Pointer Sisters* LP was released less than a month after our Troubador debut, Blue Thumb took out a full-page ad in *Billboard* announcing our arrival. The reviews were rapturous. Music critics raved about our versatility, range, and ability to dazzle. One called us "the most exciting thing to hit show business in years." Can I get a witness? Amen!

Later that summer "Yes We Can Can," reached the Top 10, and our follow-up single, Willie Dixon's "Wang Dang Doodle" (backed by the rowdy Hoodoo Rhythm Devils and featuring the scorching guitar work of John Rewind), also charted. By the time our album was certified gold (500,000 copies sold), The Pointer Sisters had toured the U.S.A. several times over (sharing a double bill with Chicago) and became the most talked-about act of the year. It wasn't long before fans started showing up in droves at our concerts wearing their own thrift-shop attire. They had themselves a ball singing and dancing along to our songs and routines.

After a performance at Roseland Dance City in New York, none other than R & B legend Stevie Wonder paid us a backstage visit, acting very flirty (mostly with Anita) and offering not only effusive praise, but to write songs with us. Eventually he came through with two numbers: "Sleeping Alone," which appeared on our 1975 album *Steppin',* and the jazzy "Bring Your Sweet Stuff Home" on 1977's *Having a Party.*

In Europe, folks like Rod Stewart, Ron Wood, the Kinks' Ray Davies, Traffic's Jim Capaldi, and Neil Sedaka all paid their respects as did jazz great Annie Ross, who was personally invited by David to "see what she had spawned." We dedicated "Little Pony" to her at our show in London, and she was near tears by the end of the song.

By the end of that tumultuous summer, The Pointer Sisters may not have been a household name like The Beatles or Speedy Alka Seltzer, but, as Bonnie famously quipped, we definitely were "the biggest thing to come out of Oakland since the Black Panthers."

I didn't give a hoot in hell about politics, but I was happy to give a black power fist pump to that sentiment.

CHAPTER FIVE

Fairy Tales and Financial Nightmares

FAME STRIKES, COMING OUT OF NOWHERE AT WARP speed sometimes. It doesn't really matter how long you've worked hard for it, planned for it; it still blindsides you. Struggling to make it big takes everything out of you. It's like pushing an imperfect stone up a steep hill. It's a cold, hard, relentless, exhausting climb. You have to stop, regroup, and find your mojo to deal with that one step forward, two steps back thing. You just never feel like you are truly getting anywhere, although somewhere inside you know that you are.

But then something happens, a pivotal moment when something inside of you transcends the struggles. You begin to notice the summit, and you find renewed strength within yourself to keep pushing until you get there. When you do, you look out and it seems that the world is yours. Every valley you trudged through, cried through, fought through now lies beneath your secondhand heels. Your world becomes redefined. The you that you used to know becomes riddled with the pride of success, a false sense of security, and the knowledge that you can make it if you push your body hard enough up that mountain. And then the high hits you like a lack of oxygen at its peak. For me that high lasted years, messing with my head as crevasses threatened to trip me up. I often found myself tumbling down the backside, sometimes just barely hanging on with my fingertips along the edge, ready to fall, with the illusion that there was something warm and cushiony ready to pick me up and carry me to safety. In reality, you snowball down that mountain, with little to break your fall through the forest canopy of fame and addiction. It slowly and painfully breaks you.

I began losing myself in drugs, alcohol, and parties pretty much from the start. Everything was happening at rocket speed once we hit. People were everywhere, many terrible influences, and it was open season on the superstar. Nobody wants to admit how impressionable she is, especially when you're an adult who thinks she is grown up with pretty good street sense. The Pointer Sisters were on the road so much, there was hardly any time to reflect and get centered. I was being shoved along, going with the flow, getting deeper and deeper into hard partying. Everybody was doing it. It was like you were the odd person out if you didn't get blazed, drunk, or worse. I had been the strange one—the odd duck, the preacher's daughter—for so many years, and I didn't want to be the strange one anymore. So I did what everybody else did to fit in. I also did whatever it took to keep the train a-rolling, sometimes at great personal sacrifice.

But at the time, it didn't matter. The gravy train kept rolling in as fast as I threw it out.

The Tonight Show folks kept pushing to have us on, and finally we settled on a date. One week before the show I had to have emergency surgery for a ruptured cyst that had to come out along with one of my ovaries. I walked out of the hospital in San Francisco and was driven straight to the airport for a flight to Burbank. When I got to NBC Studios I wondered why I'd bothered, because Johnny Carson wasn't hosting that night. Bob Newhart was subbing for him. He was a very nice man, but not the "King of Late Night TV." For the taping, I performed sitting on a stool with the stitches still in my abdomen and my hospital band around my wrist.

If it sounds like I'm jaded or not very starry-eyed, that's certainly not the case. Being able to make a living doing what you love is the ultimate fantasy for anybody, but behind that fantasy are misconceptions. It's not only lonely at the top, but it's also lonely on the road. The high point of each 24-hour day was the 60–75 minutes spent on the stage. Everything else was more or less drudgery. There was lots of air and bus travel and plenty of interviews, radio station promotions, and hotels (we got very familiar with the Holiday Inn chain), and somewhere along the line you had to find time to eat and sleep. The last two were low priorities. So, by the way, was privacy.

Despite the rocket-ride to stardom and our high public profile, we played a lot of strange places and stayed in a lot of joints for which the word "dump" would be a compliment. We embarked on our first tour in rented station wagons with tour manager Linda Rogoff and roadie Marc Vogel. We only had four pieces of luggage, and one case for our wardrobe. We developed a system to alternate whose clothes were going to be on the bottom; and whoever had their clothes on the bottom had to do some serious ironing when they got to the hotel.

Our first stop on the two-shows-a-night tour was The Cellar Door in Washington, D.C. We were booked to stay at a place called the Harrington. It was not exactly a fleabag, but it wasn't the lap of luxury, either. We had two rooms with just a single bed in each one, which meant we would have to double up—something we hadn't done since we were kids. While we were grumbling about that to one another, our roadie Marc, a very large guy who wore an oversized cowboy hat and didn't mince words about anything, was getting into it with the hotel staff because nobody seemed very interested in taking our luggage up to our rooms. Things got so intense that we ended up getting back into our cars and looking for different lodging before things got out of hand. On top of that our hired wardrobe girl, Stephanie, started crying and decided that she couldn't do the job and went home. It didn't seem like a rosy start to our tour, but we found a really cute place called the Royal Dutch Inn off the beaten path in nearby Jamestown, Virginia. It was a quaint modern-style inn with a very gracious and accommodating staff we liked so much that every time we had a show in the nation's capital we made it a point to stay at the Royal Dutch and always looked forward to it. One time I accidentally left behind a favorite jacket of mine, and when we returned the following year, it was waiting for me. They had kept it in storage, and the jacket even still had a dried flower corsage in the lapel.

Our opening act at The Cellar Door was comedian Martin Mull. Over the years we've given many comedians wide exposure. In addition to Mull, Roseanne Barr, Arsenio Hall, Ellen DeGeneres, Sinbad, and Byron Allen have opened for us. The Pointer Sisters were big fans of Mull and thought he was hilarious, but his cerebral humor didn't go over with our crowds. How do I say this properly? They were a little bit more street and urban than what Martin had in mind if you know what I mean. Under the terms of his contract Martin was obligated to spend at least 20 minutes on stage, and at one of the midnight shows as soon as his time was up he ran off after what had been a very rough outing. The promoter sitting backstage hadn't fully understood the dynamics of the situation, but he did hear the tumultuous applause as Mull fled into the wings.

"Hear that?" he shouted at Martin. "They love you! Get back out there!"

"No, no," gasped Mull, sweating bullets. "You don't understand—it's my *exit* they're applauding!"

The promoter turned Mull around and shoved him back out for an encore. As poor Martin got to the footlights, a woman in the front row glared at her male companion and said in a voice loud enough to be heard out on the street, "I told you not to clap so loud!"

From Washington, D.C. we made the trek to Boston's Paul Mall in a blizzard. After the show, we discovered our band's coats had been stolen and they had to walk back to the hotel in the freezing cold and were shivering by the time we got to the lobby. It put a bad taste in our mouths for Beantown for several years. From there we played at the famed Continental Baths in New York (where we cemented our bond with our gay followers). After that we headlined at Mr. Kelly's in Chicago, got stiffed by the owner, and were forced to sue to get our money. We sure played some shady places and paid serious dues in those early days.

There are so many things you don't know when you get into this business, and a lot of people in this industry are not hesitant at all to take advantage of your ignorance. We had plenty of that. We figured that our growing celebrity entitled us to plenty of freebies—limos, hotel rooms, champagne, clothes, jewelry. But everything has a price tag of one kind or another. It wasn't unusual to find out that in addition to paying for things we thought were on the house, there was a special "celebrity tax" tacked on. One time a "dry cleaner to the stars" who'd gotten a fabulous write-up in *Vogue* magazine charged us $1,200 for cleaning 15 dresses. We had to sue him to get a more reasonable deal.

If I'm leaving the impression that we spent lots of time poring over contracts and invoices, tapping calculator keys, and consulting lawyers and accountants, that's my bad. We were too busy living it up and thinking it was all on somebody else's dime. We cleaned out many a mini-bar and ordered room service whenever we felt like it. We went on some shopping sprees that put Imelda Marcos to shame. On those occasions we usually told our road manager, Linda Rogoff, to whip out the plastic and charge everything to David. I suppose it was our juvenile way of "sticking it to the man," but it was just another thing that came back to bite us in the ass. David was our friend and manager, but he was nobody's fool. His 20 percent management fee came right off the top of what we were paid. That was free-and-clear income for David. The remaining 80 percent sounds like a lot until you factor in all the bills and overhead that were our responsibility, not David's. Anything left had to be divided four ways. We weren't sticking it to him, but to ourselves.

Often as not I'd come home from the road and have no money—literally none—because I had spent it all whooping it up and living the high life.

Here's how bad it got: when we did our Las Vegas show at the Mirage years later, we had to actually take out a loan to pay for everything we needed—including new costumes, dancers, musicians, a stage director, a choreographer, a PR firm, ramps, hydraulic lifts, smoke, and lasers. You don't go to a thrift store with a list like that. And every cent came out of our end of the purse.

Show business is also very hard on personal relationships, and I have the five marriages to prove it. My relationship with Carl Abram, my second husband, was going just fine until success entered the equation. Carl was there for me when I was escaping the clutches of my first husband, Larry Woods, offering an abundance of love and protection that I sorely needed at the time. We were tight and had a good thing going until The Pointer Sisters exploded.

Carl was friendly with Lenny Williams, the lead vocalist for Tower of Power. They used to sing together in high school, so he wasn't totally unfamiliar with the music scene and intimately knew the ups and downs of the business. Carl hadn't been nuts about me joining my sisters in the group when they initially approached me.

"Don't count your chickens before they hatch," he warned when I first broached the idea.

"Well, I did some sessions and made some nice money," I reminded him. "It's much easier than my current job, and now we have a record deal. I think I'm going to give it a shot."

"Your sisters aren't doing *that* great," Carl sneered. "Besides, I still pay enough of the bills to be the boss around here."

It was the early '70s, and the women's lib movement was chugging right along—if you were a white chick, anyway. That "I am woman, hear me roar" stuff didn't go over so big in the hood. The dude was the breadwinner and the boss; in addition to that mindset, I think Carl was worried about losing me to another man if The Pointer Sisters took off. When we did make it big, Carl began to resent that I wasn't around so much for him—and to *really* resent the kicks I was having on the road.

When people made a fuss over me, Carl would put me down or say or do something idiotic to call attention to himself. I'd take him on press junkets, to studio sessions, and backstage on TV shows, and he'd embarrass me or just get pissed off and act like it was all an inconvenience. Sometimes he'd just stay in our hotel room and watch TV while I did my thing, and eventually I started preferring that arrangement myself. I think it also boiled down to that Carl was scared to death of becoming known as "Mr. Pointer," and that would be a tough pill for any man to swallow.

But there were more important considerations. Shortly after Carl and I got married in November 1973, I became pregnant. The Pointer Sisters were riding the crest of our first wave of fame; we were in the midst of recording our second album, planning a live recording at the San Francisco Opera House, our first Las Vegas engagement, and a musical festival in Zaire, Africa. We were booked solid for the entire year, and at that time I felt that I had no time for a child. I sure as hell didn't want to be the one responsible for stalling The Pointer Sisters' momentum by going on maternity leave. I told Carl I wanted an abortion. He was against it, but I was adamant.

Carl rode with me to the hospital where the pregnancy was terminated. He cried the entire way. Not one tear fell from my eyes.

The show must go on, right?

David pulled out all the stops for The Pointer Sisters' sophomore effort. A collection of vintage pop, swing, jazz, R & B, and country songs, the album *That's a Plenty* continued us in the jazz-baby élan/schmaltzy/high-camp direction he had mapped out. I went along with some reservations. The new songs just didn't move me. Believe it or not, the main criticism aimed at The Pointer Sisters in the early stages of our career was that we didn't sound "black" enough. I hate to say it, but there was more than an ounce of truth in that, which is why we made sure to do lots of benefits in and for the African American community. We did shows for the NAACP in Los Angeles, Operation Human Kindness in Washington, D.C., and the Urban League in San Francisco.

What concerned me musically was that we were so enmeshed in using our voices as musical instruments, offering up an array of styles and avoiding getting labeled, that we lost focus on what made us so effective as sisters—rocking hard and singing deep from the soul.

I could understand David's point of view. He wanted to stick with a formula that had most certainly worked for us. It succeeded and generated money. That sound and image he pushed established us, but I didn't want it to strictly define us then and forever. My fear was that if it was already getting stale for me, the public would eventually feel the same way about it.

But I was a team player and chose not to rock the boat (that would occur much later on). What the heck—there was no doubting that from a show business standpoint David was a freaking genius. The nostalgia razzamatazz appealed to the masses and certainly made us stand out from the other musical acts of the day. Besides, it wasn't like we were butchering the material David selected for us. In fact, we were tearing it up and hit our stride in the studio.

Those particular sessions, recorded in San Francisco, Los Angeles, and Nashville, featured two-dozen musicians, many of them famous in their own right. They included Herbie Hancock, Jesse Ed Davis, David Briggs, Harry "Sweets" Edison, and Ron McClure. A white girl with a mane of flaming red hair named Bonnie Raitt played slide guitar on the number "Grinnin' In Your Face." Bonnie was super cool, and it turned out that she was the daughter of Broadway musical star John Raitt (*Oklahoma*, *The Pajama Game*) and pianist Marjorie Haydock. So she came by her amazing musical chops honestly, although she played that bottleneck guitar like she was channeling the greatest black blues masters of all time.

That's a Plenty was even more diverse than our debut album, delved further into our multiplicity and inventiveness of musical styles, and included songs by Duke Ellington, Dizzy Gillespie, and Peggy Lee. (Bonnie sang Peggy Lee's "Black Coffee" on the album and in our live show. It was as if she channeled the spirit of Billie Holiday. She just killed that song.) Over the years lots of fans have told us this is their favorite Blue Thumb release. The cover introduced the iconic Pointer Sisters logo, which depicted four silhouetted figurines on bended knee, pointing a finger. In this case, our fingers were pointed toward another gold album, my personal misgivings about the material notwithstanding.

The album demonstrated our vocal virtuosity and sonic savoir-faire. It also showcased our famous array of musical styles—but this time, there was one difference: nestled between the finger-snapping jazz of "Little Pony" and the moody scat of "Black Coffee" was a bona-fide country-western tune, "Fairytale," written by my sisters Anita and Bonnie. It became The Pointer Sisters' second Top 20 hit and garnered us our first Grammy in 1975 for Best Country Performance by a Group or Duo. Bonnie and Anita also earned a Songwriter of the Year nomination. A year later, Elvis Presley covered "Fairytale" on his album *Elvis Today*. He performed it in concert right up to his death, and often introduced it as "the story of his life." No one was prouder of my two sisters than me.

David had us record the song at Quadraphonic Studios in Nashville and arranged to have us backed up by some of the best musicians in town: David Briggs (piano), Norbert Putnam (bass), Weldon Myrick (pedal steel guitar), Ken Buttrey (drums), Robert Thompson (acoustic guitar), and Norman Spicher (fiddle). "Fairytale"'s out-of-left-field success made us the toast of Music City. Thanks to it we were invited to sing at the Grand Ole Opry later that year—making us the first black female act to perform at "The Mother Church" of country music. Everything about that trip was memorable, beginning with the plane ride to Nashville from L.A. We were the only African Americans on board, and our presence clearly made more than a few of the white passengers uncomfortable, including the woman in the seat next to mine. She maintained a stony silence throughout the flight and made sure I wouldn't contaminate her by constantly arranging herself and her clothes so that nothing came into direct contact with me.

When the plane landed and we walked into the Nashville airport a battalion of paparazzi rushed up to take our pictures. Ms. Tight-Ass, walking ahead of us, wheeled around and demanded to know what all the fuss was about. I politely told her we were The Pointer Sisters, and she actually said, "Well, if I'd known y'all were *somebody*, I'd've talked to ya!"

When we took the Opry stage there was an older gentleman dressed in a cowboy hat, checkered shirt, and blue jeans sitting in the front whose eyes almost bugged out of his head. "Hot damn!" he shouted. "Them gals is *black*...sing it again!" And we did. We sang "Fairytale" in its entirety once more. That was a first. Those country people don't play!

After the show there was a party scheduled in our honor at a private residence. When we arrived the man who greeted us at the door led us around back into the kitchen, where we sat for 45 minutes. We could hear people partying in the living room and wondered when someone was going to come get us so we could partake in the festivities. Finally David showed up, red-faced and furious, and we found out what was going on. Because we were black, the person who'd answered the door had automatically assumed we were there as hired help and led us to the back door. David went ballistic and marched us out of there, but my sisters and I just laughed and shrugged it off. It took a lot more than Southern-fried stupidity to get us riled up. That wasn't the first time we had come face to face with racism, and it sure wouldn't be the last.

And it wasn't confined to the Old South. We had been denied service in motels and been pointedly ignored by waitresses in restaurants plenty of times.

One memorable night when we were on tour with the rock group Chicago in 1974, the manager of the bar at a Kansas City hotel we were all staying at refused to serve us. They asked us for more than two forms of identification, which we provided, and they still refused. We just politely told the cracker to blow it out his ass, but the fellows in Chicago indicated their displeasure by totally wrecking their rooms. TV sets were tossed out the window into the swimming pool, furniture was nailed to the ceiling, and when they checked out the next morning the walls of the guys' rooms had even more holes in them literally than there were figuratively in the head of that moron bar manager.

In April of '74, we recorded our first and only live double album at the War Memorial Opera House in San Francisco. It was another milestone for The Pointer Sisters as we were the first contemporary act to perform in the building that was built in 1932 by architect Arthur Brown Jr. The event was sold out three weeks in advance, and the tuxedoed and evening-gowned audience paid $10 a head to get in. We were backed by a 36-piece orchestra under the musical direction of the handsome and talented Tom Salisbury, who was also our pianist.

What was really special about that night was that our folks and our 83-year-old grandmother, Roxie Silas, saw us perform for the very first time. When the limo pulled into the driveway to take them to the venue, Grandma Roxie—who'd never taken a limo drive before—sat on the floor and put her

feet up on the seat. My mom tried to help Grandma Roxie
up but didn't have much luck because they were both laughing hysterically. They got tangled up and spilled out onto the
ground. We saw them and almost fell over laughing ourselves.
It was one of the funniest sights I've ever seen in my life.
When they finally got to the venue, Grandma was so excited
as she took her seat she told Mom, "Hold my legs down,
child, otherwise I'll be jumping up and down all night!"

The show commenced with a seven-minute instrumen-
tal called "Overture: Prelude to Islandia," composed by Tom
Salisbury. We hit the stage prancing one at a time like runway
models, carefully disarming ourelves of furs, hats, feather boas,
and gloves, placing them on an antique coat rack that was a
staple on our set at the time. It was crazy sexy, as we took our
places at the four standing microphones. We launched into a
hypersonic interpretation of Dizzy Gillespie's "Salt Peanuts."
We didn't let up for the next 75 minutes. We ended the night
with a faultless a capella and people standing on their feet
and cheering.

It was without a doubt the greatest night of our professional lives. *Live at the Opera House* was released later that
fall. If I can toot my own horn, it remains an awe-inspiring,
indispensible recording of four sisters in their prime.

Around that time Carl and I were able to rent a home
in Sausalito, as did Anita. Bonnie and June upgraded their
digs as well but opted to remain in San Francisco. Even more
satisfying, all four of us sisters chipped in to buy our parents
a home in picturesque Novato, about 30 miles north of San
Francisco in Marin County. The four-bedroom home enabled
everyone—my parents, Faun, Malik, and Anita's daughter,

Jada—to live under one roof. My hope was that Faun and Malik were finally going to have some stability in their lives after years of being uprooted and moved around.

Ever since Dad's ouster from the Church of God, my mother had worked full-time as a janitor in a public library to help make ends meet. Even more than the personal drama and substance abuse issues in my life, the toughest thing to endure at that time was watching our parents spend their "golden years" working themselves to the bone and living in virtual poverty. To buy them a decent place to live was one of the most satisfying and personally fulfilling things we ever did.

I'll tell you what else was very satisfying. Now that we were The World Famous Pointer Sisters, the same ungrateful folks at the Church of God in Oakland who'd sent Dad packing actually had the nerve to ask if we would do a benefit show to raise money for the congregation. The Bible instructs us to turn the other cheek, but I don't think it's the one I told those holier-than-thou hypocrites to kiss when they came sucking up to us. God Almighty, it felt great!

Everything felt great. It seemed that The Pointer Sisters could do no wrong. Which brings us to another relevant biblical injunction, this one from Proverbs 16:18:

"Pride goeth before destruction, and a haughty spirit before a fall."

CHAPTER SIX

Lead Us Not into Temptation

YOU KNOW THAT KING OF THE MOUNTAIN STUFF I was rapping about last chapter? Well, it sure didn't take long for the Pointer Sisters to head down the other side of that mother, head over heels.

Pride is a dangerous commodity. And in the music business, that's what it is—a commodity. It's bought and sold, used and abused; it's guaranteed to make money, and it's guaranteed to leave you more than arrogant.

It's the you that you leave behind to lighten your load as you trek up that mountain where the views from the top are both magnificent and perilous, reserved for an elect few. You get to look down at the rest of the world, and for a moment you sigh, soaking it all in, feeling blessed until you realize that you've shed the things you've held dear in life: your morals, your values, your family and friends.

Suddenly you're unsettled, but stuck, with nowhere to go but down when your pride of accomplishment becomes enticingly wrapped in the smell of green, the taste of booze, and the lines you cross in the white dust.

Then it becomes impossible to breathe where the air messes with your head and where the truth of justification is rare. There's little sweetness in the pride that slips into that abyss. It's just a dark, self-serving entity that pushes you to your limits and where the fall can kill both your spirit and your body. But you don't see that when you're standing on top of that opulent mountain, where no man or beast can touch you.

We appeared infallible. But behind the scenes The Pointer Sisters were a dysfunctional bunch, and while we looked after each other, we had to cover for June a lot throughout our career. But it's what we knew. As I mentioned earlier, June's rape sparked a downward spiral whose magnitude the rest of us weren't hip to for years. She was also the baby of the family, which means that our mother and every one of her siblings went out of our way to protect and spoil her. It was a natural inclination but in hindsight clearly not the best thing for her damaged psyche. As a result, June's emotional maturity was stunted and she dealt with complex issues by reacting like a child. She'd withdraw, retreat, or just throw a tantrum until she got her way. I recall one time when she didn't like one of her stage dresses; she burned it in the hotel bathtub. When she was in that mindset, trying to reason with her was a fool's errand. As all-knowing and powerful as we thought David Rubinson was in those days, even he couldn't snap her out of it. Sometimes she'd become unreachable.

In hindsight, June was just 20 years old and probably bipolar. But even if we knew then what we suspect now, mental illness (or rape) wasn't something that was publicly—or privately—discussed, much less dealt with, the way it is now.

Our relentless touring and 12-hour workdays—not to mention all the extracurricular fun—really started to get to June. Her skeletal appearance (she was down to 90 pounds at one point) and increasingly detached attitude had us all worried. She had a history of nervous breakdowns, and the frenzied showbiz pace, along with our nonstop partying, took their toll. June was admitted to San Francisco's Mt. Zion Hospital several times. Then, just prior to our first stint at Caesars Palace in Las Vegas, June collapsed again—her third such episode in a year's time.

Our two-week engagement in Vegas came on the heels of a chaotic European tour and was our first grab at some real money: $100,000. That's a cool $1 million in today's dollars. That princely sum came in addition to complimentary hotel suites, executive chefs, limo service, the house orchestra, a 1,200-seat state-of-the-art showroom, and billing on the marquee towering over the famous Strip that read THE POINTER SISTERS in letters the size of a small person. Speaking of which, headlining the show at Caesars was Paul Anka, the 5'6" onetime teenage heartthrob and still a draw in Vegas.

A lot was riding on this gig for us, and everyone knew it. In hindsight, we were pushed and shoved into doing the Vegas thing, and managers will often make you feel like you're riding that train to glory and if you don't cooperate, your career will be wrecked. It was too soon for this kind of show, but none of us knew it at the time. June joined us in Vegas, but then announced that no way was she going to perform. She didn't even want to leave her suite. We begged, pleaded, cajoled, screamed, and threatened, but it was like talking to a deaf person. We went so far as to bring Mom to Vegas to try to coax June into cooperating. They spent hours alone in the suite, and when Mom came out she said calmly, "I'm taking my baby home." Her tone left no doubt that it wasn't up for debate. Mom knew there was more to June's issues than we could see at the time. I get it now, but I wasn't so wise then.

The hotel staff whisked Mom and June to the airport and they caught the next plane home. When they landed, June was admitted to Mt. Zion where she was officially diagnosed with nervous exhaustion. As Mom and June flew west, headed our way from Los Angeles toot-sweet were representatives of Gibson & Stromberg, our publicists, coming to handle damage control. They floated just about every ailment out to the press they could think of to explain June's absence: kidney problems, mononucleosis, exhaustion, nervous breakdown. In a last-ditch effort to engender sympathy they even told the media about June's rape when she was a teenager.

We were in a hell of a fix. When June left it was literally just hours before the curtain was supposed to go up. Now songs on which she sang lead had to be dropped or rearranged, choreography needed changing, and virtually our entire show was revamped at the eleventh hour.

It looked it. The audience was miffed, and the reviews were the worst of our career—and justifiably so. It was like amateur hour on the Caesars Palace stage that night. It was not good.

Something else that didn't help then or throughout our two weeks there was the fact that Paul Anka was, to put it as nicely as he deserves, an unmitigated prick. We quickly came to know why a musician who'd played with him once referred to that time as his sentence to "Ankatraz."

Anka suffered from a severe case of "little man's disease." His towering ego and "my way" attitude were insufferable to us and everybody else unfortunate enough to spend time around him. On stage he introduced us as "One of the most exciting acts to come along in years," but always in a way that made it clear he didn't think that at all.

The high point of the whole two weeks for us was the night our roadie Marc Vogel, who had more balls than brains, actually walked out on stage during Anka's performance and plopped on the startled singer's noggin a McDonald's paper hat emblazoned with "You Deserve a Break Today!" The little guy almost went ape shit.

Anka has hated us ever since, and in his 2013 memoir he even took time out from bashing Frank Sinatra, Sammy Davis Jr., and the other Rat Packers who mentored him to take a cheap shot at us, too.

Anyway, when our engagement was over, Caesars Palace cut us our checks and gave us an escort to the airport. It would be many years before we were welcomed back. I don't have any hard evidence that The Pointer Sisters were officially blacklisted by the casinos, but surely Paul Anka's Shit List wasn't the only one with our names on it.

It would be very convenient for me to let poor June shoulder the lion's share of the blame for this, but the sad fact is that she wasn't the only screw-up with the last name Pointer. Several months after I married Carl, I stepped out on my marriage. It wasn't cool, and it sure wasn't pretty.

In my defense, if you can call it that, Carl had stepped out first a few years earlier. We were living with his sister Helen in Richmond, California, and one evening I walked into our bedroom and there was Carl in bed with another woman. He actually had the balls to get indignant, like I was the one who'd stepped over the line, and ordered me out of the house. As I left the room he proclaimed that he and Whatsherface were now a couple.

Helen loved me like a sister, and I felt the same way about her. She was ashamed of her brother's behavior and said I didn't have to leave the house. I had no place to go, anyway, so I moved into her daughter's room, right next door to where Carl and his new thang were basking in the afterglow. I not only had to listen to them bump uglies again that night but repeatedly for the next several months. His actions were baffling to me not only because he knew the hurt I had suffered at the hands of my first husband, but also, frankly, because Ms. Thang was one ugly heifer. She lacked class, too. What the hell kind of woman openly plays around with somebody's man when that somebody is in the bedroom right next door?

Dennis Edwards, I suppose, was my opportunity to give Carl some much-needed karmic payback. I never really bothered to take the time to consider the damage that was being done to me, or the damage I was doing to Carl. I lived by the credo, "The heart wants what it wants." In time, I learned what a foolhardy sentiment that was.

It happened in the summer of 1974, when we made our eighth and final appearance on *The Helen Reddy Show*. As we stepped onto the NBC soundstage, I heard the faint sounds of a music group rehearsing. Those voices were magnificent and somewhat familiar. Then it suddenly dawned on me: it was The Temptations. Oh, Lordy! Chills went up and down my spine because The Temptations had always been one of my favorite groups. I think every African American woman from that era will agree that The Temptations were our "Black Beatles." With their detailed choreography, distinct harmonies, and flashy wardrobe, not to mention a treasure chest full of classic songs, they were beloved by the black community in those early Motown years. In my opinion, there has never been a guy group as talented and sexy as The Temptations.

When Dennis Edwards replaced David Ruffin in 1968, The Temptations were in the midst of a musical makeover. They switched gears from white-glove R & B to "psychedelic soul" and adult contemporary R & B, thanks in part to the direction and production of the talented Norman Whitfield. They started tackling current social issues such as racial integration, ghetto life, and Vietnam, and as a result scored many more hits and accumulated a second generation of listeners.

Dennis sang the soulful, gritty, and gospel lead vocals on "I Can't Get Next to You," "Runaway Child, Running Wild," and Motown's first-ever Grammy award-winning single, "Cloud Nine." But he was really thrust into the spotlight after "Papa Was a Rollin' Stone"—which The Temps had originally been reluctant to record—reached No. 1 on the charts and netted them their second Grammy.

The Temptations had fired Ruffin after he got into drugs and started acting like he was bigger than the rest of the group. After Dennis came in as Ruffin's replacement he started down the same road and became a large pain in everybody's ass. But when I saw him for the first time that day on the Reddy set, my legs (and other parts) started quaking. After I put my eyes back in my head and recovered the power of speech, I did something I'd never done before: I asked him for his autograph.

At 6'4" (6'8", if you counted his Afro) and a strapping 200 pounds, Dennis was one fine brotha. He was definitely my type in every way—tall, brown, and handsome—and that voice put the quiver in my belly.

On the Reddy show our groups taped separate performances, but the whole time I was watching theirs, Dennis' eyes were laser-locked on mine. The electricity that crackled between The Pointer Sisters and The Temptations led to our opening for them at the Universal Amphitheater.

The show went very well, and afterward The Temptations invited us to a Beverly Hills home owned by a friend/Realtor where they liked to go to unwind after. After a few cocktails, the fellas proceeded to sit us down and give us a lesson in the music business. The Temps had broken away from the Motown label a few years earlier, and now, after all the hits, million-selling singles and albums and nonstop touring, they were still struggling and hustling to make ends meet.

At Motown no artists were allowed to have outside agents or attorneys, and the in-house agency, International Talent Management Inc., ran the show. They played the roles of booker, accountant, banker, financial planner, and lawyer—with all services nonnegotiable and subject to a 10 percent commission on royalties and box-office proceeds. Then, of course, there were the deductions—the cost of studio time, the manufacturing of records, the storage of master tapes, and the musicians' pay. The kicker was that Motown kingpin Berry Gordy even owned The Temptations name (as he did all of their other acts, including the Jackson 5). When the Temps confronted Motown with a claim for $300,000 in unpaid royalties, Gordy turned it over to his lawyers and accountants. But The Temptations didn't back down, and eventually Berry signed The Temptations name back over to group founders Otis Williams and Melvin Franklin in hopes of softening them up. Then he suggested that they do one more album for Motown, and after that they could go their separate way with no hard feelings.

Gordy was, in effect, showing one of his most successful groups ever the door. And that $300,000 in back royalties? When Otis and Melvin personally served papers on Berry at his palatial Los Angeles estate, he decided it was time to take off the kid gloves and teach them a lesson. He counterclaimed that The Temptations owed him at least that amount in record advances that were never earned back, and he never bothered to enforce it until they legally came after him. The case went to court and ended with a settlement in Gordy's favor. Checkmate, Berry Gordy.

"Pay attention to every detail, and trust no one" was the message The Temptations sang loud and clear to us that night.

That really made us start to think. David had never told us anything about finances or the label, which was then involved in litigation involving David and several other clients. However, he had no hesitancy about spilling his guts to *Rolling Stone* magazine regarding The Pointer Sisters' finances. According to David, we had grossed $360,000 in 1973 and were on track to earn $1 million in both 1974 and '75. He estimated that we grossed about $50,000 a month, with operating costs of around $20,000.

He also disclosed that at the same time he was getting 20 percent off the top of everything we earned, he had a four-year personal services contract with Blue Thumb Records that paid him $100,000 annually. Since David was also producing and managing several other acts (including Herbie Hancock and Dave Mason) and had a similar claim of 20 percent of their gross, he was really livin' large.

That was good to know, although at the time none of it mattered all that much to me because all I could think about then was the beautiful music Dennis and I could make—in the bedroom, not a recording studio. The opportunity finally came not long after the Universal Amphitheatre gig when we teamed up with The Temptations for a mini-tour. Before our first show Dennis came into our dressing room, and as I was applying my makeup he gently grabbed me from behind and pulled my head back for a kiss.

"Wait for me after the show," he said.

I made whatever sound a melting pile of goo makes, and after Dennis left my sisters were quick to remind me that I was a married woman. I vaguely recalled something like that, but to tell you the truth I'm not sure I'd have even recognized poor Carl if he'd walked in the room right then. That's how blinded I was by that four-letter word that begins with "L." I mean lust, of course. No one knew that for years I had had a thing for Dennis, and now it was coming to fruition.

After the show I hung back to wait for Dennis. When he finally appeared he grabbed me around the waist (I had one then), and before hustling me out and into a waiting limousine he covered his head with a towel. At the time I thought it was a touchingly gallant attempt to shield us from any paparazzi hanging around, but I came to realize it was actually so that the stage door groupies, of which there was never any shortage, wouldn't recognize him.

When we got to the hotel I couldn't shake Bonnie, who probably figured she was going to protect what was left of my virtue. It was a nice thought and a very sisterly thing to do, but her and what army? She yammered at Dennis the whole time about the wedding ring on my finger, sometimes thundering about God's law just like Daddy used to in the pulpit. He'd have been proud.

"But I want Ruth," responded Dennis in a cool, measured tone of voice that signaled the debate was over and she had lost.

Bonnie dejectedly left us to our adulterous fun. Finally I excused myself and went into the bathroom to get ready for the Main Event. When I came out, Mr. Temptation was already under the sheets.

"Would you mind if I took off my wig?" I shyly asked.

"As long as you don't mind if I take mine off, too," Dennis said.

We both howled with laughter. Then we just howled.

After that first night with Dennis, as they like to say in the hood, we were "on and crackin'."

CHAPTER SEVEN

Rumble in the Jungle

I AIN'T GONNA LIE TO YOU. THERE IS DEFINITELY AN upside to being a celebrity. Fame opened up doors to countless countries, opportunities, and cultural experiences that have sustained me for a lifetime. Through my travels I've met U.S. presidents, aristocrats, royalty, diplomats, professional athletes, and the biggest names in Hollywood. Even more satisfyingly, fame also allowed us to meet and befriend so many of the musical heroes the Pointer Sisters looked up to when we were making our bones. We're talking Ray Charles, Stevie Wonder, Buddy Guy, Chuck Berry, Diahann Carroll, Dolly Parton, Cher, Annie Lennox, Robin Gibb, Miles Davis, Cicely Tyson, Keith Richards, Aretha Franklin, B.B. King, Etta James, Tina Turner, Lionel Richie, Diana Ross, Mary Wilson, Patti LaBelle, Harry Belafonte, Smokey Robinson, Dionne Warwick, and Quincy Jones. Later on, that honor roll expanded to include Paul McCartney, Michael Jackson, Natalie Cole, Bruce Springsteen, Willie Nelson, Chaka Khan, Bill Wyman, Ron Wood, Alice Cooper, James Ingram, Billy Joel, Donna Summer, and Whitney Houston. All great entertainers and cultural icons, to name a few.

But if forced, gun to my head, to choose the most memorable and awe-inspiring acquaintance we made I wouldn't hesitate to name "The Greatest" himself, the incomparable Muhammad Ali. And I'll bet he's at the top of a lot of people's lists. In addition to being an outrageously good-looking man, Ali had magnificent charm and more natural charisma in his pinky finger than Carter had pills. He single-handedly took boxing to its greatest heights and then transcended the sport as a symbol of goodwill and big-heartedness. He was kind, playful, and considerate of others—and not just to members of his own race, but people from all walks of life.

It wasn't always that way, though. Today Ali is one of the most revered and beloved figures on the planet, but after he "shook up the world" by winning the heavyweight title from Sonny Liston in 1964 and then announced his conversion to Islam and changed his name from Cassius Clay to Muhammad Ali, the white power structure did its best to take him down. In 1967, when he was at the peak of his boxing powers, politicians that resented his outspokenness about racial matters and the Vietnam War stole his title after Ali refused to be drafted into the U.S. Army on religious grounds. He was not allowed to fight again in his own country for several years. Both black and white commentators called what happened to Ali a "legal lynching." Only after the U.S. Supreme Court unanimously overturned Ali's conviction in 1971 for violating the federal draft law by refusing to be inducted into the military was he allowed to resume his boxing career. He didn't waste any time battling his way back to the top.

We first crossed paths with Ali in early September 1974, when The Pointer Sisters co-hosted *The Mike Douglas Show* for an entire week. The daily talk/entertainment show was taped in front of a live audience in Philadelphia and widely syndicated throughout the country. One of the perks as co-hosts was that we got to select a few guests for each show. With our eclectic tastes, that made for one interesting roster. Our selections included Ali, Angela Davis, The Staple Singers, and our cousin, Paul Silas of the Boston Celtics. On the show Paul gave us a couple of basketball tips. We weren't really prepared to take him on as we were wearing our best vintage clothing, but we did ditch our heels and change into high-top tennis shoes to give it the old college try.

A very nice and considerate gentleman, Mike must've wondered what he'd gotten himself into when we invited Angela Davis on the show. There was no more controversial and demonized woman in America than Angela, who had close ties to the radical Black Panther and American Communist Parties (she would twice run for vice president on the ACP ticket) and in 1970 had been tried on charges of complicity in the armed takeover of a California courtroom that resulted in the deaths of four persons. She was found not guilty. A year before that, then-governor Ronald Reagan had unsuccessfully tried to have her fired from the faculty of the University of California Los Angeles because of her radical left-wing politics.

We didn't necessarily agree with all her political stances, but it seemed only fair to offer a platform to a beautiful black sister whose unbridled passion for social justice had made her a punching bag for opportunistic politicians. Viewers tuning in to the show that day expecting to see horns protruding from Angela's mammoth Afro were disappointed. She was articulate, rational, and funny and just about charmed the pants off Douglas. I wouldn't have been surprised to see old White Bread Mike jump up and join her in a Black Power salute.

(At the opposite end of the charm spectrum, by the way, was actress Loretta Swit, a guest during our co-hosting week chosen by Mike. She played the haughty, overbearing "Hot Lips" Houlihan on the popular TV series *M*A*S*H*, who had contempt for everybody but her pipsqueak boyfriend Frank Burns. Turns out Swit took the role, or at least the attitude, to heart. When the cameras rolled she was sticky sweet to us, but during the commercial breaks you could've chilled a warm beer on her.)

The highlight of our week on the Douglas show was having our parents join us on the set on our last day as co-hosts. It was their first time on national television, and it was my dad's first-ever plane ride. Mom really impressed him by showing him how to work the button to recline the seat.

"Your mom is a genius!" Dad declared when we picked them up at the airport. "She showed me how to work the seat. I'll bet she could fly that plane if she put her mind to it." We loved that about Dad. He was so easily amused.

But the highlight of that episode was seeing the look on Dad's face when Muhammad Ali joined us on stage. Ali was one of Dad's heroes, too. The former champion was on a promotional tour to hype his October 30, 1974, match with then-champion George Foreman in Kinshasa, Zaire, on the African continent—as if it needed hyping. The "Rumble in the Jungle" was the most anticipated and celebrated boxing match in years as the 32-year-old Ali looked to regain his crown from the menacing Foreman, 25, a former Olympic gold medalist who'd become the ring's latest superman by knocking out Joe Frazier and Ken Norton—both of whom had defeated Ali. Norton, in fact, broke Ali's jaw in their fight a year earlier, and on paper at least the very forbidding Foreman figured to hurt him much worse than that.

Nowadays everybody knows Big George as the cuddly teddy bear with more money than God from hawking his "Lean Mean Fat-Reducing Grilling Machine" on TV. The young Foreman, though, was a nasty thug of a man most people didn't want to get caught looking sideways at, much less get caught by one of his sledgehammer fists. But while George may have worn the championship belt, Ali proclaimed himself "The People's Champion" and wasn't awed a smidge by the prospect of getting in the ring with the man whose straightforward, one-gear-only boxing style he ridiculed by calling Foreman "The Mummy."

We didn't know it at the time we taped the Douglas show with Ali, but The Pointer Sisters would have a special connection to the historic fight. Soon after, we were booked to perform at a three-day music festival in Kinshasa conceived by trumpeter and family friend Hugh Masekela and producer Stewart Levine as a co-feature of the championship bout. The festival, called "Zaire '74", combined American soul and authentic African music and encouraged cross-cultural connections. In addition to The Pointer Sisters (minus June, who wasn't up to the trip), the all-star lineup included James Brown, B.B. King, Bill Withers, Etta James, Celia Cruz, The Fania All-Stars, Miriam Makeba, The Spinners, and a then-unknown group called Sister Sledge. The historic concert (think "Black

Woodstock") was held in a refurbished soccer stadium in front of 80,000 people—the largest audience of our career.

The festival was an impactful socioeconomic moment for all involved. It introduced African American and Latin musicians to Africa and African musicians amid Ali's black-power politics and a glittering array of music, sports, and literary figures and two documentary film crews—Leon Gast's *When We Were Kings* and Jeff Levy-Hinte's *Soul Power*. For The Pointer Sisters and many of the other artists involved it was a spiritual quest to connect with our native land and its people. Everybody involved with the festival felt like they were part of a movement and that something magical was going to take place. And it did.

"Zaire '74" was hastily put together, although the intentions were pure: to hip Westerners to African music and return the beat to its roots. We could just imagine James Brown singing to an African audience, "Say It Loud—I'm Black and I'm Proud." And when it happened, everybody got the chills.

While "The Godfather of Soul" was the consummate showman and provided many magical moments on stage, James gave the promoters all they could handle. The Pointer Sisters didn't fly into Zaire with the other entertainers because we were on tour in another part of the world. But I later learned as their charter flight was being loaded up, James showed up with about 32,000 pounds of additional equipment because he had booked himself a couple additional shows in Africa and said he wouldn't set foot on the plane until the extra equipment was put on board. He was the headliner of the festival, so of course the concert organizers caved and James' shitload of gear, one of which was a full-sized organ, was crammed into the cargo hold. The rest of them weren't exactly traveling light, either, and I'll bet there wasn't a single passenger not holding his breath as that over-stuffed bird lumbered down the runway for takeoff. But they achieved liftoff, as they say, which almost wasn't the case after they refueled in Madrid. As the plane heaved itself into the sky there it actually swiped the top branches of some trees.

The funny thing is that when we got to Zaire the production crew learned that the country's electricity ran at 220 volts, not the 110 for which our American-made equipment was made. The United States government came to the rescue, though, as a bunch of 110-volt generators that had been donated to Zaire by the U.S. Agency for International Development were rounded up. Thank God for good old American foreign aid!

We were a little bummed about not being on that plane with so many great artists and friends, but that actually turned into a blessing in disguise when we learned what happened during the 27-hour flight to Zaire. For a while everything was happy-go-lucky, with everybody singing songs, playing instruments, drinking up the bubbly, and just enjoying each other's company. But as the long, cramped hours dragged by the Kumbaya vibe evaporated like the haze of reefer smoke in the cabin and it was every man for himself. The tensest moment came when James Brown and Bill Withers got into it. Withers had been grumbling about James since the plane left the U.S.A. He used to work at an airport, and when he saw all the extra stuff Brown insisted on bringing along he was genuinely worried about their safety.

As I later learned it from one of the passengers, James and his crew were sitting up front, and the pilot asked them to move to the rear of the plane to balance the load. James stayed put, and that's when supposedly Bill Withers pulled out a dagger and started waving it around in Brown's direction. Several passengers started screaming, and a bunch of brothers leaped up to intervene before there was bloodshed. For the remainder of the flight you could've cut the tension with—you guessed it—a knife. I'm sure everyone was super relieved when the plane finally landed in Kinshasa even though it was two o'clock in the morning and 100 degrees out, with matching humidity.

When we got to Zaire's Ndolo Airport (if you could call it that—it looked like a cheap strip mall) it was like walking into a sauna. But as we stepped onto the tarmac there were lots of locals waiting for us with all sorts of handmade items to sell, including carved art, snakeskins, ivory, and malachite in all shapes and sizes.

The capital of and largest city in Zaire (now the Democratic Republic of the Congo), Kinshasa was a vibrant place of over five million people located on the Congo River. The lingering effects of the dictatorship under Leopold II of Belgium, who made a fortune for himself turning the country into a slave labor camp for the harvesting of wild rubber, still seemed evident in Zaire. It's been said that Leopold was responsible for the deaths of up to 10 million Congolese Africans in the late 1800s. It wasn't until 1965, when Joseph Mobutu seized power, that the country started to make any progress, although Mobutu was a dictator, too, and his own reign was also marked by massive corruption and human rights violations. He paid $10 million to host the fight and pumped in untold millions more to spruce up Kinshasa for its big turn in the world's spotlight.

Mobutu touted Kinshasa as a modern city, but it was as Third World as it got. I didn't see any sidewalks, and all of the roads were dirt. The city did have a couple of flea markets, and as soon as we got a load of the shopping opportunities, The Pointer Sisters planned to do our part to help kick-start the gross national product.

The sights and sounds of the Congo were unlike anything I had ever experienced: women clutching their children and balancing baskets of food and water on their heads; actual monkey paws stuffed with vegetables—a native delicacy; camouflage-suited soldiers in red berets armed to the teeth; street musicians on almost every corner; men in dashiki shirts, bush jackets, and pinstripe suits; children playing soccer barefoot, tribal members wearing spectacular colored clothing, and a bus so jammed with people that the driver used his foot to shove them all inside so he could shut the door. It was so cartoonish that it made us all laugh. Everything was there on display in Zaire, once considered the cradle of civilization.

A chartered bus took us to an outlying villa composed of several two- and three-bedroom cottages. The Spinners stayed in a cottage across the courtyard, which helped alleviate some of the tedium of being stuck out in the sticks.

You'd think the most fearsome beast in Africa would be a lion, tiger, hippo, or gorilla, but in fact it's something called the Machango worm. In addition to the required eight shots we had to get before entering Africa, we had to watch a film on the dreaded Machango. The film expressly warned not to hand-wash any clothing in the sink lest it end up infested with the Machango, which apparently makes fleas, crabs, termites, lice, ticks, and poison ivy look like Little Leaguers when it comes to dealing out misery.

Our villas came with telephones evidently imported back in the 1930s that worked some of the time and TVs that broadcast only two hours a day. There was just one channel, and all it showed was political crap designed to impress viewers with what a great man President Mobutu was.

An hour after we'd ordered breakfast from room service on that first morning, a native-looking man came to our cottage holding an uncovered plate over his head. I think it was eggs.

Luckily we weren't that far from the Hotel Intercontinental, by far the nicest place in Kinshasa and a full-on freak show where local and international eccentrics seemed to crawl out of the woodwork. In addition to the boxing and musical entourages, every time we turned around we bumped into famous writers (most notably Norman Mailer, George Plimpton, and Hunter S. Thompson), professional athletes, poets, musicians, politicians, bureaucrats, wealthy businessmen, jet-setters, artisans, Peace Corps kids, and people from all walks of life who just wanted to be a part of the manic atmosphere and energy of what was dubbed "Kinshasa's living room."

Our publicist Gary Stromberg wasted no time buying himself a striped robe that he wore the whole time he was in Zaire. With his long, flowing locks, beard, and that colorful native robe he looked like Jesus Christ himself to make heads spin everywhere he went. But not as much as the old dude sitting in the corner of the lobby on a huge basket that contained newspaper-wrapped bundles of weed so amazing that we thought we'd died and gone to heaven.

I'd have been perfectly happy to just sit in the bar watching the nonstop action. But Ali liked to have us watch him train every day at his compound a few miles upriver in Nsele. I don't know if it was because he enjoyed our company or that he considered us a good-luck charm, but every damned morning he sent for us with a car. God knows we loved that man to death, but more than once we prayed, *Please don't let Ali send a car for us today. We want to go shopping!*

The shopping was unreal, and while driving around one day we discovered a currency worth more than money. We idly tossed some flyers about the big fight out the bus window, and people dove for them like they were gold. Aha! Next time we hit the markets, we took the flyers and Ali T-shirts so we could trade for precious stones and other African artifacts. Part of the fun of shopping, after all, is getting a good deal.

The music festival took place September 22–24 at the 20th of May Stadium. It was supposed to start two days before but was postponed due to the fact that major renovations to the venue ordered by Mobutu hadn't been completed.

All over Kinshasa billboards proclaimed, "Black Power Is Sought Everywhere in the World. But It Is Realized Here in Zaire." It was a stirring sentiment, but there were other signs that things were not as copacetic as the government wanted the outside world to think. An ominous one was the bars over the windows of the stadium dressing rooms. The story goes that a Mobutu-ordered dragnet had rounded up a thousand of the country's worst criminals. They were put into the makeshift stadium cells, and upon Mobutu's arrival everyone was herded into the stadium proper and 100 of the worst desperados were executed on the spot. Then El Presidente warned the rest that that's what was in store for them if they didn't behave while the eyes of the world were on Zaire. Believe me, we didn't so much as drop a gum wrapper on the ground while we were there.

He may have been the heavyweight champion of the world, but even George Foreman himself found out who the big bossman was in Zaire after he suffered a cut over his eye while sparring on September 15, ten days before the championship bout was supposed to happen. The injury necessitated a five-week postponement of the fight, although the musicians and artists weren't told this information until we landed. Foreman wanted to go back home to heal up, but Mobutu refused to let him leave Zaire and had George's passport confiscated, essentially holding him under house arrest until the rescheduled fight went off on October 30.

That didn't apply to all the high rollers, and with the fight on hold a lot of them left the country. That and the fact that tickets to the big concert were way overpriced kept attendance down the first two nights. But on the final night the government gave tickets away and the 80,000-seat stadium was filled and rocking. What a beautiful communion of artists and music lovers that was; we found ourselves as much in awe of the audience as they were of us. Our final performance and backstage footage was recorded for posterity and can be seen on a 40-minute DVD called *The Pointer Sisters in Africa* (rereleased in 2005 as *All Night Long*).

I'd like to say it was one unforgettable party, but the fact is that due to the virtually limitless availability of booze and weed, of which we took full advantage, there are some gaps in my memory of it. I do know that when all the musicians cleared out they reportedly left behind a $225,000 hotel bill. Concert producer Stewart Levine was under house arrest, but after several days in custody he managed to sneak out of the country on a flight to Italy.

I cheered madly in Sausalito on October 30 when my dear friend Ali made Foreman look like a chump, knocking him out in the eighth round of their fight to regain the heavyweight title and cement his legend as "The Greatest of All Time." Was there ever a more enthralling athlete? To know Ali was to love this marvelous, generous soul. I did then and I still do now.

But now I had my own big rumble ahead, in the marital ring. I was so swept away by my wild and free lifestyle that I decided there was no point staying married to Carl anymore. I just hoped he wouldn't put up a knock-down, drag-out legal battle that would make that historic dust-up in Zaire look like a game of patty-cake.

CHAPTER EIGHT

Things Go Better with Coke

I've never been very good at hiding the truth. To this very day, whenever I do something wrong I look like the proverbial cat that swallowed the canary. So it really came as no surprise that Carl was on to my affair with Dennis Edwards almost instantly.

He was the jealous type to begin with, and Carl's antennae were really twitching that very first night I spent with Dennis. Carl rarely called me when I was on the road, but he did when Dennis and I got together. It was immediately obvious to him that something wasn't right. I said we'd talk when I got home.

The 90-minute flight from Los Angeles to San Francisco seemed more like 90 hours. What was there for me to say to Carl, really? I didn't want to be sneaking around with Dennis, but why should I have to? I was a grown-ass woman and could do whatever I wanted, marriage vows be damned.

Ezekiel 16:8 says, "I bound myself by oath, I made a covenant with you...and you became mine." I had made a covenant all right—to me, myself, and I, the unholiest trinity of them all. It would take me years to understand that marriage is a balance of give and take, requiring a selflessness that allows you to come out of yourself to another person in both body and spirit. I was light years from that point. Dennis was exciting and new. The whole Zaire experience made me feel alive. Carl was, well, Carl. I didn't want the status quo any longer. I wanted that adrenaline I felt with the onset of something out of control, the rush and risk of the unknown. Dennis provided that in spades.

I decided the direct approach was the best way to go, and the minute I walked through the front door of our home I came clean with Carl. He didn't take it well, and the shit really hit the fan when I announced my intention to spend the weekend with Dennis, who was playing a gig with The Temptations at the Circle Star Theatre in nearby San Carlos.

"If Dennis Edwards thinks he can show up in *my* town and sleep with *my* wife, he can kiss my natural black ass!" Carl said with the sort of rage I'd never seen in him before. "I'm either gonna take him out or kill my own damn self."

Then he looked at me like he never had before and added: "But you'd better count on the first scenario as the most likely to go down."

Was I scared? Shitless. But did that stop me from keeping my rendezvous with Dennis? Oh, hell no. Fact is, the element of danger actually added a little extra spice to our lovemaking that weekend. It turned out Carl was just spouting off, anyway.

In case it isn't already obvious, I had a very skewed and immature take on love and relationships with men. At the time most of my relationships were like an elevator in that they'd take me to a certain level and then I'd get off and wait

TV appearance, circa 1980. My hair was short after a New Zealand hairdresser didn't know how to perm it properly. I decided to cut it all off and my sisters called it the "Q-Tip."

I may have looked fresh as a daisy in this 1981 Love Boat appearance, but I was coming down off a night of smoking crack and wanted to throw myself overboard after working all day on the set.

Posing on the red carpet at the 1985 American Music Awards. We won that year for Favorite Soul/R & B video artist.

By the mid-1980s, I had hit the wall after years of almost 15 years of drug and alcohol abuse. In this 1985 photo, taken in Switzerland, I can see the darkness in my life. Luckily, I got clean and sober.

THE POINTER SISTERS
Neutron Dance
Copyright © 1984 by Paramount Pictures Corporation
All Rights Reserved.
Courtesy of Paramount Pictures

MTV ad for "Neutron Dance." The television video network helped an '80s audience rediscover the Pointer Sisters, but in this video I tipped the scales around 185 pounds. Regrettably, I looked as big as a linebacker.

Cover photo for Hot Together, *our 1986 album. This was taken about a year after I got sober and shed all those unwanted pounds.*

Up All Night *was an hour-long network television special we did with actor Bruce Willis, which was aired in January 1987. Bruce was super cool and we share a special connection: we were both born on March 19.*

By the early 1990s, the music industry had changed dramatically. Only Sisters Can Do That, *our last album of original material, was recorded in 1993.*

One of the perks of fame is getting to meet your idols, and Muhammad Ali has always been one of mine. In this photo we are attending a fundraiser in Los Angeles sometime in the 1990s. You can sense the mutual warmth is sincere and heartfelt.

Hanging out with basketball great and Los Angeles Lakers guard Magic Johnson after a show in Atlantic City. Watching him play during his prime was like witnessing an artist paint on a canvas.

I had my look together when I started dating Mike Sayles. Mike was a trainer at the gym where I worked out in Malibu. After a disastrous first date, our relationship dramatically improved.

My wedding day, September 8, 1990. I'm surrounded by sisters Anita and June and daughter Issa (far left) at our Malibu home. Mike and I have been married for more than 25 years.

for the next elevator to lift me up to the next one. Kind of like coke. You always look for the next high to be better than the last. Men were the same way. But what I couldn't see (or maybe didn't want to admit) at the time was that both coke and men were only means to mask the self-doubt that plagued me as a teenager and through my years as part of The Pointer Sisters. I still didn't trust myself. I told myself that I did, and that did nothing to help me make better choices with men.

I have a problem with the popular theory that says women are always looking for someone just like dear old dad. None of the men I've been with came close to my father. There's just no comparison. My dad was the most loving, patient, and sweetest man in the world. The guys I've gone after have been charming, attractive, talented, and flashy, but very few had that spirit of faithfulness, human respect, and drive to live a wholesome, clean life. Since I wasn't exactly a paragon of virtue myself, that suited me right down to my toes.

Once you have low self-esteem, it's tough to rid yourself of it. So you replace your self-esteem with the superficial and the lies you tell yourself to make you feel like you are making the right choices in life. It's just like being in a cult. You get sucked in, disembodied. You separate yourself from family and true friends. You can't see life for what it really is. You rely on the high provided by the new instead of the comfort of those who truly love you.

And a new romance is as powerful as any narcotic—trust me, honey, I'm plenty experienced with both—and has the same warping effect on your reason and emotions. After that weekend with Dennis, I made up my mind to leave Carl and move to L.A. to be closer to Dennis, who had a house in

Coldwater Canyon. That meant also ditching my two kids, my parents, and sisters. It made no sense at all, but at the time I felt that if two people in a marriage weren't happy the only solution was divorce.

The trouble was, I was the only unhappy one in my marriage. Sure, he'd been an a-hole for taking up with that troll, but Carl still loved me in his own way and was willing for us to try to work things out. But to my mind our elevator had gone as far as it could and Dennis was in the next one calling, "Going up!" It just about crushed Carl when I filed for divorce in February 1975, but I just rolled with it basically because that is what I did at the time.

On the musical front, The Pointer Sisters' nostalgia act was starting to get a little stale. Singing that Chattanooga Choo Choo stuff and wearing those vintage clothes night after night, even though it made us easily identifiable and successful, put us at risk of being labeled a one-trick pony. While fun at first, it really wasn't who we were. Artistically we felt straitjacketed, but David stuck with his "if it ain't broke, don't fix it" formula until I put my foot down after one day a young fan knocked me for a loop by saying, "Ms. Pointer, you guys are great singers and we love your live shows. We just don't know how to dance to your music." From the mouths of babes....

It was definitely time for us to break out of our cookie-cutter mold and start gettin' real.

Steppin' was The Pointer Sisters' third studio album for Blue Thumb but the first that actually showed the public who we really were, the kind of music we liked, and our true spirit.

The album also signaled the start of our march toward artistic independence from David Rubinson.

When The Pointer Sisters first started in the business we were actually afraid to say what kind of music we wanted to perform because we would have been told to shut up because we didn't know anything. So we played the game and tasted some success and eventually wanted a little more creative control. We had now reached the point where we wanted and had the smarts to pick our own material and do the things we had been paying others to do for us. *Steppin'* was our way of saying, "Here we are—moving and grooving and growing!" Its style was contemporary, fitting squarely within the genres of R & B, soul, and funk. And if I do say so myself, it boasted one of the era's coolest album sleeves: Converse-style high-heeled tap sneakers, which symbolized the funk/disco movement just taking off in music and pop culture. The album was a mother, and for me it was the high point of The Pointer Sisters' 1970s output.

Two key reasons for our growth were the maturation of Anita and Bonnie's songwriting skills and the fact that June was back with us and healthy. The groove-laden "How Long (Betcha Got a Chick on the Side)"—the subtitle was David's creative addition—with Anita singing seductively on lead vocal was our first single off the new album. Released in May 1975, *Steppin'* helped us to tap into and finally establish a rapport with a black listening audience. "How Long" became a No. 1 R & B hit—our first—and peaked at No. 20 on the *Billboard* Hot 100. It was a steamy syncopation of soul, funk, and nascent disco. And, by the way, it also accurately depicted the frustrating aspects of our personal relationships with the opposite sex.

Allen Toussaint wrote "Going Down Slowly" for us after we met him in New Orleans and thanked him for allowing us to record "Yes We Can Can." We asked if he had anything else as good as that. Allen was never short on good material, and the song gave us another R & B hit, peaking at No. 16.

"Sleeping Alone" was the song Stevie Wonder promised to write for us a few years before. He wanted to work out the arrangements of the song and so stayed the night at Anita's condo in Sausalito. I was also living there at the time. Being around Stevie was a wonderful but kind of surreal experience. When I got up the next morning I walked past the bathroom and groggily wondered why the lights were off but the faucet was running. *Who the hell is washing up in the dark, or did someone just leave the water running?* Then I remembered our famous houseguest who had no need of lights.

Later in the studio, Stevie played his trademark piano on this clever marriage of rock and smooth jazz. His participation in recording it was a result of my move to Los Angeles from San Francisco. I lived at the Beverly Terrace Hotel, directly across the street from the Troubadour. It was the only part of L.A. I was familiar with, and Stevie's brother Calvin often drove me around town in his cute Mercedes convertible. We'd frequently drop by Crystal Sounds Studio in Hollywood, where Stevie was working on his classic double album, *Songs in the Key of Life*. It was a huge eye-opener watching this genius at work and hearing early incarnations of "I Wish," "Isn't She Lovely," and Stevie's tribute to the late Duke Ellington, "Sir Duke."

The Pointer Sisters gave our own nod to the legendary artist with "I Ain't Got Nothin' But the Blues: A Medley in Tribute to Duke Ellington," but actually we did that more to appease David Rubinson than anything else. The same could be said for our reworking of the 1940s-style hit "Save the Bones for Henry Jones," the comical Nat King Cole/Johnny Mercer ditty about a man who doesn't eat meat.

Herbie Hancock returned to lend a hand (and his beautiful clavinet) on Taj Mahal's "Chainey Do," and Isaac Hayes' "Easy Days" (co-written with Anita and Bonnie) was a melt-in-your-mouth slice of easy listening R & B with some Latin overtones thrown in for good measure. June took lead vocals on Burt Bacharach and Hal David's "Wanting Things," originally from the Broadway score of *Promises, Promises*. Her singing on this tune was so beautiful that it makes me cry every time I hear it.

On *Steppin'* we sang our way through nostalgia, torched our way through ballads, and got down with funky rhythm and blues and mid-period soul. We planted our flag as true song stylists with plenty of sweet and sass. We had a lot of fun recording *Steppin'* and were totally engaged with the material. We felt our days as a gimmick act were coming to a close. Sales-wise, the album performed more than admirably, charting at No. 3 on the R & B charts and No. 22 on the *Billboard* 200—an affirmation that we could be successful and creative artists by being ourselves.

As for me, I was having a ball immersing myself in the fabled Hollywood lifestyle. Now free from the constraints of my marriage to Carl and direct responsibility for my kids and my parents, I felt like a teenager heading off to college for the first time, and Tinseltown was my campus. Champagne, limos, palm-tree-lined roads, sunshine-filled days, boogie nights, the Pacific Ocean, and beautiful people everywhere you turned—L.A. was a groovy and dynamic adventure. It had everything I wanted, including my new man Dennis. Being in love made everything so much better.

There was a growing contingent of black celebrities in Los Angeles at that time, and naturally we gravitated to each other. My pals included Flip Wilson, Cher, Chaka Khan, Redd Foxx, O.J. Simpson, Sammy Davis, Jr., Stevie Wonder, Donna Summer, Natalie Cole, Mary Wilson, Smokey Robinson, Louis Gossett Jr.—and the funniest man I ever met in my life, cutting-edge bad-boy comedian Richard Pryor.

Today the black culture whose seeds were planted and cultivated by all those talented musicians, actors, stand-up comedians, and professional athletes in the 1970s is inextricably woven into the fabric of society. To have witnessed and even been a part of its genesis back then is one of the proudest things in my life.

But other things happened that I'm not so proud of, chiefly my escalating drug habit. While San Francisco has historically been mostly a weed and acid town, 1970s Los Angeles was definitely fueled by cocaine. That wacky dust took Hollywood like Grant took Richmond, devastating countless lives and deviating many a septum in the process. It was everywhere. You'd go to a restaurant, club, or party and a bowl of snow would materialize and get passed around just like an appetizer. While stopping short of endorsing its use, *Time* magazine was among several news outlets reporting (incorrectly, it turned out) that cocaine was not addictive and so wasn't as bad for you as alcohol. Who was I to disagree with such learned authorities?

And when I found out that coke helped keep my weight down, that magical white powder became one of my main food groups.

I got my fill at one of Richard Pryor's soirees. Richard lived in a fashionable residence on Sunset Plaza Drive, high above the famous Sunset Strip, with a panoramic view of the valley. There was a gold-plated sign next to his doorbell that always cracked me up when I visited. It said, "If you did not make an appointment to be at my home, and if you were not invited here, get your motherfucking ass off my porch."

Around people he didn't know Richard was quiet and almost painfully shy. On the flip side he was utterly charming, supremely charismatic, and hysterically funny. When you were hanging with the comedian Jerry Seinfeld would call "the Picasso of our profession," the sky was the limit and anything he had was yours for the asking. Including that lovely white powder, although at Richard's place you never had to ask for it. I remember one wild party where the music was pumping (he had a killer sound system in his house), there was barbeque chicken cooking on huge grills, and elegantly-dressed waiters with white gloves endlessly circulated among the guests offering trays of hors d'oeuvres, booze, and heaping helpings of the finest cocaine I ever snorted.

The thing about cocaine is that it's not as much fun doing it alone. When Dennis and I were together that wasn't an issue. In the beginning we thought it enhanced our personalities, making us chattier, wittier, and much more engaging. Everything—including sex—seemed better with coke.

In time we started to depend on it for all those things, and whenever we were together coke always seemed to be within arm's reach. Then, inevitably, it dominated our lives and thoroughly kicked our asses. Especially when we started freebasing the stuff—heating it in a jar to concentrate the drug into a rock and get a high that was totally (and almost literally) out of this world. The initial 30-second rush is usually followed by a two-minute high so euphoric it renders you speechless. The urge to smoke more grows stronger with each toke, to the point where your brain demands *more, more, more.* The psychological addiction sinks its claws into you and turns gregarious stoners into loners, renders millionaires into paupers, changes beautiful chicks into $20 tricks, and brings grown men and women to their knees. When you mess with freebase (crack), it's like tapping on the devil's shoulder. You're not just asking for trouble; you're begging for it.

I am not proud to say that if you saw me on television, in concert, or in any public setting during that period, more likely than not I was, to put it mildly, in an "altered state of consciousness" and feeling no pain. The pain—as bad as I ever felt—came when I was coming down from the coke. So I pretty much adopted that popular 1970s credo: avoid hangovers—stay high.

L.A. turned this girl from the streets of Oakland into a full-on cocaine cowgirl. And I rode that sonuvabitching horse nonstop well into the next decade.

CHAPTER NINE

Having a Party…and Breaking Up

YOU'VE HEARD THE MORBID CLICHÉ THAT THE moment a person is born he begins to die, right? It's that way in the music industry, for damn sure. With few exceptions such as the Rolling Stones, U2, Rush, and ZZ Top, most music groups break up the moment they form…they just don't know it at the time.

In the music business, beautiful beginnings historically are the setup phase that leads to inevitable endings. If you review the demise of any band it is easy to chart the similarity in the rise and fall and eventual end of most hit groups. First and foremost, if you want to break up any band or musical group, just let them have a taste of success. Almost without exception, this is when the trouble begins. The money, fame, and adulation, in concert with the inevitable sharks, wolves, and worms who come out of the waters, woods, and woodwork, begin to immediately erode age-old friendships and relationships that up to that point have stood all the tests of time and seemed as solid and permanent as the Rock of Gibraltar.

A very odd thing happens in that what was once a dedicated group of people who mutually worked together for years to pull something big off begins to fragment as individual members maneuver to establish their singular importance in the group and jockey for increased time in the spotlight. Suddenly everyone adopts a me-first attitude, and the spirit and camaraderie that brought you together in the first place is splintered. Individual managers and lawyers begin fighting over issues such as getting their clients their "fair share" of publishing rights, royalties, media coverage, and product endorsements. Even who gets the most fan mail or gets asked the most questions at a press conference can become a problem after egos have been stroked and members of the group start buying into what the label's PR machine churns out about them and thinking that the rave notices are really just for them. It may not happen for years, but these seeds of destruction are planted and germinate in a band's formative stages.

And I haven't even introduced drugs, alcohol, and being cooped up on the road for hours on end into this potent mix of musical mayhem.

The Pointer Sisters shared an innate bond, naturally, and being sisters made us that much stronger than most. If you messed with one of us, you messed with all four of us. Just ask Lisa Lansky about that—if you can find her. Lisa was a road manager assigned to us by David, and we didn't like her from the get-go. For one thing, she had a major-league superiority complex and acted like she was "Ms. Massa" of four little slave girls. For another, she was dating one of the musicians in our backup band and, according to the grapevine, buying him lots of fancy dinners, clothes, and musical instruments—and even a boat, for God's sake. All of it paid for, of course, with the company credit card. In other words: our hard-earned money.

Once we collected dead certain proof of that, Anita and I confronted Lisa at the Watergate Hotel in Washington D.C. Her response was to call us a "pair of ungrateful nigga bitches" and to push Anita into a glass table so hard the glass shattered and cut Anita's leg. Blood gushed everywhere, but not all of it was my sister's. I went full ghetto on Lisa, stomping that bitch to the floor and then booting her repeatedly in her dumb-ass head. I was beyond caring if I killed her and was kicking away at Lisa like a Rockette when I was yanked back by some just-arrived metro D.C. cops. After we explained the situation they arrested Lisa. We had a concert at the Carter Barron Amphitheatre, and rather than miss the show, Anita wrapped her wound in gauze and we foolishly kept the engagement. We told Bonnie and June what had happened, who were waiting in the lobby, ready to catch a ride to the venue. They were very upset, but mostly because they hadn't gotten in their own licks on Lisa. The last we heard of Ms. Lansky she had completely lost her mind and been institutionalized. Too bad, but it would've been a hell of a lot worse for her if the police hadn't shown up when they did, and the Watergate scandal that took place a few years earlier would have paled by comparison. (Anita's cut got severely infected and she finally got medical attention on our next tour stop in Oakland, Michigan. It was a good thing she did because the doctor said the next step would have been amputation.)

We loved each other dearly, but we were only human and were susceptible to the constant strain of nonstop touring, professional commitments, and having to be "on" all the time. ("The Pointer Sisters" exuded excitement and energy, and when the cameras were on no matter how low or tired we felt we had to instantly magically transform ourselves into "them." More than 40 years later we're still expected to do that.)

Despite *Steppin's* commercial and critical success, by the end of 1975 we were torn, frayed, and tattered. You can't keep up the accelerated pace we did—two albums a year, rehearsals, frequent television appearances, concerts, nightclub engagements, photo sessions—without burning out. Some held it together better than others, but we were all just plain wiped out.

June was the first to hit the wall. After yet another hospitalization, physicians said her crippling panic attacks were triggered by a heart condition called mitral valve prolapse. It was a cardiac abnormality affecting the upper and lower chambers of the left side of her heart and their ability to close properly. The condition was first described in 1966, and it was estimated that up to 3 percent of the population suffered from this rare condition.

Doctors prescribed medication and June started popping three tranquilizers a day, which pretty much zonked her out most of the time. Eventually (and predictably) she became addicted to them. Under the circumstances, June had no choice but to bow out of the touring grind in November 1975.

In January of '76 the rest of us headed to sunny Florida for two weeks of work and play. First up was a weeklong double-bill with The Temptations at Bachelors III, a Fort Lauderdale bar/nightclub co-owned by football great Joe Namath, Bobby Van, and Ray Abruzzese.

Like "Broadway Joe" himself, the club was classy and flashy. It featured both a disco and rock section. We received standing ovations every night and some of the best reviews of our career.

Joe was super cool and even more handsome in person. His reputation as a player off the field rivaled his achievements on it, but the man I got to know that week was funny, polite, articulate, and conversant on just about any topic. One night we all sat around in his special booth, taking in the sounds of Gloria Estefan and just enjoying each other's company. I have always thought highly of Joe and have never forgotten his charm and hospitality.

I feel the same about Burt Reynolds, who we met around the same time. He was a real music enthusiast, mostly a country and western fan, but Burt also loved him some Pointer Sisters. Burt and Dinah Shore were a couple then, and she was one of the most genuine, warm, and funny people we ever met in the business. Dinah had us on her daytime chat show several times over the years, and by far the most memorable when we appeared with the great Sammy Davis Jr. and actor Jim Nabors, star of *Gomer Pyle U.S.M.C.* Nabors played a loveable doofus on-screen, but he was wickedly funny and had us in stitches during a commercial break describing a recent visit to the White House, where he sang at a state dinner by personal invitation of President Jimmy Carter. The night before, Jim said, he went on a cocaine toot and as a result was dragging ass the next day. As he was introduced to First Lady Rosalynn Carter before the dinner, surrounded by Secret Service and dignitaries, Jim let loose with a giant sneeze that caught him so unaware he was helpless to stop the snot rocket that landed on Mrs. Carter's jacket lapel. Jim's hilarious anecdote ended just as the cameras started rolling again, and America caught the entire crew and the rest of us laughing hysterically. Needless to say, Dinah didn't ask Jim to repeat the story on the air.

That same evening we were invited to Liza Minnelli and Jack Haley Jr.'s wedding reception in Los Angeles by Sammy Davis Jr., who co-hosted the event with Liza's father, Vincent. We were still living in Sausalito at the time and reluctantly told Sammy that we had already booked a flight back home and couldn't stay. But he insisted we spend the night with him and his wife, Altovise, and accompany them to the reception.

When we called home to let Mom and Dad know, we put Sammy on the line so they would know we weren't shining them on. Of course he charmed their socks off. Sammy and Altovise were living in a palatial Georgian-style brick mansion once owned by movie mogul David O. Selznick, in Beverly Hills just off Benedict Canyon. The place was a shrine to Sammy and all his accomplishments. The walls were covered with his gold records, civic and industry awards, and photos of him and important people and celebrities.

The wedding reception was held at Ciro's nightclub on Sunset Boulevard. For the occasion Sammy borrowed from one of the studios a white sequined gown worn by Marilyn Monroe in one of her classic movies so that Altovise could look stunning. We sat with them and tried hard not to let our mouths hang too far open as a who's who of celebrities paraded up to say hello to Sammy: Mae West, Jack Benny, Elizabeth Taylor, Ryan O' Neal, Rock Hudson, Goldie Hawn, Eva Gabor, Gene Kelly, Raquel Welch, Shirley MacLaine, Johnny Carson, Ruta Lee, Sid Caesar, and Shirley Jones come to mind.

The next morning Sammy had a driver take us to LAX, and for quite a while after we got off the plane we were still flying pretty high.

We maintained our friendship with Burt Reynolds over the years and he had me on his game show *Win, Lose or Draw*, which was syndicated from 1987 to 1990. It was basically Charades with paper and markers, and I was pretty good at it. Burt had a competitive streak a mile deep, and did his best to make sure we were on opposite teams. One time he wasn't scheduled to show up, but when he knew I was coming, he made a point of being there. I always got a huge kick out of beating Burt at his own game.

When we finished at Bachelors III we went to the Miami Convention Center to tape a television special called *Super Night at the Super Bowl*. The auditorium was decorated like a football stadium, and Jackie Gleason and Andy Williams headed up the long list of performers on the show that included us, Burt and Dinah, Bob Newhart, Mary Tyler Moore, Jimmie Walker, and a musical group then just starting to come into their own: the fabulous K.C. and the Sunshine Band. The place was packed with 1,400 people.

Their jaws and those of the millions watching on TV must've hit the floor when The Pointer Sisters came out looking like black Scarlett O'Haras. Whose brainstorm it was to dress us in *Gone with the Wind* gingham country couture (including parasols) to sing "Fairytale," I don't really recall. But we thought it was cute and fun to dress up, and we loved those costumes.

The 90-minute CBS prime-time special aired on the eve of Super Bowl X, pitting the Dallas Cowboys against the

Pittsburgh Steelers in Miami on January 18, 1976. It was one of the first major events of the United States' bicentennial year celebration. Football historians say the game was one of the greatest Super Bowls of all time, with the Steelers defeating the Cowboys 21–17. I'll have to take their word for it because I was busy that weekend making whoopee at what this party historian considers one of the greatest bashes ever.

I remember lovebirds Burt and Dinah always holding hands, O.J. Simpson leaping into our limo to escape a throng of teenaged girls, Anita hooking up for the weekend with Dallas Cowboy Thomas "Hollywood" Henderson, and K.C. and the Sunshine Band shaking their collective booties.

Oh yeah, and snorting up some of the finest Peruvian flake cocaine I've ever had in my life.

In addition to our recording and concerts, that year we broke into the movies thanks to our publicist, Gary Stromberg. At the time he was dating Aida Chapman, who was an associate producer for Don Cornelius on *Soul Train*. She lived a floor above me in an apartment complex in West Hollywood, and we became friendly. I went up to visit Aida one night when Gary happened to be there. Gary said he was getting into film business, starting as an executive producer of the 1976 comedy film *Car Wash*. The movie featured an all-star cast including Richard Pryor, Garrett Morris, George Carlin, Bill Duke, and Antonio Vargas. When I found out what Gary was up to I buttonholed him the first chance I got.

"Write a part for The Pointer Sisters," I begged him. "We'll find a way to make it work."

Gary and screenwriter Joel Schumacher obliged, and we were cast as "The Wilson Sisters," the glamorous entourage of suave and smooth-talking ghetto preacher "Daddy Rich," brilliantly portrayed by Richard Pryor. It wasn't a big part, but it was great fun. We'd step out of a white stretch limousine with Daddy Rich to preach the money-grubbing gospel according to the "Church of Divine Economic Spirituality" ("For a small fee I will set you free, nearer my God to thee!").

Before the cameras rolled Richard did a run-through with us to make sure his impromptu spiel passed muster with church folk (or at least their offspring). When he intoned, "I shall not be moved" one of us jumped up and testified, "Like a tree planted by the water!" Richard was thrilled. "Can I say that?" he asked. "Can I use that in my sermon?" Oh, hell yeah.

Richard didn't really need our help. He was so spellbinding as a golden-tongued preacher that the best pulpit-pounders I ever heard would've sold their own souls to the devil for just an ounce of Richard's natural-born charisma.

One time The Pointer Sisters opened for Richard in Cherry Hill, New Jersey. We loved his humor so much that we rushed through our set and quickly changed our wardrobe to get into our regular clothes to sit in the audience and watch his show. Richard spotted us in one of the first few rows and gave us major props.

"How about those fabulous Pointer Sisters?" he'd say to rip-roaring applause. "Those girls can sing, can't they? But they just won't give me no pussy!" Along with the entire audience, we howled until our ribs hurt. Richard was crazy as a road lizard.

As good a time as we had on-screen, you can bet your last dollar it was even better off camera. Director Michael Schultz ran a loose and free-spirited set, and we often passed around my antique flask filled with Remy Martin as we sat in the limo between takes. Richard would stand up and poke his head out the sunroof and tell us, "Now hold my legs, 'cause I might fall down when they make the curve." Lord, those were some good times. I remember my sisters singing the theme to the Mighty Mouse cartoon ("Here I come to save the day!") and Richard was freaked out that we knew the words…that was it. We were forever bonded.

In the picture we sang "You Gotta Believe," a Norman Whitfield–penned tune. The song was another Top 20 R & B hit for us, and was included on the movie soundtrack and on *The Best of the Pointer Sisters*, a double LP that coincided with the film's release. We'd really had our hearts set on recording the movie's theme song, "Car Wash," but Whitfield gave it to the group Rose Royce, which he happened to manage and was grooming for stardom. It shot straight to No. 1 that fall, and the soundtrack double album went platinum. At least I had the satisfaction of overhearing Whitfield haranguing lead singer Gwen Dickey during a rehearsal, "Why can't you sing like The Pointer Sisters? Come on! Put some guts into the song!"

After *Car Wash* The Pointer Sisters made several appearances on the popular PBS children's television show *Sesame Street*. Our renditions of "Hush Little Baby," "The Alphabet Song," and especially "Pinball Number Count" were replayed often and today are fond childhood memories for a generation of viewers. Faun, Malik, and Anita's daughter, Jada, sang with us on "Pinball Number Count," which makes it an especially precious moment for all involved.

We returned to the studio in late 1976 to record our final Blue Thumb album, *Having a Party*. Noticeably missing from the album were June (who contributed to only the title track) and the nostalgic sound that had defined our earlier work. Still, I thought it was a decent contemporary R & B and funk album injected with The Pointer Sisters' signature harmonies and boisterous energy. The latter, I must say, was pretty much chemically induced, as I was out of my freakin' mind by then. Just getting us to sit still long enough to shoot an album cover photo proved near impossible. David arranged for the photo shoot at a beautiful art deco train depot in Los Angeles. Dennis and I had just moved into a six-bedroom house in Hancock Park, and the very next day he left to go on tour.

All by my lonesome in that big house, I got good and loaded and stayed that way. When the driver sent to fetch me arrived, I was still in bed. I managed somehow to get myself together enough to look like I was having a good time at a party in the album cover art.

For all that, I still think the album is a fun romp and will defy anyone to listen to our rollicking version of the 1962 Sam Cooke good-time anthem "Having a Party" and not get up and bust a move. Stevie Wonder's collaboration with Anita and Bonnie on "Bring Your Sweet Stuff Home to Me" was an outstanding effort. "Lonely Gal" hinted at the rock offerings that producer Richard Perry would coax out of us in the coming years, and "I Need a Man" was a clever combo of funk and blues.

I contributed "Waiting on You," written with Melvin Ragin, better known as "Wawa." It was one of the first tunes I ever put to paper. It happened when The Pointer Sisters were playing the Bottom Line in New York. It was the middle of a sound check, and my sisters had gone on to the dressing room. The band was jamming and I stayed behind to listen. As the music got to me I was spirit stricken. I started scribbling lyrics about my increasingly frustrating relationship with Dennis. More and more he'd tell me he'd see me later, but then wouldn't show up. It seemed I was always waiting for the man.

Having a Party represented a series of lasts for The Pointer Sisters: it was the last album to feature Bonnie, the last album produced for us by David Rubinson, and our last album for Blue Thumb. The label delayed its release for several months, and when it finally came out in November '77 it landed with a big, fat thud. Blue Thumb had been purchased by ABC-Dunhill in late 1974, and three years later it was practically a ghost operation. There were no resources to promote the record, and it lacked a hit single to kick it into high gear. So *Having a Party* sank without a trace.

Any loyalty we felt toward David went overboard with it. His big cut of our pie had always been galling, and his controlling ways had gotten way out of hand. I recall one session where we were auditioning drummers for our live band. One of the prospects had played with Warren Zevon and had some serious musical chops. David asked him to play "Salt Peanuts," musically a very difficult number with lots of tempo changes, to see what kind of player he was. The guy had barely gotten started when David exploded: "You call yourself a jazz drummer? You can't hold a tempo! Don't you know better than to come to an audition and not be prepared? This is jazz, man—jazz! Pack your shit and get out of here!"

It was humiliating and unnecessary, and the rest of us looked away because we were embarrassed for the poor guy. We were simply tired of David, and the quick disappearance of

Having a Party was the final straw. At that point in our career we didn't agree on much anymore, but the vote to divorce The Pointer Sisters from David Rubinson was unanimous.

I suppose we looked like ungrateful bitches for dumping the guy who steered us to the top, but in fact we were and still are very grateful to David for investing in us and even mortgaging his home to get things off the ground. Clearly there would be no Pointer Sisters without David's investment, input, and guidance. But you know what? He made his $100,000 investment back many times over and continued to derive royalties from us for a couple of decades. David managed several other groups, and was in a hell of a lot better condition financially than we were. He was going to be just fine.

When it came time to give David the pink slip we brought along our new attorney, Jim Walsh, to do the dirty work. David was stunned and then angry, and some of his office furniture got rearranged. I hated when that happened. I felt better a couple years later when David told a newspaper reporter: "As far as the parting, it wasn't amicable because I was spoken to very harshly by someone who hadn't put in five years and every dime he ever had in the world. I felt bad about it. But now they're breaking new ground, they're stretching past the normal limits and they're working with top people, which is where they belong."

It's taken me years of 12-step work to sort out my feelings about David, who today lives in rural France. I'm at peace now with the knowledge that we came together at a crucial point in each other's lives and actually needed each other. Money comes and goes, as it has all my life, but David was a paramount figure in The Pointer Sisters' history. For that reason alone, I will always love him. Peace be with you, David.

Who would be the next one off the Pointer Merry-Go-Round? Bonnie, it turned out, when she announced that she was going to pursue a solo career. It was a bolt out of the blue, and Anita and I were very irate, especially after we discovered Bonnie had been egged on to leave us by her new boyfriend, Motown executive Jeffrey Bowen. This was the same weasel who convinced Dennis to record a solo album behind the backs of his fellow Temptations. We know how that turned out. In 1978—the same year Bonnie signed with Motown to a two-record deal—she and Bowen got married. It was a double dagger to the heart.

Going from four to three Pointer Sisters had been manageable, but Anita and I weren't exactly The Doublemint Twins. We played a New Year's show in San Francisco, just the two of us, and we were just okay in spite of the great turn-out that prompted one critic to observe, "It was so crowded you could only see two Pointer Sisters!"

Over the course of several months, we met with various managers, producers, and songwriters, and even got desperate enough to consider hiring two singers and palming them off as members of the family. I did this carrying my three-month-old offspring with Dennis, Issa, in a backpack-style baby carrier. Five years after our big breakout, The Pointer Sisters were on the ropes.

CHAPTER TEN

Pointer Sisters 2.0

···

IS THERE ANYBODY WHO DOESN'T LOVE A GREAT comeback story? I sure do. Of course, the word "comeback" implies that your career has crashed and burned or you've taken a giant ass whippin' and had to crawl under a rock to get yourself together for a shot at redemption.

In 1977, I was under one hell of a rock. A landslide, in fact.

The original Pointer Sisters were kaput. I was just about broke and severely addicted to cocaine. I had no life plan, no fallback position, no career prospects, and no idea how to get out from under.

What I did have were two young mouths to feed and a third on the way. I also had parents to support, rent to pay, and a shopping jones almost as big as my coke habit. When Dennis found out I was with child, he abandoned me in that big six-bedroom house and moved in with another woman, leaving me high and dry. Our daughter, Issa Kuren Edwards, was born on January 22, 1978. Happy New Year!

When you're in show business, about the worst thing you can do in a situation like mine is let people know how bad off you are. Instead you put up a brave front so the sharks don't smell blood and go for the kill. So I held my head up, gritted my teeth in a semblance of a smile and took any work I could find. I have always been a hard worker and wasn't too proud to beat the bushes for any gig available, no matter how small or anonymous.

Even at the height of The Pointer Sisters' fame we had done session work for Alice Cooper (*Muscle of Love*), Bobby Lamm (*Skinny Boy*), and Bill Wyman (*Stone Alone*). Now I got us on Rick James' "Little Runaway" literally by posting a guns-for-hire notice on a bulletin board at the Record Plant in Sausalito. I was that desperate. Issa was almost a year old, and Christmas was just around the corner. My mother needed money very badly to continue raising our kids, who were facing a yuletide without presents. Rick saved our hides, paying Anita and me two large apiece. Speaking of hides, Rick definitely wanted mine. At the time we recorded the song he had too much respect for Dennis to make a big play for me, but years later when Dennis was out of the picture and Rick was in "Superfreak" mode, he made several aggressive passes at me. Rick was an absolute genius in the studio, and I loved being around him, but I didn't think of him in that way.

That kind of stuff paid the bills for a while and helped me get my footing back in the L.A. music scene. I was then living with my best friend, Carolyn Washington, in the Larrabee Apartments located in West Hollywood. She and I had met through her boyfriend, Jimmy Eagle, who was Dennis' assistant at the time. Carolyn was sweet, down to earth, and, like me, a single mother. And she had the most impressive record collection I'd ever seen. We loved the same kind of music and listened, sang, and danced to records for hours on end. We're still that way with each other. When we hear something that stirs us, we'll call each other on the phone and say, "Girl, have you heard that song?"

Carolyn practically nursed me when Dennis left and when The Pointer Sisters were falling apart. She got me unconditionally and still does to this day. She is one of a handful of God-fearing, praying women I go to when I'm in emotional pain.

It was my turn to return the favor after Jimmy started physically abusing Carolyn. I encouraged her to move out immediately. I asked if she would be interested in sharing a place with me so I could get back to L.A. Living with us in the studio were her son Houston and my daughter Issa. Looking back, that was a very special time with Carolyn. Houston is no longer with us, but he's never far from my thoughts.

In the summer of '78 our new manager, Forest Hamilton, set up a meeting with producer Richard Perry. Richard was one of those guys with the Midas touch, and in the 1970s everything he touched turned to gold. His work with Harry Nilsson (*Nilsson Schmilsson*) earned the singer four Grammy nods and the trophy for Best Male Pop Vocal. Perry also produced Carly Simon's global smash "You're So Vain" and pulled Ringo Starr's career out of the doldrums with two singles that topped the charts in '73 and '74, "You're Sixteen" and "Photograph." He also produced albums for Fats Domino, Ella Fitzgerald, Barbra Streisand, Tina Turner, Martha Reeves, and Diana Ross.

But it was his work with British singer Leo Sayer on the 1976 album *Endless Flight* that really blew me away. Richard teased two No. 1 hits—"You Make Me Feel Like Dancing" and "When I Need You"—out of Sayer, and the album went

Top 10 in both the US and UK and stayed on the *Billboard* charts for more than a year. By the end of the decade Richard was in a position to write his own ticket and proceeded to do so with his new label, Planet Records.

The timing couldn't have been better for us. Richard needed a name artist to launch his label and we needed a hard-charging, creative producer to relaunch our career.

Anita and I met him at his Sunset Boulevard office and we hit it right off. Richard was a Jew from Brooklyn, highly intelligent and a no-BS kind of guy. What really helped was that he was flat-out crazy, just like us. In no time we were all laughing and carrying on. There was an instant air of familiarity, and eventually he became a part of our family, and vice versa. I'm not sure if we saw each other more in the studio or at his house. Richard's mother, Sylvia, basically adopted us. She already had three sons—Richard, Fred, and Andrew— and we happily became her "daughters." And just like a mom she didn't hesitate to critique all of our men. Most of the time she was right, too!

Sylvia attended almost every show we performed on the East Coast, and afterward we'd get together for dinner or just to hang out. After Sylvia moved to Washington State later on, the Perrys held an annual family reunion in Los Angeles. Richard would always call and say, "The family's getting together. Y'all gotta be there!" Of course we obliged; we loved all of them.

Richard could see right off that Anita and I were hungry, eager to please, and ready to get back to work. He didn't mess around with artists who didn't match his ambition, and he knew we were determined to get back to the top. What was so encouraging was that Richard had a definite vision for us and wanted the group to have a new style and sound—a commercial mixture of pop, rock, and R & B. No one had ever seen or heard black women sing straight-ahead rock and roll, and we would give it to them with all our heart and guts.

When Richard said he would make us the flagship artists of his new label, it was music to our ears. But he had two conditions for us to meet before our partnership was sealed.

The first one was that we ditch Forest Hamilton as our manager and replace him with Jerry Weintraub, the mega powerful concert and film producer. Yikes! It was clearly a smart move, but Forest was the one responsible for getting us in to meet Richard in the first place. How crass and unseemly would it be for us to now kick him in the teeth? We must've agonized over that one for a whole second or two. What the hell, Forest still managed Isaac Hayes and Wayne Henderson, so he wouldn't starve.

Meeting Richard's second condition wouldn't be that easy. He wanted a third Pointer Sister.

Asking Bonnie back was definitely out of the question. Not only had she defected from The Pointer Sisters to commence her solo career, but then she and Jeffrey Bowen got married and moved somewhere back east to start their new life and record her first album, *Bonnie Pointer*. Thanks mostly to her controlling and manipulative husband, Bonnie was impossible to reach; we didn't even know where she was living. We would be out of touch with her for several years.

June's health had improved enough for her to go back to work, but damned if she hadn't also gone and fallen under the spell of a manipulative son of a bitch. She married William

Oliver Whitmore that same year. He was a computer programmer, but as soon as they were hitched, Mr. W.O.W. appointed himself "June's manager," and in order to get to her we had to go through him.

Bill was all for her rejoining the group. I could tell by the dollar signs bulging out of his eyes like he was Daffy Duck. But first he laid down his own conditions for reuniting The Pointer Sisters. Planet Records would have to put out a solo album by June (*Baby Sister*), and we would have to accept his annoying presence on the road.

Done. Next?

With all the pieces in place we were ready to get to work on our first album—*Energy*—under the Planet Records banner. But at the studio door Richard Perry laid down the law.

"I have just one rule," he said to the three of us. "You gotta do what I tell you to do."

By then we damn well knew record producers were pretty much cut from the same cloth—they were all control freaks. David Rubinson gave us our first taste, and Norman Whitfield a big second helping. But Richard took it to a whole new level. His mantra was "Just stick to the demo!"

He was a perfectionist to the *nth* degree and even went so far as to correct our grammar during sessions and put the brakes on the musical ad-libbing we were used to doing. He demanded perfection, and with that came a large set of rules. We would get frustrated with this over time, but there was no arguing with Richard's track record. He produced major hit songs, and we desperately needed his magic touch. So we caved (at least in the beginning).

For all his rigidity, Richard's recording sessions were mostly engaging and fun, with the musicians loose and swinging from the rafters. I wish there would've been a video camera rolling in the studio to capture the mood. On *Energy* we had the cream of the L.A. session artist crop. It included Jeffrey and Michael Porcaro and David Hungate (Toto), Danny Kortchmar (James Taylor), Davey Johnstone (Elton John), Randy Bachman (Bachman-Turner Overdrive), Waddy Wachtel (Linda Ronstadt), and James Newton Howard, who later became one of the most recognized music scorers for motion pictures.

You never knew who might drop by to join in on any given day. The list included Tina Turner, Diana Ross, Barbra Streisand, Burt Bacharach, Carol Bayer Sager, Carly Simon, and Linda McCartney. I came to especially like and admire Linda. She was just a sweet lady with no pretense or agenda. We were always flattered by the likes of Diana Ross, Mary Wilson, or Tina Turner, who occassionally showed up at our live shows and watched us from the wings. Tina even commented once that I reminded her of herself. That was and still is one of the most treasured compliments I've ever received.

While learning to sing without Bonnie was difficult at first, we got the hang of it, and Richard was amazed not only by the sound we produced but how quickly we memorized the material and stylized a song to make it our own. We could hear a song and know exactly where the melody and harmony should go. If we needed to make a change, we could do it on a dime.

Richard was especially helpful when it came to shaping our new sound by dropping the multiple layers of harmonies and allowing our individual vocals to stand out. Funny thing was, he never gave individual credit for lead vocals on the album liner notes, so the public and especially we ourselves would always think of us as a single, cohesive entity.

Richard was uncommonly generous in other ways. For instance, most producers will never allow you to see the studio enhancements they use to make a record stand out. In the past, whenever we'd asked, "How'd you do that?" you'd have thought we were prying into state secrets. But Richard happily showed us exactly how he sweetened our recordings and what the potential could be. Once he even brought us to a record pressing, something we'd never seen before.

Best of all, Richard allowed us to choose half the songs for *Energy*. Some of the songs we picked were "Lay It on the Line," "Echoes of Love," and "Happiness." Richard's tastes were geared more toward rock, and he chose "Dirty Work" (Walter Becker and Donald Fagen), "Hypnotized" (Bob Welch), "As I Come of Age" (Stephen Stills), "Come and Get Your Love" (Russ Ballard), "Angry Eyes" (Kenny Loggins and Jim Messina), and most notably, "Fire," by Bruce Springsteen.

The way he heard it was that Springsteen wrote the song after he saw Elvis Presley live at the Philadelphia Spectrum in May 1977. He sent Elvis a demo of "Fire," but Elvis died before the tape arrived. Then Bruce recorded the song himself, but somehow it didn't make the cut when he put together his 1978 album, *Darkness on the Edge of Town*. How Richard got a hold of the song I don't know, and at the time I also scratched my head about why he figured this slow rockabilly number was right for us. But he called the shots, and this one was a bullseye.

We gave "Fire" a slyly suggestive and gospel touch, layered with the Pointer Sisters' (another Richard touch: dropping "The" before our name) distinctive voices. I knew it was a hit as soon as I heard the finished product, but I had no idea just how big it would become.

"Fire" became our first gold-certified single and steamed up the *Billboard* Hot 100 all the way to No. 2 (behind Rod Stewart's "Do Ya Think I'm Sexy?"), even besting everything Springsteen had put out to that point in his career. It became one of our signature songs and was an international smash, topping the charts in Belgium, The Netherlands, South Africa, New Zealand, Australia, Austria, Canada, Germany, and the United Kingdom. That song totally revitalized our career.

Our follow-up single, "Happiness," another humdinger by Allen Toussaint, was a Top 40 hit. It has become a huge fan favorite over the years and is still our opening number at all our concerts.

Released in November 1978, *Energy* went to No. 13 on the *Billboard* 200 and No. 9 on the R & B album charts, and it became our first gold LP in three years. Its title summed up what Richard felt was special about us: we infused audiences with energy.

He salvaged our career, helped us cross over to a mainstream audience, and gave us a fresh introduction to a new generation of fans, to whom we will always be deeply grateful for their support.

The Pointer Sisters went on to tear up the charts with a string of Top 10 hits, stylish videos, gold- and platinum-selling albums, and a slew of awards and accolades topped off by three Grammys. Over the next decade, thanks to Richard's astute guiding hand, we became the second most successful female act of all time, right behind The Supremes.

We were riding high once again—unfortunately, in more ways than one.

CHAPTER ELEVEN

Gangbusters

THE FIRST HALF OF 1979 STARTED OUT GANGBUSTERS. "Fire" was riding high on the charts, and our second album for Planet, *Priority*, was taking shape. We had the whole year mapped out, and it was good to see the calendar filled with tours, gigs, and promotional appearances. It was nice to be working steadily again, and even better to have some Benjamins in the bank.

My personal life was a different story. As a parent I was pretty much AWOL, having left my kids with their grandparents to chase after Dennis and the great show business god, Success. Thanks to my cocaine habit I was what we now know as dysfunctional. A study published just as I'm writing this says that coke alters the circuits in the brain in a way that prevents users from learning from their mistakes. Bingo. What's crazy is that most of the entertainers I knew then were in the exact same boat, and when we'd swap stories it seemed like dysfunction just came with the territory. I had no clue how messed up I was until years later when I got sober.

The Pointer Sisters debuted their new live sound that January with a straight-ahead rock and roll band: Tony

Eisenbarger, lead guitar; Will McFarland, rhythm guitar; Scott Chambers, bass; Eric Bikales, keyboards; Jim Langknecht, organ; and Bobby Guidotti on drums. We unleashed our look and sound in London first with a one-hour showcase performance at Ronnie Scott's Café that was so enthusiastically received we were asked to sing on *Top of the Pops* on the BBC. We followed that success with a triumphant performance at the MIDEM festival in Cannes, France, a leading international music business event where global distribution and music deals are struck and sealed. We won standing ovations from the primarily industry-oriented audience and went on to make appearances on German, French, and Dutch television programs that were equally well-received.

If you're smart and really pay attention, you'll notice that European audiences are more studied and loyal than their American counterparts. The European audiences not only know your songs, they know what album they're on, the order in which they appear, and even some of the B-sides or non-album cuts. They know who wrote the song and definitely know all the words. With a foreign audience you hardly even have to sing at all because they're singing right along with you the whole time and it just blows you away. We love playing there.

We enjoyed our first expedition to New Zealand and Australia in early 1979, although getting there was the hard part. On the eve of our scheduled departure I was up all night smoking crack. When the limo pulled up in front of my place in the morning I was butt naked, whacked out of my mind, and had packed nothing for the trip. My sisters had to dress me, and they did it with an eye to speed, not fashion. I left the house in dirty blue jeans, a yellow cable-knit sweater, boots, and a cowboy hat. After they packed my bags, off to LAX we went.

I slept throughout the 18-hour flight and woke up in Auckland, New Zealand. The first thing I did was panic because I was completely unprepared for the show. What I needed most was a perm. But where the hell would I get an African American perm in New Zealand? I called a few salons and found one that claimed they could do a black girl perm. I was doubtful, but time was short so I headed on over. They applied some kind of white folks' perm solution to my hair, then pulled and mashed it in a hopeless effort to straighten it out. My hair just laughed at that stuff. Finally I told them to just give me a nice cut and blow-dry my hair out. I ended up with a very eye-catching 'do my sisters and I called the "Q-Tip."

I sobered up during that three-week tour and realized what a hot mess I'd become. It was the one time I recall hearing talk of my being replaced in the group. That got my attention. I had three children to support, and the band was my only source of income. I got it together and fell in line quickly.

Some of our shows Down Under were our wildest and most risqué. We got downright raunchy. At some supper clubs in Australia we wore chains and leather and writhed around on the floor. I'm not sure how that went over with the folks tearing into their steaks, but we had a great time.

Back home, we honed our more contemporary sound on a series of dates all over America in the spring and summer of '79. The audiences and reviews were fantastic, but all that was offset by the news of our father's death from brain cancer on June 9. He was 78 years old.

While we lived to please our parents and make their lives as comfortable as possible, money alone couldn't ease the pain of growing older. As much as he basked in our success, Dad's last years were not kind. Following his dismissal by the church, gainful employment was elusive. After months of depression he became a parks security guard. I think that was arranged by someone who knew him from the church days and felt obliged to help. Dad didn't really have anything to do. He'd go to a job site but would end up sitting in his car and falling asleep.

Dad's eyes started going bad, and while driving he struck a pedestrian in a crosswalk. A few years earlier he'd hit a young girl. She survived, but this time the person Dad struck died. It was one of the few times I ever saw my father cry. There were no charges filed against him, but his driver's license was revoked. Now he had to rely on others to get around, including me. I'd run him to the grocery store or the bank, and sometimes he'd just want to get out of the house for a while and accompany me on my own errands. I wish like hell I could say we had some great father-daughter times doing this, but the fact is that I was too into myself to think much about Dad's comfort or needs and would get angry when I had to take him around. The poor guy had nothing to do and just wanted to spend time with me, and I acted like I'd just as soon be doing anything else. I was always in a big fat hurry, and Dad moved so slowly it got on my nerves. I'm so sorry, Daddy. I'd give anything now just for one more day with you.

The Pointer Sisters were performing at the Circle Star Theatre outside of San Francisco on the night he passed. We'd actually thought about canceling the show because we had a feeling that was going to be the day. We were onstage and all of a sudden looked at each other and just knew he was gone. We cut the show short and in the dressing room called home. Mom was crying. We went to be with her.

Daddy's funeral service was held at the Church of God, the place he and Mom built with their own hands, whose trustees later kicked them to the curb. Their ringleader was a self-righteous and uptight bitch named Addie Reeves, whom I have always believed had the hots for my father. Back in the day she openly flirted with him in front of my mom's face. Addie was also the one who, after she led Daddy's public lynching, pestered my mom for tickets for our show at the San Francisco Opera House. Addie Reeves had even more brass than ass, though it was pretty damn close.

At the funeral, who should waddle up to the pulpit to give Daddy the grand send-off but that pompous old troll. When I saw Addie standing there I just about lost my cookies. I grabbed Aaron and Fritz and hissed, "Get that woman off the stage, or I will drag her off by her hair in front of this entire congregation! She gets to say nothing today!" They knew I meant business and hurried up to speak to Addie. She promptly left the pulpit, sat her ass down in one of the wooden pews, and stayed there. No way would I allow her the satisfaction of having the last word where it concerned Daddy. (Years later she did come to visit my mother and apologized for her prior behavior. I have forgiven her.)

After the service, nothing was the same in the Pointer family. Daddy's death was a major blow to his wife, his children, his grandchildren, extended family, and the spiritual family he guided over a quarter-century. His passing was especially heartbreaking for me, his eldest daughter, who thought he created the stars and the moon. He was the kindest man I ever knew and was the epitome of goodness. Jesus had a very loyal disciple in Elton Pointer and never had a finer shepherd of His flock.

When Daddy died I did what I always did in the face of adversity—buried my pain in work and play, not allowing myself to focus on my true feelings and emotions. The studio had always been the Pointer Sisters' safe haven, and the beauty of Richard Perry's system was that he always meticulously planned everything out, and all we had to do was come into Studio 55 and sing our parts.

If we caused a puzzled ripple of amazement with our rock and roll Planet debut, then we almost certainly broke the dam on the ballsy, bluesed-out *Priority*. Taking rock covers to the next level, we delivered our most sophisticated set yet. We tackled songs by tried-and-true rockers and old- and new-wave writers, such as "Happy" (Mick Jagger and Keith Richards), "Turned up Too Late" (Graham Parker), "All Your Love" (Bob Seger), "(She Got) the Fever" (Bruce Springsteen), "Blind Faith" (Gerry Rafferty and Joe Egan), and "Who Do You Love" (Ian Hunter). Such material might seem odd for an R&B group, but not only did we hold our own, but our gospel-influenced styles were exceptionally suited for the various styles of music. Richard Perry would go so far as to call *Priority* one of his favorite albums, saying: "The musicianship is incomparable. That was a great rock and roll band. Those tracks I enjoy as much as anything I have ever done before."

While Richard's judgment concerning *Priority* was right on, I thought he was out of his freakin' mind when it came to make the album cover. At the time our preferred off-stage wardrobe was a wild brand of funk-punk, rock, and disco: leopard skin patterns, tight blue jeans, outrageous colored socks, suede boots, sometimes hot pants and high heels. That's how we showed up one day for rehearsal, and as soon as Richard got a gander at us he exclaimed, "I like the way you look! We're going to take a picture today, and it's going to be the album cover."

Sweet Jesus, we didn't even have any makeup on. But Richard insisted, and a photographer was rounded up. Anita and June were cool with the idea, but if you look at my face on the album cover it's obvious I was not a happy camper. What next—candid shots of us getting out of bed in the morning, or coming off a coke bender?

For all of its strengths, *Priority* didn't have a muscular lead single to give the album a big push upon its release in September 1979. Two singles were issued, "Blind Faith" (my first lead vocal on a single) and "Who Do You Love," but neither reached the *Billboard* Hot 100. As a result, the album fared poorly in sales, peaking at No. 72 on the *Billboard* 200 and No. 44 on the R & B albums chart.

But I go along with Richard. *Priority* was one of our finest albums to date, an interesting and vibrant step in the band's development whose mess of contradictions made it all the more intriguing. It received universally positive reviews but ran into trouble at radio stations that refused to accept a black female trio as a legitimate rock act during the height of the disco era. It also left many of the group's old fans unsure where the Pointer Sisters were headed next.

I had that same feeling regarding my relationship with Dennis Edwards, who was back in my life again. In no time we were stuck in our sick pattern of getting high together, which was bad enough. Even worse, often we would freebase in front of our daughter, Issa. Eventually she was placed in my mother's care. Sometimes we'd get to feeling guilty about that and send for Issa and resolve to do better, but the coke always came first, which meant that common sense and normal parenting instincts were never part of the equation.

That finally changed the night I had a fight with Dennis. Issa was with us then, and I fled with her to a friend's house in Santa Monica. Other people were there having a high old time, and of course I joined in and in no time forgot all about my problems with Dennis. But I also forgot about little Issa, until someone I barely knew came into the living room where we were singing, dancing, and acting goofy and told me, "Your daughter is in the kitchen messing around with some bad shit."

When I ran in there I found Issa playing with an open container of toxic insecticide she'd found under the sink. She had soaked a towel with the stuff and was wiping down the refrigerator. I freaked, snatched her up in my arms, and we got the hell out of Dodge. I drove a green Porsche convertible at the time, and we got back to our house in record time considering that I was high, extremely upset, and crying all the way. What a wake-up call that was. On account of my negligence and drug habit, my beautiful little girl almost ended up very sick and might have even died. On top of that, my driving under the influence could've killed us both.

It was time to change.

I pulled into the driveway determined to give Dennis an ultimatum. We either stopped the freebase right now, or I was leaving.

He was sitting on the side of our bed, with the torch and pipe on the nightstand.

"Dennis, I'm done—I can't do this anymore," I announced. "Either you and I are getting clean together, or I'm leaving. I've got to stop."

He didn't bat an eyelid. "I don't have a problem," he said very calmly as he reached for the pipe.

I must've known that's how it would go down because I had left the car running in the driveway. "Goodbye," I said. I drove with Issa straight through to my mother's house in Novato, in northern California. I stayed there for a few months and mostly wallowed in depression. As for Dennis, we didn't see each other again until about a year later.

I don't know if it was a fluke or some sort of weird karma, but it seemed that whenever my personal life was in shambles (which was oftener than not), things started going great for the Pointer Sisters. That's what happened now as we went back into Studio 55 with Richard Perry to cut our seventh studio album, *Special Things*, in the spring of 1980.

A sparkling mix of up-tempo tunes and ballads infused in a contemporary pop/soul vein, *Special Things* slid into mellower waters, the hard-rocking riffs replaced by pronounced basslines and bright brass punches shaping the group's new R & B stylings. Richard also brought synthesizers to the front of the action, putting the Pointer Sisters smack in the middle of a musical revolution on the verge of explosion. Our timing was near perfect as the new synth-heavy sounds paved the way for '80s mainstream radio.

Special Things took longer to record than past albums, but it was enjoyable because we had grown to the point where we felt more free and easy in the studio, and because of our blossoming relationship with Richard. Vocally we were at our peak, and I think the album captured some of our best performances ever. We actually went into the project with a bit of an attitude, knowing that in the wake of *Priority*'s lukewarm reception we'd settle for nothing less than smash material. We listened to a lot of tunes, and any that didn't knock our socks off we passed on.

The nine-song album features a couple of songs written by Anita, the title track and one she co-wrote with album arranger and associate producer Trevor Lawrence titled "Could I Be Dreaming." She wrote the latter when, just like me, she was going through hard personal times and after a bad breakup had also ended up back at Mom's. She gave a standout vocal performance on that song with a believability that I'd never heard before. Anita also co-wrote a song with me, Trevor Lawrence, and our friend Mario Henderson called "Movin' On," a strong declaration of female independence. Our rocky relationships with men yielded an authentic ocean of tunes on that subject. Sometimes it felt like the Pointer women were cursed. We sure did know how to pick 'em, by which I mean we sure *didn't* know how to pick them. I had a ton of experience with men by then, but it sure didn't wise me up as I eventually racked up five husbands before I found the right one. Later on I would get laughs by calling myself the "black Elizabeth Taylor." For a while Liz and I were neck and neck in the marriage derby. But she was a lot smarter than me—she hung on to her diamonds, while I got stuck with mostly fool's gold.

Special Things included two new songs from Burt Bacharach and Carol Bayer-Sager ("The Love Too Good to Last" and "Where Did the Time Go"). We were big Bacharach fans and loved what he did for Dionne Warwick's career. I remember all of us catching one of his shows at The Diplomat in Miami. We sat there and cried, "We want to sing songs like that."

"We've Got the Power" was another great song from that album. We pulled it from the *Roller Boogie* soundtrack and sang the song as a show opener to promote the album. One memorable night we opened with a medley of "We've Got the Power" and "Special Things" at a 650-capacity club called The Attic in Greenville, North Carolina. Whoever decorated that joint had serious issues or a very warped sense of humor. The club logo was a hanging rope and noose and they seemed to be everywhere—on the walls, T-shirts, programs and concert stubs. As if that weren't unnerving enough, the lights over the stage hung so low and were so hot that my wig actually started to smoke during our performance. We were taping a live performance for *Standing Ovation*, a new TV show on NBC, and I had to exit the stage super quick while the cameras were still rolling. I ran to the bathroom where I snatched the wig off my head and threw it into the sink before it was fully engulfed. My "show must go on" instincts must have kicked in because I fluffed out my little natural Afro and ran back out onto the stage to finish the show. Then we smoked on out of there as quickly as possible.

The album's first hit single, "He's So Shy," written by Tom Snow and Cynthia Weil, was originally meant for Leo Sayer and called "She's So Shy." Richard no longer was connected with Leo, and saw great potential in the song for the Pointer

Sisters, so it underwent a gender change. Richard originally intended for Anita to sing the lead vocal because "He's So Shy" seemed best suited for her voice. She actually recorded a version of the song, but Richard said, "I think I want June to record this." Richard had a special relationship with June, and it proved to be a great choice. June's infectious joyfulness gave "He's So Shy" an extra bump. It was a smash, peaking at No. 3, and stayed on the Top 40 charts for 26 weeks while the album climbed to No. 13, notching us another gold-certified single and album. The song gave us a new level of exposure and came back to Anita after June's death. I love the way she performs it today.

My best recollection is that "He's So Shy" was the Pointer Sisters' first music video. It was a primitive affair, just the three of us dancing and lip-synching to the song inside the Bradbury Building in downtown Los Angeles. Lots of stairs and elevators, but we made it work. The video was made just before the dawn of MTV, and so there weren't many outlets available to show it. Luckily, it has found a permanent home on YouTube, where millions can view our pioneering effort.

After the album was released in August 1980 and "He's So Shy" took off, we sang it on NBC's *The Midnight Special* and for an episode of the hugely popular ABC series *The Love Boat*. The night before we taped the show, who showed up at my door but Jeffrey Bowen, Bonnie's husband. I hadn't seen either one since they vanished almost overnight a few years earlier. But I'd heard plenty about them, and none of it good.

Jeffrey considered himself quite the badass gangster, dressing flashy, acting tough, and talking out of his ass most of the time. Whenever the Pointer Sisters were in Philadelphia,

Atlantic City, or New York, we'd invariably bump into people looking for him and Bonnie because they owed them a ridiculous amount of money. My sister and her husband wreaked havoc wherever they hung their hats. Bonnie was later sued for a half million dollars by a musicians' union for failing to pay wages owed to contracted musicians. She had repeated problems with unpaid hotel bills, and her agent Robb Cooper ended their longtime association after she stiffed him for $2,500 in advances. In September 1981, after Jeffrey and Bonnie defaulted on a commitment to record an album for Motown, Berry Gordy Jr. slapped them with a $6 million lawsuit alleging extortion and threats to his life. The suit was dismissed in '82, but their reputation in the industry was crap.

The fact is, I felt sorry for Bonnie and believe Jeffrey controlled her through drugs, physical threats, and his bottomless pit of empty promises. Their marriage was bizarre from the start. The wedding ceremony had taken place at our folks' house in Novato, with our mother presiding. And immediately after exchanging sacred vows the newlyweds adjourned to the master bedroom to smoke crack.

I'm probably the last one who ought to be casting stones about that, especially since I had absolutely no use for Jeffrey until he showed up at my door that day before *The Love Boat* taping and said it was time for us to smoke a peace pipe— filled with crack. By then all my good intentions about getting clean had been forgotten. Cocaine had become too expensive for my taste, but the crack epidemic was now upon us, and when what you cared about most was a decent high it was, as Captain Stubing and his merry Love Boat crew might say, any port in a storm. So Bowen and I got to smoking, and after a while he came to the point.

"What are you guys doing with Richard Perry, anyway?" he asked, though it was more of a sneer than a question. Jeffrey and Richard had known each other going back to the Motown days, and I don't know if Jeffrey's problem with Richard dated back to then or he was just jealous of Richard's success as well as ours. By that time he had produced two albums for Bonnie and both of them had gone nowhere, despite ranting that Bonnie would outshine us all one day.

Even in my stoned condition it was clear that making peace was the last thing on Bowen's mind. But I put up with his bluster until the crack ran out. If he even half seriously entertained the notion that we'd desert Richard and throw in with him, he was suffering from terminal self-delusion. Our manager then, Jerry Weintraub, was one of the best in the business and no man to be trifled with by the likes of Jeffrey Bowen. Jerry was good pals with Frank Sinatra and no shrinking violet himself. He had some mind-blowing industry stories, and no one in Hollywood was a better storyteller. He was one helluva classy gangsta. I still got major love for Jerry Weintraub and mourn his passing.

After Jeffrey finally slunk away at dawn I was in pretty sad shape. I was spiraling down from the crack high, and if given a choice of singing on *The Love Boat* or throwing myself overboard, it would have been no contest. But I managed to get through the taping.

By this time, Dennis was back with The Temptations after they booted him a few years before, and the group had returned to Motown after the two albums they'd done for

Atlantic quickly deep-sixed. It was a point of pride for Berry Gordy to woo them back to the label where they had both achieved greatness. Their days of consistent hit-making were behind them, but the Temps were still a big draw on the road.

When Dennis turned up again it took about a nanosecond for us to take up right where we'd left off—getting good and loaded. One day I withdrew a mess of money from the bank and bought about 20 grams of crack. (I didn't mess around. I bought in bulk!) Then I purchased a beautiful Gucci briefcase and stashed the crack and remaining cash inside. That evening I brought out the briefcase, opened it, and watched his eyes damn near pop out of his head. Then I went for the kill.

"Why don't we just go to Vegas and get married?" I purred in my most seductive voice.

"Okay," he shrugged, as if I'd asked if he wanted to watch TV.

We checked into a seedy motel near LAX and smoked crack until the break of dawn, then hopped into a cab to catch our early flight to Vegas. After checking into Caesars Palace we purchased a couple of wedding rings and went to our room and filled the bathtub with champagne. We drank and smoked that entire night.

The next morning, December 21, 1980, we headed down to the justice of the peace and tied the knot. We laughed throughout the ceremony, like two fools getting a rush by leaping off the Empire State Building.

CHAPTER TWELVE

So Excited...and Disappointed...

THE HONEYMOON OF MR. AND MRS. DENNIS Edwards lasted about as long as one of our crack highs. The marriage itself, maybe six months. We moved into a lovely home in Burbank after our nuptials and proceeded to turn it into our personal garbage dump. Vacuuming, doing dishes, tidying up—that was for normal people, and the norm for us was getting and staying stoned as much as possible. When The Temptations came over to the house, we never even bothered cleaning up for them. We didn't care. Our solution was to just shut off parts of the house as they became unlivable. It got so bad that we had a massive invasion of rats, although frankly I'm not sure if it was an actual infestation or just a manifestation induced by the crack. That's how crazy it was.

Dennis and I had become crack fiends, smoking almost 24/7. I was right there with him most of the time, keeping up a pretty blistering pace if I say so myself. Soon Dennis was once again on the outs with The Temptations. The other guys had grown tired of him constantly missing rehearsals and group meetings and showing up for concerts looking way worse for the wear. He was fined so much the amount even surpassed the tally racked up by his predecessor, David Ruffin. Temptations gatekeepers Otis Williams and Melvin Franklin finally had enough when they learned that Jeffrey Bowen had secretly approached Dennis about doing a solo album. He was all for it, of course, and started recording *Wings of Love* while negotiations with Motown were still ongoing. Dennis completed the album, and it was an absolute masterpiece. The only problem was, he ended up demanding too much from Motown and the project was shelved. Then Otis and Melvin booted him out of The Temptations.

Dennis didn't much care. That was the beauty of freebase—it cured all your ailments and made you forget all your problems. Dennis, crack, and I were a steady threesome. If we weren't working we could freebase day and night, and frequently did. In addition to the obvious side effects—paranoia, psychosis, sensitivity to noise and light, irritability, and suppression of appetite—the drug did some serious physical damage. The crack infected my gums and sucked all the calcium out of my teeth, and I had to have a total dental reconstruction. Dark bags formed under my eyes and my skin turned dry and itchy. Scariest of all were the cardiac palpitations. My heart would flutter nonstop and I'd have trouble catching my breath.

But none of that even slowed us down. One time the glass pipe burned Dennis' leg bad enough to leave a permanent large scar. I don't think he even flinched.

It didn't take long before Dennis started disappearing for days on end. When he went out on tour I got reports he was causing problems if he even bothered showing up for gigs at all, and that he was seen cavorting with groupies.

Let me be real here: I don't think Dennis and I would have ever gotten together in the first place had it not been for the drugs. Sure, we genuinely liked each other and had a lot of laughs. He was good to all of my sisters, especially June, and we had a lot of things in common, chiefly the music. But what we ended up as was drug buddies, no more, no less. Maybe we could have been good friends and even sustained a long-term marriage as healthy as the next person's, but the cocaine and crack smashed any prospect of that all to hell.

I definitely had my own issues, and he sure had his. Dennis was an only child who was spoiled by his mother. He was naturally selfish and didn't like to share anything (especially his dope). He felt he never had to answer to anyone, including the guys in The Temptations who gave him a hand up in the business. At the heart of it all was the fact that Dennis was insecure and couldn't deal with success. And really, was that so surprising? Take a young poor boy from the country and throw him into a goldfish bowl situation where he's constantly worshipped and scrutinized, and that'll mess with his head big time. I don't care who you are or what your family background is, fame is a bitch and can and will take you out unless you're constantly on guard.

Its list of victims is long and distinguished: Jimi Hendrix, Janis Joplin, Jim Morrison, Elvis Presley, Keith Moon, Kurt Cobain, Dee Dee Ramone, John Entwistle, Amy Winehouse, Ike Turner, Chris Kelly, Whitney Houston, and Michael Jackson. I knew and loved a few of these rock stars that ended up rock casualties. How in the hell Dennis and I didn't make that list ranks as one of the true miracles of the age.

According to State of California records, we were officially divorced in 1983. I looked it up. At the time I was too out of it to know or care.

Brace yourself now for the following announcement: I still have great affection for Dennis. We share a beautiful daughter, Issa, who inherited his charisma and towering talent. David Ruffin, Eddie Kendricks, Richard Street, all great members of The Temptations started slipping away. I was concerned for Dennis and wanted to connect again before anything happened to him. I'm very happy to report that Dennis has been clean and sober for many years. When the chips were down, Dennis called his mother in St. Louis and moved in with her. She gently but firmly pushed him to get right with God again. Dennis has finally found peace, and I'm so happy for him and his wife, Brenda.

In the mid-90s, the Pointer Sisters were on tour promoting *Ain't Misbehavin'*, and during a stop in Washington, D.C., I took time out to attend a charity fundraising event hosted by Eunice Kennedy Shriver at her home in Potomac, Maryland. Eunice and I were chatting when all of a sudden I heard Dennis' unmistakable voice belting out one of The Temptations' classic hits. Unbeknownst to me, they had been booked to perform at the event. My stomach had butterflies and my knees almost buckled. I hadn't seen Dennis since the divorce. Eunice noted my shocked expression and asked if I was all right. I mumbled that I had been married to Dennis for a spell back in the '80s—whereupon she took my hand and led me into a large tent set up outdoors and up to the staging area. When he spotted me, Dennis announced, "Ladies and gentlemen, I have two wives in the audience, one of which is a Pointer Sister with whom I share a lovely daughter. The other is my current beautiful wife. One of them sings, so I'm gonna ask if she'll join me up here. No disrespect, Brenda." I forget what we sang that night, but not that any hard feelings remaining between us were instantly washed away.

I didn't have the luxury to sit around and sulk after our breakup because the tour-record-promote grind never seemed to stop. In retrospect, I'm truly amazed at not only our output then but by the high quality of our work. It didn't get any better than our 1981 album *Black & White*.

The title held special significance because we were sick of being categorized. *Black & White* basically meant, "This is it… this is who we are. You're going to have to accept a little country influence in our songs, a little rock and roll, some R & B, do-wop and whatever else we decide to sing." Our singing style had always obscured racial boundaries and what was so wrong about that?

The reality was our sound at that time had evolved into progressive black contemporary pop that was positive, sophisticated, and accessible. We wanted mainstream success, and got our wish with *Black & White*.

"Slow Hand" was the song that got us there. The sultry and seductive song with Anita handling lead vocals wasn't even written for us, according to John Bettis, who co-authored it with Nashville-based collaborator Michael Clark. "The Pointer Sisters were the furthest act from our minds," he told *Billboard* magazine. The demo Richard heard had a very country-soul flair, and he instantly knew it had the potential to be one of our biggest hits.

An unexpected by-product of "Slow Hand's" success was a controversy stirred up by some ultraconservative critics who felt the lyrics were too shockingly bold and aggressive:

I want a man with a slow hand.
I want a lover with an easy touch.
I want somebody who will spend some time
Not come and go in a heated rush.
When it comes to love, I want a slow hand.

According to those laughably uptight and neurotic naysayers, women just didn't put it out there like that about how much they enjoyed the art of seduction and making love. One idiot who probably never got to first base with a dame in his life went so far as to call our song a "license for date rape." Really?! Where was his mind....

What no one could debate was the song's success. In America the song zoomed all the way to No. 2 on *Billboard's* Hot 100 and stayed there for three weeks in the summer of 1981, kept only from reaching the top by Diana Ross' and Lionel Richie's mega-hit duet "Endless Love." It also reached No. 7 on the R & B charts, our first top-10 since 1975. It performed equally as well in Canada and many European countries including the United Kingdom, where we finally broke into the Top 10. A year later "Slow Hand" was covered by Conway Twitty and sailed to the top of the country charts. Funny, but I don't recall any reviewers clucking their tongues over Twitty's version. In any case, I'm happy that today ours remains a staple of adult contemporary radio stations all over the world.

Our follow-up single, June's bubbly "Should I Do It," was an ode to the early '60s girl groups in the vein of The Shirelles and The Chiffons. It reached No. 13 in the spring of 1982, making *Black & White* the first Pointer Sisters album to yield two Top 20 hits. The album itself reached No. 12 on the *Billboard* 200 and was certified gold a month after its release. It was our fastest-selling work to date and gave us two consecutive hit albums as well as a pair of Grammy nominations for Best Pop Performance by a Duo or Group with Vocal and Best R & B Performance by a Group or Duo. We felt we were really hitting our creative stride, and I even proclaimed to *People* magazine that if we didn't win a Grammy that year I was going to slap somebody silly. We didn't win a Grammy, but our album was such a success without it that "Sugar" Ruth Pointer kept her hands to herself.

With another long tour under our belt, I went to my mother's place in Novato to spend time with her, Faun, Malik, and Issa. My kids really flourished under my mother's care; she gave them plenty of love and attention and a heaping dose of spirituality. This was clearly the best place for them. Mom hated what I had done to myself with drugs, of course, but, God bless her, she never went off on me about it. In fact, she pretty much kept her opinions to herself when it came to my lifestyle choices. She never got in my business but always hammered home two points: she loved me unconditionally, and she was praying for me nonstop. Her loving manner and gentle message always stayed in the back of my mind, and eventually they would bear fruit.

When it was time to get back to work, Anita allowed me to live in her Burbank condominium while I saved up to buy my own. A few months later I purchased a condo just two doors down from Anita's, on Sarah Street off Pass Avenue, at which point Mom gently suggested I might want to try giving parenting another shot. She was getting older, after all, and taking care of her house and my kids was getting to be too much for her. We had all chipped in and hired Rose Gibson to help. Rose had been a member of my dad's church in Oakland and was one of the few who'd stuck with them after his ouster from the pulpit. Rose was in a very abusive relationship and I suspected she was gay. She was definitely on the masculine side. Back then the gay pride movement was in its infancy and older gays preferred to stay in the closet. My parents never judged, and their natural warmth drew Rose like a moth to a flame and she was like family.

Rose became emotionally attached to Issa the day my daughter was born. When I showed up at Mom's all drugged out she often took Issa to her own house in nearby Burlingame on weekends to shield her from the family drama. She never said so to me, but I think Rose actually hoped to adopt Issa. Though I wasn't ready for full-time parenthood, that was never going to happen.

But now that I had my own place again I did send for Malik, who was 16 at the time. He was my "little man" and protector. We've always enjoyed a close-knit relationship. For all of my faults, Malik was always in my corner, supporting and rooting for me no matter what. My nephew Segun, Fritz's son, came to live with us and we had a blast. There was no particular reason Segun joined us, and we were delighted to have him. I loved his and Malik's youthful energy and zany antics and rarely felt lonely with them in the house.

Out on the road it was another story. Which brings us to the No. 4 spot in my marital batting lineup.

Don Boyette was the bassist in our touring band when we hit the road in the spring of '82. He was super talented, and that instrument practically melted in his hands. The fact that he was tall, fit, and handsome didn't hurt. I was also drawn to Don because he was funny, kind, and also hailed from Oakland. He was a good 10 years younger than me, but that beat 10 years older all to hell.

We had been acting flirty with each other, but that was as far as it went until we got to Amsterdam. Then I don't know if it was the tulip-scented air or fact that I was plastered, but one night after a show we met at a club and I got right to the point.

"I want you," I told him.

"I want you, too," he responded.

We hightailed it to the hotel and took care of all that wanting. You folks who've been to that part of Europe know that most hotel rooms are equipped with single beds. Don and I solved that problem by pushing the two in my room together. The next day we walked in on the maids, who were busy making our bed and arranged the sheets and pillows sideways. Don and I had a good laugh at the sight.

After the tour Don moved in with me. Everything went fine until we messed up by getting hitched a few years later.

So Excited! was our ninth studio album and the fifth for Planet Records. The album contained some of our best material to date, including the single that later launched the Pointer Sisters into the musical stratosphere: "I'm So Excited." The song was a collaborative effort by Anita, June, associate producer Trevor Lawrence, and me. We set out to write a hard-driving feel-good anthem, and Trevor started off the writing session by asking, "What do you want to write a song about? Think of something, a message that you want to give the world that represents you and who you are." People had always told us that we were exciting girls, so he said, "Think of one phrase that you say when you're going out for the weekend and you can't wait to get there. What do you say?"

Someone blurted out, "You would say, 'I'm So Excited!'" And we were off to the races.

We intended the song to roll off the tongue and be something everyone would say all the time that reminded them of the Pointer Sisters. It was one of those songs that was a perfect merging of words, melody, and the personality and spirit of the Pointer Sisters:

Tonight's the night we're gonna make it happen
Tonight we'll put all other things aside
Give in this time and show me some affection
We're goin' for those pleasures in the night
I want to love you
Feel you
And wrap myself around you
I want to squeeze you
Please you
I just can't get enough
And if you move real slow
I'll let it go
I'm so excited
And I just can't hide it
I'm about to lose control and I think I like it
I'm so excited

The song starts with a driving drumbeat followed by a charged-up piano melody. Trevor thought placing the piano part there was a mistake and said, "I'll fix that," but my sisters and I loved it.

"Are you crazy?" we said. "We love that little jump right there. Don't you mess with it." And so it stayed.

My big contribution was the line, "And if you move real slow, I'll let it go," which was inspired by my own sexual experiences. Fellas, what's the big freakin' hurry?! Slower is better.

We shot the video for "I'm So Excited" a few months later. The video revolution was really kicking into high gear then, with high-tech production values and scripted storylines that embellished the message of the songs and played to the artists' best qualities. For "I'm So Excited," director Kenny Ortega first captured the essence of each Pointer Sister by shooting us getting ready for a big weekend. He filmed me primping in front of a mirror, June splashing around in a bubble bath, and Anita applying her makeup.

The video's big party scene took place in a posh nightclub—the kind of place, Kenny said knowingly, where we would raise holy hell. Toward that end, as we were seated at a dining table while the cameras rolled, all of a sudden he suggested, "Why don't you just turn that table over?" We happily complied, and the slow-motion footage of us overturning our table perfectly captured the "let's get excited" spirit of the song lyrics and made the video a classic.

We all felt another potential blockbuster hit was "I Feel for You," written by a young up-and-comer named Prince Rogers Nelson. We actually met Prince in the late '70s before his first album came out. Richard correctly assessed that Prince was going to break it big in the music industry and thought we should meet him. He was performing with his band at a hotel near LAX, and Richard suggested we go and hear him play. Prince was a sight to behold and I'll never forget his look: long pageboy haircut, white pants, white shirt, red suspenders, and tall boots. Even though he was a relative unknown at the time, he was definitely a rock star. After the set, we went over and introduced ourselves and wished him well.

"I Feel for You" was perfect for the Pointer Sisters and an opportunity for us to really turn it loose. That, however, would have required souping up the original arrangement, and as always Richard insisted that we keep it as close to the demo as possible. That really irked me. What was wrong with at least trying out the interpretation of the material as we heard it play in our own heads? We respected Richard's expertise as an accomplished producer and absolutely loved him as a person. He was fun, cool, funny, and energetic. But Great God Almighty, he could be stiff and uncompromising when it came to the music.

I remember when the great singer and my longtime friend Patti LaBelle asked us how we crossed over into the musical mainstream. Patti was working on her album *Winner in You*, and wondered if I would mind if she asked Richard to work with her on a couple tracks. I told her to go ahead. Two things happened after that, and neither one surprised me one iota. Thanks to Richard, Patti's song "On My Own" went to No. 1, and the next time I saw her Patti exclaimed, "Lord, I don't know how you guys work with that man! I NEVER want to work with him again!"

We were the artists, and by God we had earned the right to speak our minds. After all, it was our name on the record label. We were black, fierce, and spirited, and really wanted to run wild on "I Feel for You." But Richard wouldn't budge, and we did it his way. Two years later, Chaka Khan covered "I Feel for You" the way we had wanted to do it and knocked it out of the damn park. Her version became a Top 10 world-wide hit in 1984, and Chaka's innovative video was an MTV staple for years. I was happy for her. She's been a great friend over the years, and I only have mad love for her.

Another misstep was Richard's insistence that the first single off *So Excited!* be "American Music," a mid-tempo swing song that belied the album's title and mood and harkened back to our nostalgia period. I hated it. It was safe and boring and so white bread that my current husband (who is white) told me that "American Music" was what turned him on to the Pointer Sisters. I didn't take it as a compliment. "You would love that song," I snorted.

"American Music" charted decently at No. 16 in July 1982 and became our eighth Top 20 single. But whenever we sang it on-stage it was a downer for us and therefore also the audience.

In my opinion, having it as the lead-off single slowed the momentum of the album. *So Excited!* peaked at No. 59, our most dismal showing since *Priority*. When Richard finally got around to releasing "I'm So Excited" as a single, it stalled at No. 30 and at No. 46 on the R & B chart. We were inconsolable at the time.

Our next single, "If You Wanna Get Back Your Lady," the most club-driven song on the album, stalled at No. 67, but our 12-inch mix held the top spot on the *Billboard* Dance chart in March 1983. Me and Anita still go crazy when we hear that song.

The hauntingly beautiful "See How the Love Goes," co-written by Terry Britten and Sue Shifrin, was a potential single but was shelved because it was about a woman considering an affair with her best friend's boyfriend. Richard thought it would be too controversial and nixed the idea. Hell, we *loved* controversy, and had survived the hullabaloo ignited by "Slow Hand" the year before just fine. But Richard got it his way again.

We later learned—the hard way, I might add—that Richard had switched Planet's distribution agreement from Elektra/Asylum and the WEA corporation a few weeks after *So Excited!* was released. This adversely impacted album sales as RCA had worked hard to establish Planet within the pre-existing relationships the company had with radio and retail. To make matters worse, WEA released a *Greatest Hits* compilation in November 1982, while RCA was still promoting *So Excited!* It was too much of a good thing, and the compilation stopped *So Excited!* dead in its tracks.

Every time I think of *So Excited!* and all its misspent energy and missed opportunities, my frustration boils up all over again. But you know what? As disappointing as it was at the time, at least we learned to start trusting our own instincts more in the studio. And that made the prospect of future toe-to-toe battles with Richard less daunting than before.

CHAPTER THIRTEEN

Breaking Out and Breaking Down

BEING THE "HOT NEW THING" IS A GREAT FEELING, but it's a good idea to not get used to it because there's always a hot and newer thing tailgating your ass. Even with your pedal to the metal you don't stay the hot new thing for long, because when you are the hot new thing the powers that be will run you to death.

By 1983, the Pointer Sisters had celebrated a decade in the spotlight and kept up a scorching pace that put most other acts to shame. If James Brown was the "Hardest Working Man in Show Business," then the Pointer Sisters were the "Hardest Working Women in Entertainment." When the booking agency sealed the deal, we'd show up and play anywhere—nightclubs, supper clubs, cabarets, festivals, amusement parks, benefits, amphitheaters, military bases, and even a prison or two—pretty much anyplace that had a stage and a dressing room, and sometimes no dressing room. Sometimes we were contracted to sing twice a night…and on some occassions, three times a night. I don't believe a musical voice is meant to do that and remain healthy.

There was volatility and quiet desperation to our career that drove us to work so hard: we knew that if we didn't succeed, our children and parents didn't eat. The same went for all the people on our payroll. We paid musicians, a road crew, a manager, publicists, attorneys, accountants, and a costume designer/seamstress. Our first designer was the talented and lovely Ola Hudson, better known as the mother of "Slash," the guitarist for Guns 'n' Roses. The first masterpiece she ever designed for me was "The Ruthie Dress"—a white A-line knotted front decorated in cherries with a sweetheart neckline. Very much what Marilyn Monroe would have worn in her heyday. There's actually a picture of me in the dress in the *1974 World Book Encyclopedia*. Ola also specially designed my wedding dress when I got married to Carl.

The Pointer Sisters straddled that fine line between popularity and success. We were a known entity, but we weren't selling out stadiums like the Stones. We had a few gold albums under our belt, but they paid very little in the way of royalties. We were famous but far from rich. It always seemed we were betwixt and between.

That all changed with our landmark 1983 album *Break Out*.

There are many reasons for the album's success—which I will get to later—but chief among them has to be the fact that we'd had a 14-month recording gap since our last album. It always seemed that we were threatened with a due date for all of our projects. I know the word *threatened* is pretty harsh, but that's what it felt like. The Pointer Sisters never had the luxury to take our time and create something truly special in the studio. In the past, all of our albums were crammed between tour dates and other obligations of the group. That 14-month rest was crucial to our mind, body, spirit, *and* our creativity.

How the recording process worked was that Richard would round up approximately 50 to 75 demos for us to listen to and consider. We could usually tell within the first eight to 16 bars whether or not we were interested. It's all about that first groove or rhythm and feeling a strong connection to the material. We had become quite proficient at nailing down what was right for us, and if it wasn't right it was on to something else. *Break Out* had a bumper crop of songs to choose from, more so than usual. I instantly connected with "Jump (For My Love)," "Automatic," and "Baby Come and Get It." The other songs—"Neutron Dance," "I Need You," "Dance Electric," "Easy Persuasion," "Telegraph Your Love," "Operator" and "Nightline"—were equally strong.

But when I really knew *Break Out* was something very special was the night I was at home cooking and put an early mix of the album on my stereo. The next thing I knew I was on the balcony dancing like crazy, dinner totally forgotten. And the only thing I was high on at the time was the music.

I have always had a fondness for those classic early 1970s albums featuring Marvin Gaye and Stevie Wonder where you knew all the words to the songs on *both* sides. You put the album on the turntable and played it until it was over and then you put it on *again*. Those were the kind of albums the Pointer Sisters always wanted to make, but never did. That was our goal with *Break Out*. It not only became the touchstone of our career, but I can proudly say it defined an era of pop music and dance-infused R & B.

"Nightline," a song Michael Jackson had recorded for *Thriller* but then left off at the last minute, was the tune that launched our new electro-funk-pop-dance direction that included plenty of drum machines, mini-moog, funky guitar hooks, and synth-riffs. Richard said, "This is now the template that we will use to find every other song on this album. They will all have to be as good as this one."

Richard originally wanted to take us back to our R & B and gospel roots, but all of us couldn't help but be influenced by the dance music we were hearing on the streets and in the clubs. *Break Out* signaled the dawn of the techno age that followed in the 1980s and demonstrated that warmth, soul and artistry were not incompatible with the machine-based sounds. Or as one reviewer wrote, *Break Out* was "the Pointer Sisters at their sassiest, brassiest uptempo best."

Ironically, "Nightline" was ditched after the first pressing, and at our insistence Planet issued a reworked version of the album in August 1984 that included a slightly remixed version of "I'm So Excited." We finally got our way, and it paid off big-time. The song reached No. 9 and at last got the recognition it deserved. It was a massive success and played at every major sporting event around the world, at every Lakers game when they were at the peak of their "Showtime" dynasty, and in numerous films. Today it is a worldwide anthem and without a doubt our signature song.

The album had an incredible run of six singles, starting with the smooth R & B ballad "I Need You," in October 1983, and bookended in March '85 by June's sexually charged "Baby Come and Get It." Sandwiched in between were four Top 10 singles—"Automatic," "Jump (For My Love)," "Neutron

Dance" and "I'm So Excited." And thanks to four high-stepping videos and the explosion of MTV, the Pointer Sisters found a new audience of young listeners and once again reinvented our sound and public image—this time as irresistible and charming over-the-top pop trash divas. *Break Out* was a cultural and music phenomenon, eventually selling three million copies, peaking at No. 8 and staying on the charts for approximately 18 months (*Break Out* also enjoyed a 58-week residency on the UK charts, peaking at No. 9). It also won some snazzy hardware—two Grammys (Best Pop Vocal by a Duo or Group for "Jump [For My Love]" and Best Vocal Arrangement for "Automatic") and a pair of American Music Awards.

The Pointer Sisters were on top of the musical world, and it finally felt as if we had our moment in the sun.

Break Out was also vital in reconnecting the Pointer Sisters with black audiences and radio. There was still a large chasm between the group and a solid black fanbase. Black audiences didn't see us as a "black group" and saw us as singing white music. Of course, when we released songs like "American Music," it didn't help our cause. When our new dance-infused R & B songs began permeating the radio, including an appearance on *Soul Train*, our new edginess allowed us to finally build a bridge with an urban audience. And so did our videos.

The Pointer Sisters attained a major benchmark when "Jump (For My Love)," one of four popular videos we shot for *Break Out*, landed all over MTV, making us one of the first black acts to be played in heavy rotation. MTV amplified our songs and persona, which definitely translated into album and record sales.

In a way, *Break Out* was my own coming-out party. Two of the singles—"Automatic" and "Neutron Dance," which peaked at No. 5 and No. 6 respectively—featured me on lead vocals. Both songs came to fruition in strange ways. We had *Break Out* pretty much wrapped up but felt we needed one last number to cinch things up. We were taking a break from recording in the office of Jim Tract, who was Richard Perry's right-hand man, and Jim mentioned that he had a stash of tapes we might want to listen to as long as we were taking a breather. All of us loved "Automatic" right off the bat. In fact, we all sat up straight when we first heard it and told Richard we wanted to include it on the album. Okay, he said, but who would sing the low part?

"Are you kidding me?" I said. "*I'll* do the low part!" And I made it work, baby.

When I first heard "Neutron Dance" I didn't want to sing it. I liked the rhythm and vigorous arrangement of the song, but to me the word "neutron" had a violent connotation on account of the neutron bomb then so much in the news. The song's author, Allee Willis, who wrote for Earth, Wind & Fire ("Boogie Wonderland"), Patti LaBelle ("Stir It Up") and penned the theme for *Friends* ("I'll Be There for You"), was a good friend and a real character. I told her to change the lyrics, and she told me to quit overthinking it and just sing the damn song! Luckily I shut up and listened. I gave "Neutron Dance" a gospel feel and nailed it in a few takes. I had no idea the song would become as popular as it did. We were on tour with Lionel Richie for almost three months when we found out that Paramount Pictures used "Neutron Dance" in a pivotal chase scene in *Beverly Hills Cop*, the enormously popular Eddie Murphy movie. Apparently director Martin Brest had discovered the song and temporarily put it in the rough cut of the film. The song made the scene sparkle, but producers Don Simpson and Jerry Bruckheimer wanted Richard to create a new song that no one ever heard and asked him to craft something like "Neutron Dance" for them. Richard told them it was a "one in a million song that couldn't be duplicated" and assured them that no one knew the track. They bit and put it on the *Beverly Hills Cop* soundtrack, which sold two million copies. Richard wisely released it as our fifth single a month before *Beverly Hills Cop* debuted. The song, and its outlandish video (featuring a hilarious cameo by actor Bronson Pinchot) that depicted the Pointer Sisters as ushers at a rowdy *Beverly Hills Cop* screening, helped *Break Out* move another million units.

We were at our last stop in Hawaii when the movie hit theaters in December 1984 and weren't even doing the number in our act. Lionel Richie, who headlined the tour, insisted we add it then. "People are going crazy over it back on the mainland," he said in our dressing room before the show. As soon as the opening notes of "Neutron Dance" were played at our concert that night, people rushed the stage and I almost forgot the lyrics.

So this is what a hit feels like? I said to myself. We had never experienced that level of hysteria before.

For many years I had faithfully been a team player and waited for my turn in the spotlight. With few exceptions, Anita handled almost all of the lead vocals on our singles, and rightfully so. She has a beautiful voice and can sing her ass off. June had her own special moments, including her 1983 solo album *Baby Sister*, which garnered decent play on R & B radio. June needed that ego boost, and it did wonders for her confidence. Her life finally seemed to be on an even keel. She and Bill Whitmore were in love and had a nice house just above the Sunset Strip, and June drove around in a cute black BMW convertible. It was nice while it lasted.

Meanwhile, a few of my own chickens were coming home to roost. *Break Out*'s extended run on the album charts meant that I had to be away on the road longer than usual to meet the public demand. That meant less time with my kids. Now teenagers, Faun and Malik were starting to get into trouble with drugs and alcohol. I even had to rescue Faun from the clutches of Jeffrey Bowen and Bonnie, who'd moved to Los Angeles and then, when I was on tour, invited Faun to live with them. When I returned, I went there and literally dragged Faun away. Big brave Jeffrey brandished a gun, but a U.S. Army battalion couldn't have kept me from taking my daughter back. I not only threatened his life but dared that sonofabitch to come around my children again.

I wish I'd come sooner. Faun told me she lost her virginity to Berry Gordy's son, Kennedy (later known by his stage name, "Rockwell"), in that house, after he had introduced her to pornographic materials. I shipped her ass right back to Novato. If I couldn't protect her, my mother sure as hell would.

A few years later when Mom was no longer up to the job, I set Faun up in a furnished apartment across the street from my condo. She didn't work, I paid the rent, and I thought I was being a good parent by providing for her needs. But of course I wasn't teaching her a damn thing other than how to be totally dependent on me.

By then Malik was into cocaine and crack. He had shown an interest in music at an early age, and I encouraged him to consider a career behind the sound-mixing console. I even paid for an engineer to come to the house and teach Malik how to run a soundboard. So much for good intentions. One day I came home and found Malik and Faun sprawled out on my floor, looking like they had been up for days on end. My room had been broken into, my jewelry stolen, and many other items taken and most likely pawned.

I'm busting my ass for this? I said to myself. But who was I kidding? My kids were just taking after me, following the wonderful example I'd set. Ma Barker had been a better parent than me.

My unstinting fondness for drugs and booze had taken an awful toll. My immune system was worn out. I was in Atlantic City on the Fourth of July weekend '84 when the roof caved in. I got so ill we had to cancel the show, which usually took an act of God. I had contracted viral meningitis, but managed to accompany the girls to Chicago, our next stop, before I had to be rushed to the hospital. When I woke up I had no idea where I was or how I'd gotten there. There was a doctor standing at my bedside, and his first words were, "Whatever lifestyle you're living right now needs to change, because otherwise you're not going to be around for very long."

I had a battery of tests and a painful spinal tap. They put me on morphine and Demerol, and my head felt like it had been cracked open with a hammer. The headaches were so crushing my room was kept totally dark and I still had to keep my eyes closed. When I did force them open I saw my baby Issa, then six years old; my mother; my brothers Aaron and Fritz; and a longtime family friend named David Patterson gathered around my bed. They all wore sunglasses because they were crying and didn't want me to know how touch-and-go my situation was. Even with my eyes closed I had kinda figured that out for myself.

When Mom said they had to head back to California, my body shot bolt upright. No way was I staying there alone. Come hell or high water, I was going with my family to the West Coast. Arrangements were made to have a nurse accompany me on the plane, and she shot me up with an elephant's dose of Darvon before takeoff. It wore off somewhere over Middle America, and by the time we landed I was in such excruciating pain I was whisked straight to the UCLA Medical Center in Westwood.

During the two weeks I was there the great R & B singer Esther Phillips passed away on another floor of the hospital, from liver and kidney failure caused by drug abuse. She was just 48. That beat all to hell any warning from the doctors about where I was headed if I didn't change my ways.

A second two-by-four to the head came in the form of a full-page ad in *Billboard* magazine wishing me a speedy recovery.

Oh my God, they think I'm checkin' out, I thought.

In fact, I was damned close to it. But through His grand mercy God turned things around in my body. And as I lay in that hospital bed I took a way overdue honest look at myself and saw a horrifying picture. I'd been a rebellious daughter, an unfaithful wife, an AWOL parent, a so-so sister, an alcoholic, a drug addict, and an overall pretty poor excuse for a human being.

It was time to get my act together because more than likely God, the grand operator of the universe, was getting very tired of giving Ruth Esther Pointer wake-up calls.

CHAPTER FOURTEEN

We Are the World

THERE ARE CERTAIN HARD TRUTHS WE MUST ALL face about ourselves, and sometimes what looks back at us in the mirror isn't easy to take. I'm not talking about physical imperfections, but about the emotional and psychological warts and scars we mostly inflict on ourselves. My own reflection looked like a Picasso portrait.

But at least I was alive. There was time for a full makeover.

It took me nearly three months to recover from the viral meningitis. The great blessing was that it totally cleared my system of alcohol and drugs for the first time in 15 years. Another blessing was that I had plenty of time for self-reflection, which is vital in recovery. My doctors had drummed into me that my body could not stand up to the nonstop abuse I had been subjecting it to. As I would go on to learn, drugs and alcohol were a one-way ticket to three places: mental institutions, jail, and the graveyard. I had an aversion to all three. Besides, I had children to tend to and loved ones I still wanted to be with. That was reason enough to want to live. I was only 38 years old, and, to be honest, I didn't want to die.

Anita graciously allowed me to recover in her condo those first few weeks. When I wasn't sleeping, I spent a lot of time on her couch watching the '84 Summer Olympics. Every week I went to the UCLA Medical Center for blood tests and monitoring. Those hospital visits were constant reminders of the second chance I had been given. As soon as I walked in I saw patients in the lobby carting along their IV drips on hanging poles, looking like they were knocking on death's door. *That's your fate if you go back to the way you were living,* I told myself.

I knew full well who'd given me that second chance, and I decided it was time to reciprocate.

"I want to live a safe, Christian life," I told Don Boyette one day. We weren't married yet, but that would come later on in spite of Don's palpable discomfort when I mentioned embarking on a more spiritual path. I couldn't blame him. He was in his twenties and living out the rock star dream. Since our tour had ended Don had played with Lionel Richie, and later on Cher, Stevie Nicks, Cyndi Lauper, and Michael Jackson. We had been drug buddies, too, and now I was ending that part of our relationship and talking about God. Don's unease should have raised a big red flag, but if it did I was too caught up in my own reformation to notice.

When I went back on the road with my sisters I was, to put it mildly, a giant pain in the ass. I had a lot of rules, and they weren't just for me. I posted signs in our dressing rooms banning drugs, alcohol, and even cigarettes from the premises. "Get those damn cigarettes out of here! I don't want to see no liquor, and I'd better not smell any marijuana!"

It was a 180-degree change from "good old Ruthie."

But I was in full survival mode. What I needed but hadn't developed yet were the tools to help me fight the good fight. Addiction is cunning, baffling, and always waiting on the sidelines to get back in the game, and I was afraid to look anywhere but straight ahead when I wasn't just squeezing my eyes shut and shouting "No!"

It was a very confusing time. In many ways, I was just winging it—basic things such as organizing my house, preparing meals, the proper way to act around my kids, and the simple day-to-day responsibilities were all foreign to me. I guess you could say that drugs had been the band that held all my insecurities together in the past. Now, without that to keep them from erupting en masse, I needed something else to give me solace and emotional comfort.

I found it, of all places, in food.

As I eventually learned, scientists have pinpointed a definite biological connection between alcohol and sugar. Both alcohol and sugar affect the brain by boosting levels of dopamine, the reward chemical in your brain. They both re-create the same feelings of pleasure and levels of serotonin, which the brain then wants to replicate. Just as the alcoholic loses control of his or her ability to control their drinking, the brain of a person who eats too much sugar will demand more and more of it, creating a binge eater.

Goodbye, crack. Hello, Twinkies! Now I mainlined food. Nothing good for you, of course. Junk food, room service, take-out, and what was to me the crack of candy—caramel corn. I hoovered up all I could get my sticky little hands on, and by the time we filmed the "Neutron Dance" video I topped the scale at a hefty 185 pounds. The director put me in a large padded jacket and baggy skirt to hide my girth. I looked like a linebacker for the Green Bay Packers.

Give women a choice of dying from a drug overdose or from being fat, and I'll bet you my last dollar bill 99.9 percent would vote to go out with a needle in their arm than get caught shopping for clothes at Lane Bryant. I was no exception. I loved the food but hated the extra weight. So I started using cocaine again to bring it down.

As a kid I had controlled my weight through gobbling diet pills my mother had stashed away in her bathroom medicine cabinet. Back then, diet pills—which were actually speed— were not that big of a deal. They were doctor-prescribed and readily available in most households. All you did was pop 'em in your mouth and let the speed turn you into a cleaning dervish. Women and their vacuum cleaners became Ginger Rogers and Fred Astaire. And Mom loved it when I cleaned the house from top to bottom.

Then came the sensational '70s and the invasion of cocaine and freebase. I remember Desi Arnaz in a funny *Saturday Night Live* skit playing "Raoul" Nitti in a spoof of *The Untouchables*. Dan Aykroyd, playing Elliot Ness, discovered a bag of cocaine and tells Nitti he's busted. Nitti's defense: he only uses cocaine to help him diet. It got a big laugh, but in fact a lot of Hollywood and music industry types considered coke better than Weight Watchers.

Unfortunately, I wasn't too busy stuffing my face to rush to the altar for the fourth time. I was in bed with Don one night talking about how I wanted to live a better, more normal life, and how I felt guilty sleeping with a man I wasn't married to. I must've been on one hell of a caramel corn high because almost before I knew it we were headed for the altar. We got married at Mom's church in Marin City on October 3, 1984. In fact, Mom officiated at the ceremony. I'm sure she wasn't under any illusion that the fourth time would be the charm for her oldest daughter, but she loved me and held her tongue. She also liked Don a lot.

Just three months later I pulled the plug on marriage No. 4. Don was a very sweet man, but I was a mess emotionally, hormonally, physically, and every other way. Plus, he was a full 10 years younger than me, and if, say, I ate until I exploded, I couldn't see Don overseeing my estate and tending to my children. He was more like a friend to the older ones than a parent.

When I gave Don the bad news he looked at me in total bewilderment and said, "You're really divorcing me?" I was, although the hangdog look on his face sure didn't make it any easier.

But I wasn't kicking him out of my life altogether. I liked sleeping with him too much for that. After the divorce Don moved into an apartment across the street and we continued seeing each other for several more years. Yeah, you could say it was complicated.

Once again, I was riding that weird Ruthie Pointer teeter-totter. While my personal life was sinking, professionally everything was going up. On January 28, 1985, a few weeks after we got off the road with Lionel Richie, the Pointer Sisters were feted at the 12th annual American Music Awards. That night at L.A.'s Shrine Auditorium we were among a roster of award winners that included Prince, Lionel Richie, Bruce Springsteen, and Cyndi Lauper. The Pointer Sisters received the prize for Favorite Soul Group and Favorite R&B Video Group, beating out The Jacksons, The Time, and Kool & the Gang in both categories.

To tell you the truth, winning the hardware was almost anticlimactic for us on that dazzling night. We got to open the national TV broadcast singing a medley of our seven Top 10 hits, beginning with "I'm So Excited" and closing with "Jump (For My Love)." In our futuristic custom outfits designed by Billy Blue we looked like we'd beamed down from the Starship Enterprise for the occasion. Some very acrobatic dancers joined us for a couple of the numbers, and the energy and excitement set the tone for the rest of the broadcast.

Immediately following the ceremony we accompanied many of the other award winners to A & M Studios in Hollywood to participate in the recording of "We Are the World," a charity single produced by Quincy Jones and Michael Omartian. The star-studded, one-of-a-kind session brought together music's greatest living legends in one room, including Ray Charles, Harry Belafonte, Tina Turner, Lionel Richie, Bob Dylan, Diana Ross, Bruce Springsteen, Paul Simon, Waylon Jennings, Willie Nelson, Billy Joel, Stevie Wonder, Bette Midler, and almost 30 others singers.

It was Harry Belafonte's brainstorm. The entertainer and social activist had started a non-profit foundation called USA for Africa a few months earlier to help feed starving people in Africa. Harry's idea was that a recording of this magnitude could raise money for—and, equally important, raise worldwide awareness of—this important human rights issue.

The first hour after we arrived at the studio everybody greeted and congratulated each other on their respective successes. It almost felt like Thanksgiving. June came in with Bruce Springsteen and they plopped down together on the only chair still available in the room. Since he'd given us the song "Fire," Bruce had written Anita a very sweet note saying how much he enjoyed our version and treated her like royalty at one of his concerts, providing her with VIP treatment and a backstage pass. Bruce is a special guy and the real deal.

That night provided so many "pinch me—I can't believe this is happening!" moments: Ray Charles and Stevie Wonder greeting everybody at the door and promising to drive them home if the song wasn't completed in a single take; Bob Dylan rehearsing his lines with Stevie accompanying him on the piano; Fleetwood Mac's Lindsay Buckingham chatting up Harry Belafonte and spontaneously breaking into the "Banana Boat Song (Day-O)," Harry's signature song; and the Boomtown Rats' Bob Geldof, who led the British "Band Aid" sing-along a year earlier that was the template for ours, giving us all a pep talk before the sheet music was passed out and we started recording.

It was a noble undertaking, and to ensure nobody got out of line, Quincy Jones posted a banner outside Studio A that read: "Please check your egos at the door." Just about everybody got the message, the two notable exceptions being country-western singer Waylon Jennings and my brother-in-law, Bill Whitmore.

Waylon was sitting right next to Stevie Wonder, going over the "We Are the World" song lyrics, when Stevie got the idea to have us sing a key lyric in Swahili ("sha-lum sha-lin-gay").

"I'm a country boy, and I'm not singing that shit!" wailed ol' Waylon. Instantly the entire room went silent. Then

Jennings got up and stomped out. Some of the other artists were in favor of locking the door behind him, but a few expressed their own, milder reservations about the change in lyrics. The matter was debated thoroughly and resolved, and eventually Waylon was talked into returning to the studio.

As for Bill Whitmore, June's husband/manager, he embarrassed us all by causing a scene because, as a nonsinger, he wasn't allowed inside the studio to begin with. Others such as Jane Fonda, Ali MacGraw, and Dick Clark all patiently watched on a TV monitor in another room. But that wasn't good enough for Bill. His response was to announce that if he didn't go in, neither did June. Nobody else was allowed to bring family or handlers inside, and damned if Anita or I were going to argue that an exception be made for Wild Bill. So away he marched with June just as Jones and Omartian were making assignments for the 21 solo lines in the song. Without June, it didn't make much sense to give the Pointer Sisters their own line, and so Anita and I were relegated to singing backup on one of the most culturally significant songs of the 20th century. Bill didn't give a hoot about that; the horse's ass just wanted everybody to know what a big shot he considered himself.

Our disappointment about not getting a solo line didn't last long because it was so much fun just hanging out with old friends. At one point Anita, Tina Turner, Bette Midler, LaToya Jackson, and I huddled in a corner for a freewheeling talk about men. I recall being thrown for a loop when all of a sudden LaToya asked if I could help her find a way to get away from her father and manager, Joe Jackson, who was notoriously heavy-handed with his children.

"I just don't like him managing me," LaToya said. "I've got to get away from him." Her brother Michael happened to be sitting within hearing distance, but didn't weigh in.

I stammered and stuttered around until "The Divine Miss M" jumped in and changed the subject. I always liked Bette Midler's style and spunk, especially when it came to men. Once we happened to be dating the same guy, and one night when it was my turn and he came to pick me up there were raw scratch marks all over his face. When I asked what happened he confessed that he had gotten into an argument with Bette and she had literally scratched out a victory. When I reminded Bette of that poor sap now, she smiled broadly as Tina Turner looked on admiringly.

The recording session itself lasted several hours, and the choral section was finished around 3:00 AM. Just about everybody had passed around his or her sheet music to be signed by all the participants in this unique event. Of course I forgot. Anita didn't, though, and still proudly displays her framed copy.

Released in March 1985, "We Are the World" sold in excess of 20 million copies. It topped music charts throughout the world and became the fastest-selling American pop single in history. It garnered four Grammys, two MTV Video Music Awards, one American Music Award, and a People's Choice Award. The merchandise marketed in conjunction with the project (album, video, books, posters, and simulcast) ended up raising more than $63 million, with 90 percent earmarked for African relief.

Although our part in it was relatively minor (thanks, Bill!), I will always be proud to have been a part of that humanitarian effort that brought out the best in the entertainment community. It was a night of pure magic equaled less than a month later when the Pointer Sisters received two Grammys—Best Pop Performance by a Duo or Group for "Jump (For My Love)" and Best Vocal Arrangement for "Automatic." Most of the winners that year were veteran acts that had recorded for well over a decade: Lionel Richie, Chaka Khan, Herbie Hancock, Andrae Crouch, and Tina Turner. Tina sat next to Richard Perry when her name was called for Record of the Year for "What's Love Got to Do with It." Our wins highlighted an era when artists could achieve massive crossover success a decade and more into their careers. That doesn't seem to happen much anymore.

The Pointer Sisters would not experience stratospheric success like that again. We had climbed our mountain. Now the trick would be to not tumble all the way back down.

CHAPTER FIFTEEN

12-Steppin'

BREAK OUT WAS THE SEMINAL RECORD OF OUR CAREER and a real bitch to try to follow. I wonder what went through Michael Jackson's head when he recorded *Bad*, the follow-up to *Thriller*, or when Carole King had to constantly live in the shadow of *Tapestry*? How do you continue on with your work when you know you've peaked? The answer is, you just keep on keepin' on. And so we did. The Pointer Sisters didn't even take a breather. We continued our torrid pace and had *Contact* in the can in early 1985 but then had to keep delaying its release while *Break Out* kept up its monster run on the charts.

Contact was recorded between concert dates throughout 1984 at Studio 55 in Los Angeles; Starke Lake in Ocoee, Florida; Clinton Recording Studios in New York City; and RAK in London. While we were in England filming a commercial for Diet Coke, we were thrilled to receive an invitation to perform for Queen Elizabeth II at Buckingham Palace. But once again, a once-in-a-lifetime opportunity was thwarted by Bill Whitmore.

The day after the invite came, as Anita and I spent hours in London's finest boutiques looking for wardrobe for our next video shoot, we were walking a good foot aboveground anticipating the rare honor of playing for the Queen. We came crashing down to earth when we got back to our hotel and found out that Bill had hijacked June and they were already on their way back to California. No explanation was given for yanking the rug out from under us again. Anita and I had a pretty good idea it was just Bill's Napoleonic complex again rearing its pathetic pointy head. He was a deeply insecure man who just couldn't stand having his wife and sisters-in-law get all the attention.

Once again produced by Richard Perry, *Contact* was our 11th studio album and our debut with RCA. Although it sold well—it went platinum almost immediately—it was largely an exercise in slick, edgy, syntho-pop rock. "Dare Me" hit bullseyes on various charts (No. 6 R & B; No. 11 Pop; No. 1 Dance; and a Top 20 hit in the UK and several other countries).

The song also became part of pop culture history as an outtake from the popular nationally syndicated radio program *American Top 40* in September 1985. The last notes of "Dare Me" had barely died away when host Casey Kasem began reading a letter from a listener requesting a special song dedication for his terminally ill dog, "Snuggles." A sentence or two into the sad letter, Casey stopped and launched into an angry and profane rant that concluded with the plaintive demand that the show's producer "use his fucking brain and not come out of a record that's uptempo and I gotta talk about a fuckin' dog dying!"

"Freedom" and "Twist My Arm" followed "Dare Me" as singles but ended up like poor Snuggles. I just thought the whole album had a kind of desperate air of "don't rock the boat" about it. Don't get me wrong—*Contact* has some very good music, but stylistically it just didn't seek the unchartered waters of *Break Out*.

There was a lot of coke and booze in the studio when we recorded *Contact* and people quietly slipping in and out of bathrooms for a quick toot to rally themselves for our all-night sessions. Now semisober, I wasn't nuts about that, either. But I enjoyed making the two videos we shot for "Dare Me" and "Twist My Arm."

"Dare Me" was beautifully directed and choreographed by our friend Kenny Ortega, and in the first part of the video we were dressed as gangsters (June even wore a pencil-line mustache!) as we walked into a busy boxing gym and attached ourselves to one of the fighters, portrayed by 1984 Olympic and future professional welterweight champion Mark Breland.

The filming took place in a downtown Los Angeles gymnasium, and we had a blast hanging out with Breland and shadow boxing with him in the ring. To this day I still laugh when I see the part of the video where June, Anita, and I are working in Breland's corner and instead of squirting water into his mouth June squirts it into her own. She totally ad-libbed that, and the director loved it.

Actor Steven Bauer of *Scarface* fame was also in the video, and was thrilled to be a part of the production because he was such a huge Pointer Sisters fan. It was a mutual admiration society as we were big fans of the movie and thought he was so cute and adorable. Funny man, too. We just loved Steven.

"Twist My Arm," with a scorching lead vocal by Anita, was a wacky and colorful experiment that featured cutting-edge graphics and gravity-defying antics. We enlisted comedian Bobcat Goldthwait for a cameo appearance as a nervous suitor for Anita who gets more than he bargained for. Bobcat was hilarious and entertained us throughout the shoot both on and off camera. The Pointer Sisters have always had a special place in our hearts for comedians.

Our renewed success resulted in more bookings at larger concert venues and a whopping $1 million payday for a week-long engagement at The Mirage in Las Vegas. That was the first real windfall of our career, and it enabled Anita to build from scratch a two-story home in Beverly Hills complete with a Jacuzzi and swimming pool, and me to purchase and renovate a three-bedroom ranch-style hideaway on two acres of land in the Malibu hills not far from the beach. June had fun redecorating her home in L.A., adding space for all of the things she collected over the years on her travels.

One day while Anita's home was under construction I met her there, and as we stood together taking in the spectacular panoramic view of Los Angeles I got the shivers.

"Can you believe we are doing these things?" I asked. "You are building your dream home and I am going to live in Malibu. Do you know how happy I am to be a Pointer Sister right now?"

It wasn't a rhetorical question. I was grateful for all the good things in my life. Now it was time to enjoy them cold-stone sober.

That happened on October 11, 1985. We were recording our next album, *Hot Together*, at Studio 55, and I didn't want to drive to Malibu in the dark so I hired a limo to take me home after the session. Once I was tucked away in the backseat I reached into my purse for my stash of cocaine. It was just before dawn, and I knew that if I snorted just a line or two I would be up all day. The fact is, I was bored with getting high and tired of the way I felt while coming down. One of the last times I got high it wasn't pretty. I thought I was seeing things on my ceiling and screamed, waking my new assistant Mindy Lymperis, who later became a celebrity chef to the stars. I asked her to check my ceiling for maggots and spiders. She did and assured me they weren't there. I was hallucinating after an all-night freebase session. Now I looked at the plastic bag filled with magical white powder and reached over to the control panel and pushed the lever that opened the limo's sunroof. Then I stood up, took a big gulp of that fresh ocean air, and tossed the baggie into the wind. I was done.

In 2015, I celebrated 30 years of sobriety.

My next move was to finally bring my entire family back under one roof—Faun, Malik, and Issa, as well as Mindy. As it turned out, Faun didn't stay with me long. She was still trying to find herself, and I encouraged her to take acting lessons. I had a car service pick her up a couple of times a week and take her to and from classes...until I found out she was using the service to go everywhere but class.

I quickly discovered that getting sober didn't rid you of all your problems in one fell swoop. After all, drug and alcohol addictions take years to build, and even though I'd sworn them off I still exhibited major addictive behaviors and was almost as confused in sobriety as I'd been before.

I think God sends certain people into our lives when we need them most, and at about that time He sent me a messenger named Gaby Horowitz. Some people might be surprised to see Gaby's and God's names in the same sentence, but the reason for it will become evident later on.

I met him through the great Lucille Ball, whom I knew through Dennis Edwards' landlord, Paula Stewart, a longtime friend of Lucy's. Lucy was a great dame who truly cared about people. If you were lucky enough to call her friend, you knew she had your back. She definitely had mine. She recruited me to play in her annual Lucille Ball Salem Ultra Backgammon Tournament, which benefited Children's Hospital Orthopedic Division. Back in the late 1970s and early '80s, backgammon was the rage among the rich set in Los Angeles. Most bars and high-end clubs had a couple of tables. At the time, Pips in Beverly Hills was the backgammon mecca, and Gaby Horowitz was the king of backgammon.

Back then he called himself "Gabrielle Monet." I didn't know his real name until I started writing this book, nor that he secretly wed O.J. Simpson prosecutor Marcia Clark in 1976. Gaby was to backgammon what Bobby Fischer was to chess, and to this day he's the game's most controversial figure ever. He was often accused of cheating and loading the dice, though I never saw any of that. I did see him purposely lose games so that people would like him. Accusations of cheating in backgammon are common because it is a cutthroat game usually involving players with huge egos. Gaby was blessed with a natural talent and genius for the game, and that made him a marked man in backgammon circles.

Lucy sent him to teach me how to play, and when Gaby pulled up in my driveway in a beautiful Rolls-Royce convertible and I saw that flowing mane of curly brown hair, casual jacket, collared shirt unbuttoned to show off his chest, and an entire family of black and white Pomeranians in the back seat, I thought, *Lord! Who is this guy?*

Gaby learned backgammon from his father, a diamond dealer from Poland who later immigrated to Israel. Gaby came to the States from Israel as a teen and started playing backgammon at the homes of wealthy Beverly Hills residents—and charming their socks off. He spoke four languages and had a natural charisma that even outshone his narcissism, which was quite a feat. When backgammon really started catching on in the '70s, Gaby started raking in the dough. With his earnings he bought a Beverly Hills condo, flashy suits, and expensive watches, and also supported his mother, Clara, whom I grew to adore.

Gaby's fleet of fine automobiles included his Rolls, several Cadillacs, Lincolns, Mercedes, Porsches, a Bentley, and a Maserati. Each time he pulled up to my place he was in a different one. He was the first one I knew to use a remote control key to lock and unlock his car. The gadget also raised and lowered the car windows, and I'd never seen that before, either. I was blown away. One time when I was on tour he had my black Mercedes SEL 500 tricked out just like his. When I got back we had great fun playing with our expensive toys. He was a great guy and wonderful company.

I learned much more from him than how to play backgammon. Gaby was a member of the Church of Scientology, which was neither here nor there as far as I was concerned, and told me about Narconon International, a drug rehabilitation program that had helped many celebrities deal with substance abuse issues. It turned out that Narconon was an offshoot of Scientology, but I didn't make the connection when Gaby pitched it to me. I thought it was just an independent drug and alcohol recovery program.

Narconon's eight primary phases to recovery addressed emotions, personal integrity and self-worth, a more positive outlook on life, setting goals, building constructive relationships, and finding the ability to lead a happy and productive drug-free life. The program also included a detoxification process involving exercise; low-heat saunas; a vitamin, mineral, and oil regimen; a regular diet of fruits and vegetables; and getting the proper amount of sleep.

I signed up, and every single day for five weeks immersed myself in the program for at least five hours. I even fasted for a two-week period and added colonics to my regimen. I dove into wellness as avidly as I had into drugs, only now the resulting high came from endorphins and not chemicals. The cleaner my head got the more I knew I didn't need drugs or alcohol. It was proof I was on the right track.

I was so enthused about Narconon that I enrolled Faun and Malik. Unlike me, however, they were admitted for inpatient treatment—and that's when I got second thoughts. Narconon put Faun and Malik up in an apartment complex where they were kept under constant surveillance by people with walkie-talkies. Narconon reps began showing up at my house twice a week, asking very detailed and personal questions that made me more than a little uncomfortable.

The clincher was the arrival of bills from Narconon, amounting to almost $70,000. I paid them, got Faun and Malik out of there, and gently disengaged myself from the program. Far be it from me to give a negative impression of everything I experienced, because Narconon has helped many people over the years, and it got me pointed in the right direction toward recovery. But now it was time to look elsewhere.

My new perspective made me open and receptive to things I would have blown off in the past. When my son Malik, who was bravely finding sobriety on his own, asked me to go with him to a 12-step meeting in Beverly Hills, I agreed, although with secret reservations. What I expected was to see people in raggedy clothing, maybe one step above homelessness, sitting around chain-smoking cigarettes and telling boring war stories. What a surprise to find instead that everyone at the meeting was well-dressed and successful, and they were laughing, talking, eating donuts, and drinking coffee, enjoying each other's company. Turned out I already knew some of them, including a longtime friend who worked and partied with us on a TJ Swan wine commercial. I was welcomed with hugs, handshakes, and pats on the back. It felt very warm and familiar. It was far from the grim recital of the dos-and-don'ts of sobriety I had expected. The meetings became a social experience for me, which kept me coming back. As I delved further into and began practicing the tenets of the 12-step program I was fueled by a determination to become a better person for my children and be the example and role model they needed their mother to be. I wanted them to be proud of me.

Malik and I were inseparable at this time and each other's strength. We often went out to clubs together and sipped sodas and danced our butts off. Malik has always been a people magnet; wherever he goes others naturally gravitate to him because his personality is totally infectious and he has the looks and fashion sense of a movie star. Especially, of course, the ladies. When we'd be at a club dancing and enjoying ourselves all the young ladies would give the stink eye to the cougar who'd snared the hottest guy in the joint. I loved seeing their faces when Malik told them I was his mother.

When not out on the town we'd attend meetings. We were working hard at staying sober, but as much as I enjoyed and relied on those meetings I hadn't yet taken what 12-Steppers call "The First Step" by standing up in front of everyone and admitting that I was an addict. That finally changed when I gave Malik a cake to celebrate his two-year anniversary of sobriety. Looking at him and our new life together and the happiness we shared in sobriety made me realize it was time to fully embrace the program. The prospect of standing up and openly confessing to others what was obvious frightened me. Like most addicts, I was loath to admit that I needed help. I was a *celebrity*, for crying out loud, on top of the world, a valued and worshipped commodity with lots of money—what problems could I possibly have?

That First Step was absolutely vital because, had I not taken it, it would have kept me from being my authentic self and becoming who I really wanted to be. It was scary as hell, like standing up naked in a room full of people, but I finally did it. And—hallelujah!—it was purifying and empowering. It also helped tremendously to hear everybody else's war stories—stories that I very much related to. Pretty soon I was opening up and telling a few of my own. Allowing myself to be vulnerable and totally honest liberated me in a way no drug ever came close to doing. Soon I got addicted to the truth because it will, by God, set you free.

As I racked up more and more days of sobriety the desire to do drugs and drink alcohol almost vanished completely. For a lot of addicts that desire never fully leaves but just recedes into the background, waiting to pounce. But I was one of the truly blessed ones. Sometimes even now I will suddenly smell something that reminds me of crack, but remembering how pathetic my life was when I used keeps me grounded in reality.

For sure, I have had to be constantly vigilant and especially determined to do whatever it takes to avoid what the prayer books call the "near occasion of sin." If that means getting up and walking out of a room where somebody is using, that's what I do. No apologies or explanations necessary. Stress and uncomfortable situations can also trigger those old feelings and put you in the mindset to use, so I had to learn how to destress and come up with new coping mechanisms. The meetings helped enormously with that. I would've attended three of them a day if that's what it took. The greatest gift they gave me was structure in my life that not only helped me to swear off booze and drugs, but also just to survive in this crazy world.

I have savored my sobriety and will always defend it with a vengeance. But I quickly learned that being sober doesn't protect you from the thorns that come with the roses life hands out. And in the years ahead I'd have plenty of both.

CHAPTER SIXTEEN

Hot Together

EVERY MUSIC GENRE IS A HARSH MISTRESS AND entertainment careers tend to run pretty hot and cold, especially if you're black and female. By the mid-'80s, the Pointer Sisters were the second most successful female act of all time behind The Supremes. And even they didn't have a happy ending or much money in their pockets when all was said and done. We knew better than to rest on our laurels. Resting at all was out of the question.

Hot Together, released in November 1986, signaled the start of a downturn in the Pointer Sisters' recording career. I like the album a lot, and anything with Richard Perry's name on it meant quality, but the music was no longer connecting to a mainstream audience. Music has and always will be a young person's game. They have their ear on the street, set the trends, and buy the music. *Hot Together* was a mixture of catchy songs and shimmering production that showed off our skin-tight musical unity, but it wasn't enough. It was a great party album drowned out by the advent of hip-hop, dancehall, and the New Jack revolution.

Hot Together had some great songs and harmonies, including the first single, "Goldmine," written by Andy Goldmark and Bruce Roberts. The song was the Pointer Sisters' 15th Top 40 hit but charted only as high as No. 33. The title track was another album highlight and featured a strident lead vocal by June. I loved the song's double meaning and felt it was an obvious single. We added it to our concert set list and our audience always ate it up. I don't know how or why RCA didn't think the song was a single but they struck out when they issued the June-led "All I Know Is the Way I Feel" instead. It peaked at No. 93 and then sank altogether. Unfortunately, artists were the last people who were consulted when it came to issuing singles, and it is often the "suits" that made those choices.

My favorite track and the third single issued was "Mercury Rising." Both June and Anita had taken a whack at the lead vocal, but Richard wasn't happy with the results. I told Richard the song reminded me of a Marvin Gaye tune. He asked what I meant. I sang it to him in falsetto and he *loved* it. It was in my own way, a nice tribute to Marvin with laces of "Sexual Healing" throughout. It was sensual and courtly, and I was proud of the end result. Richard later told an associate I "owned the song," which was about as big a compliment you could get out of Richard. It was nice to take on a different vocal personality, but the single only scaled the low end of the R & B charts. Still, it's worthy of a listen if you get a chance.

Hot Together's cover shot was taken by Randee St. Nicholas on top of a Sunset Strip penthouse roof. It was an all-white building and we were wearing all white. One of my best

My pregnancy at age 47 drew worldwide attention, as evidenced by this press conference in Providence, Rhode Island, for the birth of our twins Ali and Conor.

My mother, Sarah Pointer, was my guardian angel and never stopped praying for my sobriety. Those prayers were finally answered in the mid-1980s and we enjoyed a special relationship. This was taken a few months before her death on November 15, 2000.

Pointer Sisters

Misbehavin'

By Simi Horwitz

Ain't Misbehavin', the classic Fats Waller musical, was an attempt to jumpstart the Pointer Sisters' career after going hitless for almost a decade. Starting in 1995, we spent close to a year on the road and it was the hardest work I've ever done in my life. I came away with a new appreciation for the stage.

My husband Mike encouraged me to take a USO Tour of Sarajevo, Kosovo, and Bosnia in September 1999. My life was forever touched by our nation's military personnel, who fight and protect our freedoms on a daily basis.

My first USO was such a great adventure that I signed up for a repeat performance in December 1999 for Operation Starlife "Handshake" Tour. The tour included a great cast of entertainers, including model Christie Brinkley, comedian Al Franken, MTV's "Downtown" Julie Brown, and headed up by Supreme Allied Commander Wesley Clark.

One of the last pictures taken of me, June, and Anita together as the Pointer Sisters. This lineup stayed together for more than two decades, selling millions of records and creating lots of hits and memorable music for generations of fans.

Singing with my daughter Issa and sister Anita. Issa joined the group for our first Night of the Proms *tour in Antwerp, Belgium, in 2002.*

Granddaughters Onika (left) and Sedako (right) have given me lots of joy over the years.

My son Malik and I share a very special mother-son relationship. He's seen me through the good and the bad years.

In July 2009, granddaughter Sedako joined the Pointer Sisters and began rotating with Issa for the third slot. Like Issa, she has developed her own following.

I blinked and suddenly my babies, Ali and Conor, were all grown up. Now in their twenties, the twins are some fine-looking kids if I do say so myself.

My beautiful daughter Faun.

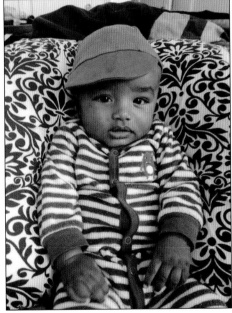

Bailan, my grandson and Issa's son.

The birth of Orland (Sedako's son) in 2015 officially means I'm a great-grandmother!

Still So Excited, *2015. (Photo by Nancy Lee Andrews)*

Sitting behind the recording console, a place where I feel very comfortable. Could there be some new music in my future? (Photo by Nancy Lee Andrews)

On a recent trip to Nashville, where I revisited the Ryman Auditorium more than forty years after The Pointer Sisters made their debut in the hallowed venue with "Fairytale." (Photo by Nancy Lee Andrews)

friends, Max D'Ifray, a Beverly Hills salon owner and stylist teased hair better than anybody in L.A. He teased ours about as high as the building where we took the iconic photo. I used to joke he was the teasers of all teasers. Max was also a standup guy. He cut and styled my hair for years and later gave me away at my fifth and final wedding.

In terms of performance, *Hot Together* paled in comparison to *Break Out* and even *Contact*, peaking at No. 48 on *Billboard.* That was surprising given all the PR juice we put into the album, including a number of interviews on late-night television; a steady stream of concerts; placement in the soundtracks for the films *Spaceballs, Stake Out* ("Hot Together") and *Jumpin' Jack Flash* ("Set Me Free"); a video for "Goldmine," and our first network television special, *Up All Night*, which aired on NBC in January 1987.

Paula Abdul choreographed some great moves on the "Goldmine" video and was a rah-rah director who could go all night and frequently did. But I suspected the perky ex-L.A. Lakers cheerleader and a few others on the set might have had some chemical help. After an all-day shoot, with midnight rapidly approaching, I was exhausted. This was in the very early stages of my drug and alcohol recovery, and I was still pretty fragile. I was no longer up for all-night partying and was simply tired. I had my assistant Mindy pull the car up to the door of the soundstage so I could make a quick getaway after one more take. Then I told Paula straight up: "Look, I'm sorry, but I'm giving you one more take. You can stay up all night if you want to, but I've got to get to bed."

Damned if she didn't want yet another take when we finished. But I just walked off the stage, out the door, and into the idling car. When I got home, Mindy carefully and lovingly tucked me into bed, fully clothed, orange hair teased to the max, with full makeup still on my face. I figured I'd deal with the makeup stains in the morning. I needed sleep!

Up All Night was a much more pleasurable experience. The hour-long special, directed by Emmy-winning producer Don Mischer, was a fast-stepping musical trip around L.A.'s hotspots, and included cameos by Bruce Willis, Whoopi Goldberg, and the McGuire Sisters.

The McGuires had recently come out of retirement the year before, and we had them on the show to sing "Cloudburst" with us at an after-hours club. We had always considered them our sisters from another mister in another era. They were musically gifted, sang like angels, and enjoyed hangin' with the sinners. For some reason, Phyllis and I really clicked. Whenever we appeared in Vegas she came to see us, and we had a standing invitation to visit her at her 55,000-square-foot mansion, which reportedly included a beauty parlor, swan moat, a 45-foot replica of the Eiffel Tower, bulletproof windows, and a 28-person staff to maintain the house and grounds. Phyllis also had more diamonds than Elizabeth Taylor had husbands and a shoe collection larger than an entire department at Nordstrom. That woman really knew how to shop. She once told Barbara Walters the home was paid for by "oil money" she invested in at the height of her career. I'd heard a lot of things about Sam Giancana, but never that he was an oil baron. Hey, whatever works. I ain't mad at 'em.

I've always had my own affinity for gangsters, which is why I need Jesus in my life! My youngest son, Conor, recently asked me what my favorite films are. I think he was expecting an answer like *The Color Purple,* or *Lee Daniels' The Butler.* What he got was *The Godfather, Scarface, Once upon a Time in America,* and *Goodfellas.* Conor has looked at his mom in a totally different light ever since.

During the filming of *Up All Night* we were getting along great with the very charming and sweet Bruce Willis (born on March 19, the same day as me). We had actually met Bruce the year before when he recorded "Respect Yourself," a cover of the Staple Singers classic, for his debut album, *The Return of Bruno.* Bruce contacted us because he was a big fan of Taj Mahal. He said, "I want whoever was singing background on 'Texas Woman Blues' on my album." Well, that was us. We also reprised it for a segment on *Up All Night.*

Everything with Bruce was cool until Bill Whitmore screwed that up with his typical skill. Bill got his undies in a major bundle when, as he was hovering around acting important, a member of Bruce's security team asked to see his credentials. Bill went into gangsta' mode and even threatened to shoot up the set, and the cops had to be summoned. Come to think of it, though, one of the high points of the night was seeing Wild Bill get run off the premises.

Our scenes with Whoopi Goldberg were shot in an old-school diner called Rae's Restaurant in Santa Monica. Getting there was the hard part. My assistant Mindy Lymperis was fairly new to Los Angeles and didn't know her way around the Valley. She gave the limo driver the address but neglected to tell him what city. When we pulled up at a lawnmower repair shop, I blew a gasket. The sun was going down, and we were losing the natural light necessary for the shoot. Time was money on a set, and this mistake might cost us dearly. June talked me out of firing Mindy on the spot, but when the driver figured out where we were supposed to go I ordered Mindy to sit up front with him and do some serious praying. We laugh about it now, but at the time Mindy was as scared as I was pissed.

We made it to Rae's, and the night couldn't have been more fun. We sang the Temptations' "Can't Get Next To You" and had a ball. Repeated takes were necessary because Whoopi would slip out of character and do something crazy. I wish we had the outtakes because they were hysterical.

We had actually met Whoopi several years before when she was doing her one-woman show on Broadway. At that time, we had the same manager, Sandy Gallin, who brought her backstage after our show. He introduced us and told us that she was up for the part of Celie in Steven Spielberg's *The Color Purple*. I lost my mind. I had that entire book almost memorized. She confessed, "I don't know if I want to do it."

"You have to do it, Whoopi!" I said. "I read the book and Celie is you! She is you, girl!" I ain't gonna take credit for Whoopi eventually taking the part (I'm sure her agent threatened to fire her if she didn't take a key role in a Steven Spielberg production), but I do get to brag that I was right on the money. Whoopi nailed that part, and the rest is history.

The evening's most memorable cameo wasn't part of the script. While we were being filmed riding down Hollywood Boulevard in an older-model white Cadillac, we stopped at a red light. As we waited for it to change, one of my sisters glanced over at a man in the car in the next lane over, did a double-take, and screeched, "Is that Sly Stone?" Damned if it wasn't. I had met him several years back when we opened for him at the Palladium in Los Angeles. He was a legend to us.

Up All Night marked my dog Langley's network debut. Langley was a three-pound Yorkshire Terrier and my constant companion. My friend Paula Stewart had several Yorkies, and I enjoyed playing with them during my visits with her. The breed is highly intelligent, sweet, playful, and their droppings are minimal—like little Tootsie Rolls. (Apologies to all whose favorite candy that was until now.) Paula found me a breeder so I could have my own Yorkie to keep me company on the road. Langley, named after Langley Wallingford, my favorite character (actor Louis Edmonds) on *All My Children*, was my constant travel companion for the next five years. That little sucker was smart and mischievous. He knew the entire Pointer Sisters' repertoire, and when he heard the opening strains of "Jump (For My Love)," our closer, he'd run from the backstage area and stand right next to the dressing room door. (Mostly he wanted first crack at June's pantyhose so he could chew the crotch out.)

Having Langley with me was nice, but even after four failed marriages and more heartache than a jukebox full of country tunes, I still believed in and hungered for a man's love. I was bona-fide sucker for guys who were tall, handsome, talented—and, as I got older, younger than me. Lamotte Page fit that bill to a tee. The one drawback was his addiction to crack.

Lamotte, whose show business handle was "Sherrick," was being groomed for recording stardom by Raynoma Gordy-Singleton, former wife of Motown founder Berry Gordy. At 6'4" tall, with a pencil-line moustache and spit curl on his forehead, he looked like a cross between Billy Dee Williams and Clark Gable. His knockout looks and silky smooth voice made women swoon, which is why Raynoma took him under her professional wing. He cut one album, called *Sherrick*, for Warner Brothers in 1987 and enjoyed middling success with the singles "Just Call" and "Let's Be Lovers Tonight." But he soon faded out of the spotlight thanks to his erratic behavior and love for crack.

I met Sherrick through Anita's longtime boyfriend, Gary Reid. He was managing Sherrick at the time. Raynoma had split from him after one too many frantic calls from Sherrick pleading for money to pay off his drug dealers. A few times he gave her car to the dealers as collateral. Sherrick put Raynoma in some real binds and scary situations, but I knew none of this until much later.

Sherrick had just gotten out of rehab for the second time when I took up with him, which took all of a hot second. Since I had some sobriety under my belt, I thought my influence and example would help him, and we started dating. That led, in turn, to the not-so-bright idea of having him move into my beautiful Malibu home.

Admittedly, Sherrick was a rebound man as Don and I were in the middle of one of our many breakups. I had been helping Don out financially to support his family in Oakland while he was on tour with Michael Jackson. I was feeling generous and bought him a brand-new sports car and even had it wrapped in a bow. He showed his appreciation by inviting me to Paris to see Michael Jackson on the *Bad* tour (which I had encouraged Don to audition for). When I got to Paris, Don wasn't there. I called his hotel room in London, and when some chick answered the phone, damned if she didn't demand to know who the hell was I and why was I calling her man. So long, Don.

My mother happened to be visiting when I decided to have Sherrick move in with me. She didn't waste a second letting me know she was dead-set against the idea. "How could you bring this total stranger into your life and your children's life?" she asked. "Think about their welfare." Mom had never interfered in my personal life before, and I was taken aback by her response. Hers was a totally legitimate and understandable comment, but it caught me so off guard and was all in my feelings.

"Do not come into MY house and tell me what to do!" I said to this sweet, caring woman who never hurt a soul in her life and loved me with every fiber of her being. It pains me to this day to remember how I talked so disrespectfully to her—especially since, as usual, Mom knew best.

Sherrick's increasingly odd behavior led me to suspect he was using again, and my suspicions were confirmed when he took off one night in my 500 SEL Mercedes and didn't return. After a few days my assistant at the time, Sue Balmforth, called to report that Sherrick was holed up in some Hollywood dump and asked what did I want her to do.

"Don't you dare bring him back here," I told her. "Bring my car back and leave him right where you found him!"

A while later Sherrick called me himself. He said he was very sorry, begged for forgiveness, and asked me to take him back.

"Hell to the no!" I said. "I never want to see you again as long as I live." And I never did.

Not long after that he disappeared again and this time was off the grid for several years. Once I heard he had been severely beaten and shot by a dealer. He eventually resurfaced, married, and had a family, and even started recording again. But in January 1999 his naked corpse was found on the beach near the Santa Monica Pier. Sherrick was just 41 years old.

As for Gaby Horowitz, whom I dated on and off for several years, his fate was almost as tragic. My relationship with Gaby was different than most. We never argued, never exchanged a cross word, and we never had sex, not even when I traveled with him to Japan for a backgammon tournament. And I ended up not even seeing him play then because I was taking advantage of the shopping opportunities in Tokyo.

It's not that I didn't find Gaby physically alluring. He was a very sexy man. But at the time I was still with Don Boyette. Gaby never once brought up the matter of sex with me, nor I with him. We respected each other, enjoyed each other's company, and shared a love that, though platonic, was satisfying enough for me to once give some thought to marrying Gaby. That didn't happen, and as the years went by our friendship gradually waned.

One of Gaby's star backgammon pupils was Bruce Roman, a strikingly handsome man and also a Scientologist. They became great friends and made the backgammon circuit together. When they were out on the town the women had to be beaten off with a stick.

Gaby and Bruce were avid gun collectors. One day in April 1989, they were checking out Bruce's collection when the Colt .45 in Bruce's hands went off. The bullet ricocheted off the ceiling and stuck Gaby in the head. Fragments lodged in his brain. It was whispered throughout the backgammon community that it wasn't an accident, and eventually police arrested Roman on suspicion of murder. But an investigation disclosed that what happened was a freak accident, and Bruce was absolved.

We were performing in Vegas when I heard what happened, and the first chance I got I went to see Gaby in the hospital. I was horrified. He was in a coma and, due to the bullet wound in his forehead, virtually unrecognizable. He would emerge from the coma, but was permanently paralyzed and unable to talk. All Gaby's possessions were sold, and he moved in with his mother, Clara, in Palm Springs.

When I later met Mike Sayles and we became engaged, I thought it would be nice to get Gaby's blessing. Mike and I drove to Palm Springs, and I will never forget the aggrieved look on Gaby's face when I told him why we had come. His mother placed a sheet of paper in front of him on which Gaby laboriously scrawled a single word: "Approve." He and his mother did attend our wedding, and I was touched by their presence. It meant a lot.

CHAPTER SEVENTEEN

Man with the Right Rhythm

FAME COMES AND FAME GOES, AND WHERE IT STOPS nobody knows…although I sorta had a clue we were heading into a Mojave Desert–scale dry spell as the '80s came to a close. Momentum is a funny thing—you can feel when it's working in your favor, and you can sure as hell feel when it's not. Less than five years after *Break Out*, our rejuvenated career had seemingly dissolved into thin air. Our next album, *Serious Slammin'*, accelerated our decline in popularity and radio play.

Released in March 1988, *Serious Slammin'* was our last album with RCA, as well as our ninth and final collaboration with Richard Perry. It was one of those changing-of-the-guard moments; I think we were all getting a little tired of each other and were ready for it to be over. Richard tried as hard as he could to develop a strong stable of artists for Planet, which included Bill Medley, The Cretones, Marva King, and The Plimsouls. After a decade, we were still his biggest and best-selling clients. Richard wanted to build Planet into another Motown, but it just didn't happen that way. Also, his duties at Planet were all-encompassing and required him to push a lot more paper, network a lot more hours, and crunch more numbers than he was used to. I think Richard was ready to go back and just produce again. I couldn't blame him for that. No one worked harder than Richard, and he needed to take a long breather.

With *Serious Slammin'*, Richard tried to take the Pointer Sisters into a harder electronic funk sound akin to the Cameo/S.O.S./Gap Band hits of the period. He wanted to reconnect us with an urban audience (how many times have you heard that already?!) with more funky, hip-hop, dance floor numbers. The only problem with trying to draw in new fans is that in doing so you usually alienate your older ones. As much as I loved and admired Richard, he didn't know funk from junk. He had an uncanny ear for commercial pop, rock, and R & B, but this genre was clearly out of his realm. My recollection that the sessions were uninspired, the tunes were tuneless, and the lyrics lame is borne out when I listen to the album today. We were so lost.

"He Turned Me Out" was the first single and the opening theme to the movie *Action Jackson*, starring Carl Weathers, Vanity, Sharon Stone, and Craig T. Nelson. We did a fun video with Carl and the beautiful actress-singer Vanity to promote the song and movie, which helped land the song on the R & B and Dance charts. Carl was such a gentleman and not at all what I thought he'd be, the cocky Apollo Creed. He was nice, very sweet, and a wonderful man.

The second single, "I'm in Love," was originally written for Ruby Turner and was a minor UK hit. Our version became our final R & B hit for RCA and made the Top 40 on *Billboard's* Adult Contemporary chart. But after that there was zip.

After the success of "Neutron Dance" in *Beverly Hills Cop* we were invited to contribute to the soundtrack of the movie's sequel. "Be There" was actually produced by '80s hit-maker Narada Michael Walden, fresh from hits with Whitney Houston, Mariah Carey, and Starship. He helped kick-start Whitney Houston's career ("How Will I Know") and practically revived Aretha Franklin's with "Freeway of Love." Narada is a special human being and artist. He is extremely spiritual, philanthropic, kind, and sensitive. Our industry only benefits with people like Narada. "Be There" was a great experience, and the song was included on the *Beverly Hills Cop II* soundtrack as well as *Serious Slammin'*.

Since this was our last album for RCA, we knew they wouldn't invest much time, money, and effort in promoting it. It showed. *Serious Slammin'* tanked at No. 152 on the *Billboard* 200 and failed to make an entry on *Billboard*'s R & B album chart. It was our worst outing since 1977's *Having a Party*.

But the Ruth Pointer teeter-totter—career up, personal life down—was about to go into its uncanny flip mode again. Even though I now had my weight under control without the assistance of cocaine, I still had eating and body image issues. So I turned to Jackson Sousa, a health and fitness guru to the jet set. His impressive roster of clients included Michael Landon, Nick Nolte, Melanie Griffith, Pierce Brosnan, Cathy Lee Crosby, Roy Orbison, Ed Harris, and Charlie Sheen. Jackson worked on film sets, whipping the stars and well-paid film executives into shape. He co-owned a gym with Mike Sayles, a recent transplant from Boston, located on Pacific Coast Highway near Pepperdine University.

Jackson focused on three areas: stretching exercises for flexibility, weight lifting for muscular strength, and cardio-vascular for endurance. But he stressed that nutrition was the most important element of a fitness program and pushed me hard to change my eating patterns. You could work out all day long, Jackson said, and then literally eat yourself back out of shape at the supper table. He recommended a diet with no fat, no dairy, and no sweets. Which to me meant no fun. Jackson dealt with a lot of self-destructive and abusive types but probably had not encountered the hardcore stubborn-ness of a Pointer Sister before. I hated going to the gym, and I had a horrible attitude when I stepped through the front door. Sometimes I didn't bother going at all. So naturally the weight didn't melt off as fast as I wanted, and I got depressed and frustrated. Jackson finally suggested that I join a 12-step group for people with eating problems. It was based in Santa Monica, and Jackson even offered to take me to a meeting the next morning. He did, and I will be forever grateful. I never fully realized the power food had over me until that day.

What I got at that first meeting was a clear and concise message: I wouldn't starve, and there was always another meal coming. It was a reassuring and positive message I needed to hear. Like everything else I did, I jumped into the deep end of diet and nutrition with both feet and never looked back. I started keeping a journal of everything I ate, weighed all my food portions on a scale, and read everything I could get my hands on about health and nutrition. I also attended meetings regularly and started going to the gym with a much better attitude, and after a few weeks the results started to show.

My confidence began to soar and, maybe best of all, my new regimen gave me a whole new reason to go clothes shopping.

A golden opportunity to unveil my new look presented itself when boxer Sugar Ray Leonard invited the Pointer Sisters to sing the national anthem at his championship fight against Thomas Hearns at Caesars Palace in Las Vegas on June 12, 1989. This was the long-awaited rematch between that decade's most exciting and charismatic boxers, both of whom were big-time supporters of the Pointer Sisters and often attended our shows in Vegas and Atlantic City. Sugar Ray once told us that he wanted us to sing the anthem at all of his fights. That was very sweet, even though it turned out he'd said the very same thing to Ray Charles and God knows how many others.

The first Leonard-Hearns fight in 1981 was a classic match between the consummate boxer—Sugar Ray—and the hard-punching "Hitman." Leonard won that one and the undisputed welterweight title with it. Eight years later both guys were a bit ringworn, but their rivalry was as white-hot as ever, and the rematch, a 12-round draw, lived up to its billing as "The War."

As much as I looked forward to attending the fight and showing off the new, improved me, as the big day approached I was missing one very important thing: a date. As far as I'm concerned, there's nothing sexier than an attractive man helping a woman climb up into a boxing ring. June and Anita had their men, but I had jack.

My dear friend and assistant Sue Balmforth swung into action to remedy that situation. It was almost comical the lengths Sue went to in order to find me a date for the fight.

Actually, it was more like a crusade. We had talked about trolling art galleries, museums, and high-end clubs, sizing up the male clientele. Then during a brainstorming session Sue threw a name out of left field.

"What about Mike Sayles?" she said.

"What *about* Mike Sayles?" I replied.

"Well, he seems like a nice guy, and he doesn't really know anyone here," Sue said. "He lives right over the hill and he's convenient."

Oh, how the mighty had fallen! I always preferred my guys flashy, charismatic, and a little cocky. "Nice" and "convenient" weren't even on my radar. Of course, look how swell that had worked out for me in the past. Now I was 43, and maybe it was time to see what dating a stable man was like.

Mike Sayles wasn't a total stranger to me. He was Jackson's partner at the gym and Oakland Raider Howie Long's best friend. He grew up with Howie and lived with him and his family in Palos Verdes for a few months after arriving in California, until he found an apartment in Malibu. We'd said hello from time to time in the gym. Mike seemed quiet, mostly kept to himself, and was respectful of other people's private space. He was cute and had a killer physique, but I really hadn't thought about him as boyfriend material.

Sue called Mike, who was also her trainer, and asked him to be my date for the fight. He said yes, but I'm not sure he fully understood what he was getting himself into. Mike had a wedding to attend in Massachusetts before the fight and had to fly to Vegas and meet me there.

Mike was naturally reserved and shy. I'm pretty sure he felt somewhat out of sorts when he stepped onto the red carpet at Caesars Palace. A championship fight is unlike any sporting event in the world. The girls and I had been to plenty of them before, but it never got old. The high rollers are out in droves: rich old white dudes and their slinky young eye-candy; leather-and-fur-clad Superflys, celebrities up the wazoo. Mike's head was on a swivel checking out the whole spectacle that night. He was so distracted that when it came time for him to help me into the ring I had to tell him, "Get up."

Mike barely said two words to me the whole night. Six of us jetted back to Los Angeles right after our show at Caesars Palace. When we landed we said good night and went our separate ways. When Howie called Mike to ask how the date went, Mike told him, "She hates my guts."

I most certainly did not. But I understood where he was coming from, that he had been a little freaked out and overwhelmed. That's why I decided to call him two weeks later. He was surprised, especially when I asked if he wanted to go out to a movie or dinner. But he agreed.

We went to dinner, and I started to get to know Mike much better on a personal level. He was actually a good conversationalist and an even better listener. I discovered he was 32, eleven years my junior, but he was as mature and together as any man I'd ever met.

On our second date we went to see the Tom Hanks and Meg Ryan film *When Harry Met Sally* in Westwood, near UCLA. The theater was jammed that night, and when the movie ended we were swamped in a sea of people as we headed for the car. Mike instinctively grabbed my hand and guided me through the crowd. When he touched my hand a surge of electricity went through me. I liked that sensation, but what I liked just as much was how looked out for and protected I felt right then. I wasn't used to that.

After Mike pulled up into the driveway we spent a couple hours talking. Subsequent dates ended that same way. One time we sat there talking and enjoying each other's company until the sun came up. None of my prior relationships had ever started out that way. They were always drug- or partying-induced or sexually inspired relationships. Some of them exploited my weaknesses and left me pregnant and alone. Mike just wanted to be my friend—a real friend. I felt very comfortable in his presence, and I opened up to him in a way that I had never opened up to anyone else.

A few weeks after we started dating, I flew to Atlanta to attend a convention. When I got to my hotel room there were flowers from Mike, and he also called several times to say he couldn't wait for me to get back.

Okay, I thought. *This is really nice.* I had been married four times, but I had never been wooed like that before in my life. A girl could get used to it.

When I returned to Malibu it wasn't five minutes before my doorbell rang. It was Mike, come to show me exactly how much he had missed me.

God, was the feeling ever mutual.

CHAPTER EIGHTEEN

Going to the Chapel

SOBRIETY, STABILITY, AND LOVE—MATURE LOVE, I should say—suited me well. I clung to all three with all of my might. My relationship with Mike blossomed, and we ended each date with a heartfelt conversation in the driveway. After months of romantic dating, Mike proposed. Of course I was thrilled, but my initial response was to ask, "Are you sure about this? I have quite a complicated history that you may not wanna be associated with."

Babe Ruth never blasted one out of the park the way Mike did then.

"I don't care who you used to be or what you've done in the past," he said. "All I know is I love who you are right now and I'm willing to take the risk."

I shed many tears, but they were tears of joy. Finally, a man who accepted me just for me. It took a lot of courage on his part because I came with serious baggage, including plenty of family drama in which he was bound to get involved. There was also the matter of the scrutiny he would face as the husband of a famous woman. Sure, fame can bring unusual perks and privileges. It can get you invited to gala events, film premieres, championship fights in Vegas—and backstage at a Paul McCartney concert.

I met Linda McCartney through Richard Perry, and when the famous ex-Beatle swung through Los Angeles in November 1989, Richard not only scored us tickets but also got us backstage. It was McCartney's first major concert tour of the United States in 13 years and he was no longer shy about playing Fab Four tunes, which got the entire music world really excited. Now, Mike is a classic rock guy—Beatles, Stones, Aerosmith, Clapton—anything from the 1960s and '70s; he has an encyclopedic knowledge of that music and era. When he found out we were not only going to the concert but also meeting the "Cute Beatle," he was beside himself.

The nearly three-hour concert was amazing, and I danced all night. About the only thing that rivaled that show was the time Richard took me to see Queen. Freddie Mercury blew me away and was probably the best frontman I had ever seen perform. Before the show, we were escorted backstage where we mingled with the likes of Jack Nicholson, Don Johnson, Melanie Griffith, Dyan Cannon, Mac Davis, Steve Wynn, and plenty of other Hollywood A-listers and industry heavy hitters. When Paul and Linda entered the room, Linda spotted me and shouted, "Ruth!" and I went over to give her and Paul a big hug. Mike had that same deer-in-the-headlights look he had in Vegas when he shook Paul's hand. Paul was pretty used to that, and went out of his way to make Mike feel comfortable. He couldn't have been nicer and more gracious. That sort of kindness is something you never forget.

It was a different story a few years later when we went to New York City to tape an episode of *Live! With Regis &*

Kathie Lee. By then the luster of showbiz had worn a little thin with Mike, and instead of coming with me to the studio, he opted to hang back at the hotel. What he didn't know until I called him from the studio's green room was that Linda McCartney was also booked on the show (to promote a cookbook) and that her famous husband was there with her to lend his support.

"*Miiiiiiiike,* you'll never guess who's with me on the show today?" I purred. "I'm here with Linda, and Paul's here, too. You should have come with me to the studio." Then Sir Paul himself took the phone with a mischievous glint in his eye.

"Yeah, Mike, you should come to the studio so we could all hang out and get to know each other better," he teased. "Sorry about that, mate!"

But back to my point—while there were perks and privileges, fame could also present an unusual set of problems for men married to celebrated women. There were issues of privacy, intrusive fans, friends with dubious motives, press scrutiny, and jam-packed schedules that meant being away from each other for large chunks of time. Men married to famous women must be strong, independent, secure, and successful in their own right in order for the marriage to have a chance of survival.

Mike understood the potential pitfalls but said the only thing that mattered was that he loved me and I loved him. Thank you, Jesus! We set the date: September 8, 1990.

So Marriage No. 5 was on deck, and I needed a home run badly because by then the Pointer Sisters were steadily striking out when it came to producing hit records.

Right Rhythm, our 14th studio album, was released in June 1990 by Motown Records. It sounded good on paper—the Pointer Sisters and Motown, the classic R & B label that birthed some of the biggest names in the music industry as well as my favorite artists. I grew up on the sound and fashion of Motown and was delighted to call them our new home. It was a one-off deal, but our expectations were high. The problem was that we caught Motown a few years after Berry Gordy sold the label, by which time, save for a handful of artists—Lionel Richie, Stevie Wonder, Diana Ross, and Boyz II Men—was at its bottom. Motown was a far cry from the powerhouse label of the 1960s and early '70s. We knew that going into the deal and hoped the partnership would be an up-by-the-bootstraps deal for both sides. But instead of stepping higher, we just stepped in it.

It started off promisingly enough. Motown assigned to us three producers—James Carmichael, Levi Seacer Jr., and Marti Sharron—and shipped us off to Minneapolis for a few days to record at Paisley Park Studios, the ultra-hip recording facility conceptualized, constructed, and financed by Prince.

Knowing we were coming to record there, Prince himself gave us a tour of the complex, and we freaked. We loved him and his music. Built to his specifications, Paisley Park included four state-of-the-art recording studios, a video editing suite, a 12,500-square-foot soundstage for band and tour rehearsals, and a museum where Prince stored his gold records, awards, and memorabilia, including his iconic motorcycle from *Purple Rain*. There was a tailor on hand full-time to make Prince's outfits at the drop of a hat. Prince's calico cat, Paisley, freely roamed the halls to give the place a homey feel.

We recorded a batch of songs there, but for the life of me I can't call to mind a single one of them. I do remember that one critic wrote the album had "substandard songs, only routine production and arrangements, and didn't sound very inspired on any number." I can't find any fault with that statement. *Right Rhythm* was rushed to market without much forethought. The only thing I liked about the album was its cover, but that didn't sell records. It helps sometimes, but not in this case.

It didn't really matter. Motown was in a constant state of turmoil at that time and had a revolving door of executives, beginning with Jheryl Busby, Gordy's successor. Claiming Motown's product did not receive adequate attention or promotion, in 1991 Busby sued MCA to have its distribution deal with the company terminated, which would explain why *Right Rhythm* died so quickly. Whatever attention the album received was drummed up by the Pointer Sisters. While on tour we did radio, television, magazine, and newspaper interviews; record store promotion; autograph signings; and everything else we could to push the product. In the end, Motown just proved to be the wrong label to recharge our career.

But you know what? That was okay. Now I had Mike to blunt those sorts of career knocks and cushion all the brickbats and blows. And I had our wedding to look forward to.

It took place in the garden of my Malibu home before approximately 250 guests, including Mom, Anita, June, Faun, Malik, Issa, and granddaughters Onika and Sadako, who served as flower girls. My friend James Watson presided over the ceremony, relieving my mother of her usual duties. That was cool with Mom because it gave her a chance to visit with actor Dick Van Dyke, who came with longtime companion Michelle Triola (whom Mike trained). My mom loved *The Dick Van Dyke Show*. It was one of the few television shows we were allowed to watch as kids. She was ecstatic to spend a few hours with him. Other notables included Natalie Cole, who has remained a good friend through the years, Mary and Betty Watson, childhood sisters who inspired the Pointer Sisters to first sing as a group, and Gaby Horowitz and his mother Clara.

Mike sported a black tux and was flanked by best man Howie Long. They both looked so handsome. I proudly wore a white dress. Wanna make something of it?

Friend and hairstylist Max D'Ifray gave me away, and he was more nervous than I was. Max more or less dragged me down the aisle, and my veil got snagged on some bushes. I had to tell him to slow down. (Shortly after the wedding, Mike and I visited Max's Beverly Hills salon to see Max. The receptionist said, "You don't know? Max passed away." I literally fell to the floor. I remember Max getting thin, but had no idea he had AIDS. He kept his illness from all his close friends, and it broke my heart. We had so many good times together, and he could make me laugh harder than anyone I knew. I still miss him SO much.)

Somehow I misplaced the tape of wedding music I had picked out for the procession down the aisle, but that turned out to be a good thing because my sisters improvised a wonderful version of "Going to the Chapel" that made the occasion even more special.

About the only thing we didn't mess up were our vows, though we did have to take a few deep pauses to collect ourselves. We had such love in our eyes as we pledged ever-lasting love to each other. The power of those feelings was so overwhelming it almost knocked me over.

Before heading to Hawaii for our honeymoon we spent our wedding night at the chic Bel-Air Hotel. While checking in we ran into actor Tony Curtis, whom I had met years before at Studio 55 through Richard Perry. Tony remembered me—or at least part of me. At the studio I was relaxing between sessions with my shoes off, and Tony told me I had the most beautiful feet he had ever seen. It was the first and last time I was complimented on my size 11 hooves. I'd always heard Tony liked his women big, but I didn't know he meant in the feet.

In addition to the usual reasons, our wedding night was memorable because I leaped off the dietary wagon and ate everything I could get my hands on. I even brought along a shopping bag full of my favorite junk food—lots of chocolate, my beloved caramel corn, and Petrossian caviar, which was top-tier stuff. It was not a time for weighing portions. Seeing me go to town, my new husband was in shock. After a while he tried to lure me down to the swimming pool, but I was right where I wanted to be. The sugar was great, but it didn't come close to the pure sweetness of the true love I'd finally found.

I wished everyone could be as happy as I was then. Especially my baby sister June.

For some time she and Bill Whitmore had been unhappy, and for very good reason—Bill was the living, breathing definition of a shitheel. During their sham of a marriage he went out of his way to destroy my sister's already fragile ego not only by having numerous affairs but also by setting up several mistresses in apartments and buying them cars, property, jewelry, clothes, and fancy dinners—all on June's dime. And the worthless sonofabitch wasn't even secretive about it. It was all pretty much done out in the open and right in June's face, including a child born out of wedlock.

I wish that was the worst of it, but as her "manager" Bill took it upon himself to work on their taxes and got them in hot water with the Internal Revenue Service. They came after the Whitmores with a vengeance, and later it came out that he had hidden money in several offshore accounts. Thanks to him, June had been bled dry.

Unfortunately, my sister was in the throes of addiction and was ripe for the taking. She was a victim of Whitmore's blatant manipulation and control for many years, and blissing out on pills, alcohol, and coke was a lot easier for her than dealing with reality. When June initiated divorce proceedings my mom, Anita, and I almost literally had to drag her to the courthouse in downtown L.A. because she was so tuned out. If not for us she probably wouldn't have dealt with the situation at all.

June ended up shedding Bill, but it cost her dearly. He had the gall to ask for lifetime alimony to the tune of almost $4,250 a month—and got it. Then the judge ordered June to pay his legal fees. I was surprised he didn't brand her with a scarlet letter while he was at it.

When sober enough to understand what happened, June thought she had been through hell. In fact, she had only just arrived at the outskirts.

CHAPTER NINETEEN

Only Sisters Can Do That

AFTER OUR HONEYMOON IN HAWAII IT WAS BUSINESS as usual for the Pointer Sisters. With Marie Osmond, Ann Jillian, and baseball great Johnny Bench, we joined Bob and Dolores Hope in December 1990 to entertain U.S. military troops in the Persian Gulf during Operation Desert Storm. It was the Hopes' final USO tour and our first. It was taped and aired on an ABC-TV *Welcome Home* special on January 12, 1991.

Bob was a big Pointer Sisters fan, and we were humbled by his invitation to join him on his 33rd USO tour. Bob was funny and nice and of course larger than life thanks to his long and storied career. Mike, who went with me this time, was reluctant to go up to Bob and have a picture taken with him. Luckily Mike was sitting in a chair when Bob sat in an empty seat next to him and a photographer snapped their picture together. That picture proudly hangs in Mike's office today.

Because we were in a war zone, there was no set itinerary. Armed military guards accompanied us everywhere we went. We stayed in a hotel in Bahrain, and for the first time since we were paraded into church as youngsters the Pointer Sisters had a dress code. In keeping with Middle Eastern cultural mores, our arms, legs, and heads were always covered up, and there was definitely no cleavage on display.

I made a special connection with the soldiers and sailors on the U.S.S. *Wisconsin*—men and women. They were all so young, innocent, and sweet. It was always "Yes ma'am," "No ma'am," "Watch your step ma'am." Such impeccable manners. I loved them all and wanted to take them home. I spent as much time with these kids as possible. Many came from single-parent and underprivileged households. A few told me that for them it had been either the military or jail. Now they were getting educations and seeing the world.

What blew me away more than anything was the women pilots. I just about fell over when I saw them in their jumpsuits, climbing up into the cockpit, strapping their helmets on, and tearing off into the sky. I loved seeing that and felt an overwhelming sense of pride in my country and in these dauntless female pioneers who proved that a woman's place was wherever her dreams took her.

I was incredibly touched by the whole experience, and one of the proudest moments of my career was when I was named a USO spokesperson in 2000. We owe such a debt to the men and women of our armed forces who put their lives on the line to defend freedom. They are true American heroes and deserve our unending gratitude.

When we returned from the Middle East it seemed our career fortunes had taken a turn for the better. Our manager, Sandy Gallin, had just taken on Michael Jackson as a client. Michael had just signed a $65 million deal—a record-breaker back then—with Sony. His album *Dangerous* placed him firmly back on the charts, and he was riding high once again. I was happy for Michael, whom I had briefly met during the "We Are the World" session and with whom I subsequently had a nice visit during the *Bad* tour, when Don Boyette served as his bassist. Michael was very childlike and inquisitive and exuded a sincere kindness.

"You're Ruth, the one with the deep voice?" he asked in that trademark gentle tone.

"Yes, that's me," I smiled. "The one with the deep voice."

"I love your voice," he said. "I think you have the most unique voice out of all of the sisters."

Michael was very complimentary of the Pointer Sisters' music and told me which of our songs were his favorites. He knew just about our entire catalog—including the B-sides and dance remixes. He had that kind of mind and range of interest. Being "King of Pop" also meant knowing what others were doing.

As he was talking, Michael was chugging on an Ensure nutritional drink. He must have noticed me staring because he addressed it.

"It's hard for me to keep weight on, so I have to drink these," he said. He had endured serious weight loss in the early 1980s and now was careful about what he put in his body. He was thin, but not alarmingly so. Our visit was brief but memorable. He was a sweet man and of course one of the great entertainers of our time. I'd never seen a performer work so hard. That boy really worked, and he left his guts on the stage every night.

Because our agent Sandy Gallin was now linked to Michael, as well as to Cher, Neil Diamond, Mariah Carey,

Barbra Streisand, and Dolly Parton, that stamped him as a real go-to guy in the business. It was right about then that Charles Koppelman, one of the principal owners of SBK Records, called Sandy to tender a recording contract to the Pointer Sisters. SBK was part of the EMI Group and was one of the hotter labels to emerge in the early 1990s. The label had several hits with Wilson Phillips, Jon Secada, Vanilla Ice, Jesus Jones, and McQueen Street. They were young, hip and vibrant—just the kind of place we wanted and needed to be.

Only Sisters Can Do That, our 15th studio album, was helmed by the talented Peter F. Wolf, an Austrian composer, writer, and producer. Peter had turned out major hits with Starship, the Commodores, Wang Chung, Go West, Heart, and Patti LaBelle and seemed like a solid bet to put us back on top.

We recorded 10 tracks at his Simi Valley recording studio sometime in late 1992. A little over a year later the place was decimated in the Northridge earthquake. But then, I was starting to feel some rumbling of my own.

Before Mike entered the picture I considered my child-bearing years over and figured the only time I'd ever set foot in a maternity ward again would be to visit someone else. But now that we were man and wife, we both wanted babies and got right to work. But not in the usual way. At 45 I was no spring chicken. I already had three children and two grand-children, and biology was not in my favor. But we were very determined and had access to some amazing doctors.

They were necessary because I'd had my tubes tied several years earlier, which is why Mike and I decided to do in-vitro fertilization. We tried that twice and nothing. From that point, we had no alternative but to go on an "egg hunt." We searched for a donor who was young, black, and somewhat resembled me. We wanted her to be tall, slender, healthy, and educated. Easier said than done. But glory hallelujah, we finally found a young woman who fit the bill perfectly. She provided 17 eggs, five of which were fertilized with Mike's sperm in a laboratory dish and then implanted in my uterus for germination. I also took hormone shots three times a day for the next two years. The shots made me very emotional; it was like going through PMS and menopause at the same time. I was living in hormone hell and poor Mike was dragged along on the bumpy ride.

Our journey took us to the Milford Hospital in Milford, Massachusetts, Mike's hometown, where we stayed at a hotel while visiting his family for Christmas 1992. We'd already had several negative results, and I couldn't deal with another, so I sent Mike to the clinic for them and waited in our room. He called me from the doctor's office and asked if I was sitting down. When I told him I was he said, "Well, good—because you're pregnant!"

Hearing that was like an out-of-body experience, and I started bawling. It was such a joyful and emotional moment, and those damned hormone shots sure didn't help.

When I hung up the phone I went to my knees on the floor and thanked God. I hadn't done that enough lately. Like most people, I usually only reached out to God in dire need. I had been extraordinarily blessed and knew it, and major thanks were in order. While I was at it I also asked Him to help me be the parent I wished I had been for Faun, Malik, and Issa.

On Christmas Day we informed the entire Sayles family that I was pregnant. It was the best Christmas present ever.

A week later came a belated gift.

We were having twins.

I remember feeling a certain glow when we started recording *Only Sisters Can Do That*. By that time I had my babies inside of me and I loved being able to sing to them while they were still in the womb. In addition to the title track, my single biggest contribution was "Don't Walk Away," a song I had originally recorded for a solo project I was trying to get off the ground with producer Andre Fisher. Written by Andy Hill and Peter Sinfield, the song was brought to me by Andre around the time I started dating Mike. He was with me in the studio when I recorded "Don't Walk Away," and he just loved that song.

My proposed solo album coincided with *Only Sisters Can Do That*, and since the Pointer Sisters was always my first priority I abandoned the project. When it turned out that another song was needed for *Only Sisters Can Do That*, I suggested "Don't Walk Away." Why waste it? The song was tabbed as our first single for *Only Sisters Can Do That*. Peter enlisted Michael McDonald as a guest vocalist, which made it memorable. But I still prefer the solo recording, which Mike still has somewhere in the vaults. One of these days maybe someone can persuade me to release the original version.

As much as I loved "Don't Walk Away" I hated the lame and anemic "Lose Myself to Find Myself," which Charles Koppelman selected as our follow-up single. I still have no clue what the psycho-babble double-talk bullshit title means, and the four-and-a-half-minute song itself sure didn't leave any clues. It was so ponderous, hokey, and vanilla it just about made us gag. But Koppelman kept pushing for us to record this dingbat tune, and to get him off our backs we finally did. We thought that would be the end of it, but it turned out it was the end of us, instead.

Before *Only Sisters Can Do That* was released, SBK flew us to the south of France to perform at a small and insignificant industry party. There Koppelman twisted our arms to sing "Lose Myself to Find Myself." We were team players, so we bit the bullet and sang the damn song. We gave it our best shot, but the applause was tepid at best. Koppelman blamed us for the lukewarm reaction and said we needed an attitude adjustment. We got into a heated argument that ended when Koppelman said he had never wanted the Pointer Sisters on the label in the first place.

"Okay, we can go now," I said to my sisters, and we got the hell out of there fast.

Meanwhile, Mike and Sandy Gallin were spending lots of time together at the gym. Mike was training him, and he told me that during their workout sessions Sandy was constantly on his cell phone, working on music deals and promoting his clients. The curious thing was, Mike said, that none of Sandy's phone conversations concerned the Pointer Sisters. Mike wasn't trying to meddle, but he was on Team Pointer, and it was obvious to him that we were not very high on the list of Sandy Gallin's top priorities. It turned out Mike was absolutely right. So we fired Gallin.

When Charles Koppelman found out that Sandy was no longer in our corner, *Only Sisters Can Do That* was dead in the water. Clearly Koppelman was just using the Pointer Sisters to gain entrée to Gallin's higher-profile clients. There was just no other way to read the situation.

We brought in Shep Gordon, who managed Alice Cooper (and still does), Blondie, Anne Murray, and Luther Vandross, to negotiate with SBK in support of the album. Shep was and is one of the few stand-up managers in the music and film industry, and he did what he could to salvage the deal. But the news wasn't good.

"Ladies, there's nothing I can do for you," Shep reported. He wouldn't take our money and suggested we find ourselves a new manager. We hated losing Shep because he was such a nice man, but we understood what he was telling us—get new blood. Mike decided to take the managerial reins until we could find someone else. Trust me, it wasn't an easy or enviable job. June was getting harder to corral and was often late for or missing shows altogether. Mike had to tread lightly, and it was a nerve-wracking few months for him.

SBK held on to the album for several months before grudgingly releasing it in November 1993. Despite critical accolades, it was a commercial disappointment. That was a shame because it coincided with our 20th anniversary in the business and should have been a triumph. It turned out to be the last Pointer Sisters studio album of original material made with June, and it definitely was not the way we wanted to go out.

Maybe it was just as well, since the timing coincided with a much more important event with a life-changing result: the birth of my last two children.

Surprisingly, it wasn't a difficult pregnancy except near the end when I was about 50 pounds heavier and ready to drop.

The Pointer Sisters, along with Fats Domino, Bobby Rydell and The Stylistics, were booked to perform at the Welcome America Festival in Philadelphia over the July 4 weekend. I was about seven-and-a-half months pregnant, and up to then had been feeling all right. But in Philly I started having pains, and Mike whisked me to a hospital. The doctors told me to get in bed and stay there.

I was not cleared to fly, so Mike made arrangements to keep me on the East Coast. Since his parents lived in the Boston area and his mother, Mary, was available to lend a hand, Mike drove us from Philly to Boston in a rental car, about a five-hour trip. Mike checked me into the Women and Infants Hospital in Providence, Rhode Island, one of the best hospitals in the world for newborn pediatrics. They welcomed us with open arms and gave me a large suite and a second room for visitors.

My situation drew international attention because I was a 47-year-old celebrity having twins, which was unheard of at that time. It was also a high-risk pregnancy. We were profiled on *Entertainment Tonight, Good Morning America, Sally Jessy Raphael,* and *The Joan Rivers Show* and in a host of publications, including two in England. *Hello!,* the *People* magazine of the United Kingdom, did a nice spread, but *The Globe,* a trashy publication that invented stories—the nuttier the better—to suit its whim, gave us the full tabloid treatment culminating in the screaming headline, "Ruth Pointer Is Pregnant with Test Tube Babies."

On July 17, 1993, I gave birth to a 4-pound, 11-ounce boy, Conor, and daughter Ali, who weighed 3 pounds, 12 ounces. They were nine weeks premature and delivered by caesarian section. Because of their low birth weights, Conor remained in the hospital for about a week, and Ali a couple weeks longer. It tore me up having to leave my babies behind. I was in emotional knots and called the nurses every morning as soon as I awoke to check on my children. I was especially worried about Ali, because she was so tiny. It was always a scary call to make. I drove to Rhode Island every other day to breastfeed her. Even after they were both home, Conor and Ali wore heart apnea monitors for eight months until they were officially declared out of the woods.

CHAPTER TWENTY

Ain't Misbehavin'

THE NECESSITY OF EXTENDED MONITORING OF THE
twins' health and our satisfaction with the quality of the professional care they were getting made our decision to stay
put in Massachusetts a no-brainer. My mother-in-law, Mary
Sayles, was a godsend. She invited us to temporarily move
into her three-bedroom home in Milford (where Mike and
his sister Linda grew up) while we were building a house in
Massachusetts. She also didn't blink an eye when we had Issa
join us from California. Mary quit her job with the State of
Massachusetts to help us out with the twins. We paid her
a salary, but she went way above the call of duty, especially
when I had to go out of town on business.

The Malibu fires of 1993, which came very close to torch-
ing our home, and the 6.8 Northridge earthquake a year later
seemed like signals from above that it was time to sell our
home on the West Coast and start over elsewhere. Besides,
Mike was starting a new career and had partnered with a business associate to develop a 100-acre lot in nearby Mendon.
Mike needed to be in Massachusetts full-time; all I needed to
continue with my career was access to an airport.

As warm and hospitable as our new home and surroundings were, going from Malibu to Milford was a whopping cultural and meteorological shock. At the time, Milford had a population of about 20,000 people, most of whom were Caucasian. Looking for other African American persons around town became an enthusiastic pastime for Issa and me. Whenever we saw one we'd scream, "Black people!" I tried to fit in as best as I could, shopping at the local food markets and clothing boutiques, eating at downtown restaurants, and making sure to be friendly to everyone. It is a nice little town, and whenever I got a craving for the quicker pulse, faster pace, and greater across-the-board variety of the big city I got in the car and drove to Boston, about 40 miles away, and found whatever I wanted. Usually at the top of that list was Starbucks and fashionable clothing.

Adjusting from the near-perfect Malibu weather and sunshine every day to the frigid, snowy East Coast was a whole different kind of challenge. Over the years I have grown to appreciate and even love summer and fall in the Northeast. I cannot say the same about winter. As I'm writing this now, our area has had over 110 inches of snow this winter alone and way below-average temperatures.

When I was ready to get back into the harness, the Pointer Sisters' first gig was singing the National Anthem at a Los Angeles Raiders home game in fall or winter '93. It turned out to be old home week, as Mike's best friend Howie Long played for the Raiders then and my brother Aaron officiated at the game. Aaron had been a professional baseball player for several years in the United States, Japan, and Venezuela. After he retired he became a top-flight gridiron referee. Before the game they took a group photo of all of us on the sidelines that hangs on my wall still.

Right around that time we recorded Aretha Franklin's "Chain of Fools" with Clint Black for a duets album called *Rhythm, Country and Blues*. The album's intent was to demonstrate there wasn't a world of difference between country and soul. Producers Don Was and Tony Brown drummed up a series of 11 duets featuring different country and R & B artists, including Vince Gill and Gladys Knight, Al Green and Lyle Lovett, Little Richard and Tanya Tucker, and Patti LaBelle and Travis Tritt.

"Chain of Fools" was right up our alley, and in fact had been in our repertoire for years. We loved Aretha Franklin, but the feeling wasn't always mutual. Until he threw her over for me, Dennis Edwards and Aretha were an item and had even contemplated getting married. So Aretha was not my biggest fan, and for a few years whenever we crossed paths she was colder than Boston in December. I didn't take it personally, though. The inspiration that I've received from her since I was eight years old is enough for me. I love the lady, and I stand on her shoulders as they say.

The session seemed to last but a nanosecond and was recorded and later aired on PBS. Clint Black was not only a real gentleman cowboy, but also a true pro. We got the song in a few takes. *Rhythm, Country and Blues* was released by MCA Records on March 1, 1994, and debuted at No. 1 on the Top Country albums and No. 15 on Top R & B/Hip-Hop.

The album was an expected smash and went platinum—our first since 1985—and "Chain of Fools" was nominated for Song of the Year by the Country Music Association. It definitely helped build some much-needed career momentum after a very long slump and also helped us snare our next manager, Jason Winters of the powerful Sterling/Winters Co. He was our manager for the next decade.

Another boost came when the William Morris Agency, our booking agents, set up a star for us on the Hollywood Walk of Fame on September 29, 1994. We were the second all-female group to receive such an honor. The first was The Supremes. The unveiling of our star was a happening, and the show got underway when the Los Angeles Rams cheerleaders arrived to warm up the boisterous crowd, followed by honorary Hollywood mayor Johnny Grant. We arrived in high style in a procession of three vintage Rolls-Royces led by police escort. The cars carried the Pointer Sisters, Fritz and Aaron, and my mother.

Estranged sister Bonnie came along for the ride, though it wasn't my or Anita's idea to invite her. At the time Bonnie was drinking and drugging it up big time, and the last thing we wanted was for any untoward behavior to detract from the occasion. It was June who pulled Bonnie into the picture at the last minute. That ride in the Rolls to the celebration was awkward, but we gritted our teeth and politely kept our mouths shut.

The crowd erupted in cheers as the Pointer Sisters, decked out in eye-catching nostalgia threads (a nod to our musical roots as well as our next big career move—starring in a traveling production of the Broadway classic *Ain't Misbehavin'*) pranced through an aisle of cheerleaders onto the stage on Hollywood Boulevard. Several friends and family members stepped up to the podium to talk about our past accomplishments, and an MCA record executive presented us with our platinum records for *Rhythm, Country and Blues.* Mayor Grant mentioned our impending foray into musical theater, unveiled our star, and officially proclaimed it "Pointer Sisters Day" in Hollywood.

It was a wonderful event and would have been even better had June not been drunk. She was of the mindset that this was a celebration, and celebration meant party time. After the unveiling we headed to the House of Blues on Sunset Boulevard where they hosted a reception for us and we previewed a song from *Ain't Misbehavin'.* Bonnie was wasted by then and hinting that she wanted to get back in the group. When June started lobbying on Bonnie's behalf, the vibe got weird and very strained. We had been a trio for so long, and, much as it pains me to say this, Bonnie no longer fit the musical mold of the group. Anita and Mike and I got very uncomfortable with Bonnie around. After visiting with my mother and a few friends, we cut our night short and quietly left.

June's behavior was really starting to concern me, especially when I thought about our upcoming tour of duty in *Ain't Misbehavin'.* We had signed on for a yearlong commitment requiring eight performances a week. I knew Anita and I were up to the physical demands that would impose on us, but June was a big question mark.

Our touring production of *Ain't Misbehavin'* would revive the popular 1978 play based on 35 songs by Thomas "Fats" Waller, the Tin Pan Alley master whose jazzy, swinging, torch songs captured the sounds of black musicians of the 1920s and '30s who ignited the Harlem Renaissance. The musical revue captures the excitement of the Cotton Club, Savoy Ballroom, and Lenox Avenue dives and honky-tonks that were the playgrounds of high society. The beloved original Broadway production, starring Irene Cara and Nell Carter, ran for four years to loud cheers.

We had performed a "Fats" Waller medley on *The Carol Burnett Show* in the early 1970s and had also sung "Tain't Nobody's Biz-ness If I Do" a time or two before, but other than that we weren't familiar with Fats Waller's musical catalog. What a pleasure it was to get acquainted with it. There is a real joy to the music that tells what life was like for him on the road and about his relationships with various people and what they meant to him.

In preparing for the musical we quickly learned what Broadway artists physically endure. It was like training for a championship fight. We'd done Vegas and some acting before, and the Pointer Sisters' choreography was, if I say so myself, as intricate and impressive as anything going. But this was very different. There were so many things to remember— including learning to not say "thank you" to the audience after each song. We had done that during every performance for more than two decades, and now cutting it out took real concentration. And in a stage play there is no ad-libbing. You recite only what's in the script so as not to throw off your fellow actors. You'd think that wouldn't be such a big deal, but it was much harder than it looked. That and the fact that rehearsals ran about eight hours a day, six days a week, and in three-inch platform shoes.

Our six-week rehearsal period started in New York City in July '95 with co-stars Eugene Barry-Hill and Michael-Leon Wooley. Arthur Faria, who owned the rights to the musical, came up with the choreography. The plan was to record a cast album, take the revue around the country, and end up on Broadway, re-establishing the Pointer Sisters as a household name.

Only two of the above happened, and it sure wasn't the two at the top of our list.

In the beginning it was a new and thrilling adventure. The investors were very generous and everything was first-class. They brought us to the Big Apple to experience what it felt like to be real "Broadway artists." We were put up in the Pierre Hotel on 61st Street near Rockefeller Center. I loved the hustle and bustle of the city, getting picked up in a town car, and listening to my favorite R & B station on the ride to the rehearsal hall. There we would run into other artists in the hallway or on the elevator. We'd hear the tinkling of the piano and actors rehearsing their lines and see dancers stretching their limbs. You couldn't help but be excited in this type of environment.

That special feeling lasted all of one week after we took *Ain't Misbehavin'* on the road.

By design, we opened in September in Green Bay, Wisconsin, about as far off the Great White Way as it gets. We didn't want the eyes of the big-city media on us until we worked out all the kinks in the show. But right off the bat we got unwanted attention of a different kind when agents of the Drug Enforcement Administration showed up at our hotel looking for June. They'd intercepted a package sent to her, and I probably don't have to tell you what it contained. Luckily for June, the agents were Pointer Sisters fans and let her slide with a warning. Sadly, she didn't learn from her mistakes and wasn't humbled or rattled at all by her close call.

She was simply beyond caring at that point. Not holding her accountable for her actions right then and there was, in retrospect, probably the worst thing for her. It meant that rock bottom still awaited June, and she continued on her not-so-merry descent.

Ain't Misbehavin' ran for 48 weeks, and June missed 211 performances—approximately 30 weeks! Most of her absences were a result of drug binges, but on one occasion she was knocked out of commission by Jeffrey Bowen, Bonnie's punk-ass husband. It happened at a Christmas Eve party at June's house. Everything was fine until Jeffrey told Bonnie it was time for them to leave. Bonnie didn't want to go. They ended up in a scuffle, and when June intervened Jeffrey broke her nose and sprained one of her fingers. Despite her slight build, June was no one to mess with. She had a temper and wasn't one to back down. June grabbed the nearest thing she could find—an ice bucket—and cracked Jeffrey over the head, knocking him out. When he came to, the police hauled his ass to jail. When he bailed out, he and Bonnie went right to the *National Enquirer* to tell them their side of the story—that Bonnie broke her own nose with the ice bucket. In court it was a different story.

In front of a judge, Jeffrey cried like a bitch-ass punk, blamed his behavior on alcohol and cocaine, and begged for forgiveness. He was sentenced to three years probation, eight months of community service, and a year of domestic abuse counseling, and was ordered to attend two Narcotics Anonymous meetings a week for 13 weeks and fined $2,000. In a development about as surprising as night following day, a few weeks later Jeffrey violated his parole and was packed off to jail for 60 days.

June ended up missing almost a month of performances due to the injury. Her understudy, Wendy Edmead, ended up making more money than June because she had to fill in so many times for my AWOL sister. Remember when Nell Carter caught grief in the press for missing a record 100-plus performances? June put that record to shame. It was such a pity because June had the best part and the biggest dance number in the play, which she performed with such natural ease and grace. She never failed to blow us all away when she put her mind to it. But that just didn't happen very often.

Wendy Edmead turned out to be quite the scene-stealer. Though more diminutive than June, she would slip on her blue dress, belt out her big number, "The Jitterbug Waltz," and seek out ways to twinkle the star quality she possessed. (Later on, when June was embargoed from the group, we hired Wendy as a Pointer Sister for some of our concerts. That didn't work out after a while because Wendy got a classic case of Big Head Syndrome and committed the cardinal sin of trying to upstage Anita and me. Her excommunication from the family was swift and final.)

As the *Ain't Misbehavin'* tour limped on we dealt not only with mixed reviews, tepid audiences, and few sold-out shows, but I was missing my husband and children something fierce. Think about it—I was married to Mike only three years, Conor and Ali were just two, and Issa was still a teenager. During a break in production I got a chance to go home. Conor was very sick with pneumonia. My anguish compounded when it came time to leave my sick child behind.

Mike did his best to bring the kids whenever it was possible. They came to Minneapolis, Denver, Orlando, and San Francisco. While in the Bay Area we stayed for three weeks in a two-bedroom suite at the Ritz Carlton Hotel and put Mom up at a nearby hotel. We took the twins to see her every day. She loved and adored them and the feeling was more than mutual.

By then we had hired Katie Keunny, a college student, as our nanny. I'm pretty sure we wore her out. The Ritz Carlton was situated on a hill, and Katie and I got plenty of exercise pushing the double stroller up and down it and the other steep San Francisco hills. And they don't call them the "Terrible Twos" for nothing. At the Ritz, Conor was forever escaping from our room. Usually he ended up in the hotel's gift shop, where there was a life-sized toy tiger for sale. He just loved that stuffed animal. Whenever Conor showed up in the gift shop to moon at it, the clerk would call our room and cheerfully announce, "One of your twins has escaped!"

Ain't Misbehavin' never did make it to Broadway. June's lousy attendance record doomed that objective. The New York media would have eaten her alive, and the show's investors would have lost a ton of money thanks to the bad publicity. Rather than risk that, they pulled the plug. That was actually fine by me. Toward the end I was marking off each day like I was serving a prison stretch.

About the only thing we managed to squeeze out of *Ain't Misbehavin'* was a 17-song "highlights" album, released by RCA in January 1996. I couldn't tell you how it sold and in fact have never even listened to it. Those are all terrific songs, but hearing them again would evoke more bad memories than good ones.

CHAPTER TWENTY-ONE

Where Did the Time Go?

WORRYING ABOUT JUNE BECAME A FULL-TIME JOB for everybody in the Pointers' camp. As much as we loved June—she was the sweetest, kindest, and most talented sister a person could wish for—it didn't take long for us to get fed up with her excuses for not showing up for gigs (when she even bothered coming up with an excuse at all) and, when she did show up, being totally whacked out on alcohol or drugs. Sometimes she'd fly alone to the town where we were working, get to the venue, and we'd already be on stage performing. Then she'd turn on her heel and fly right back home.

We knew she was hurting deep down inside. Her divorce still stung (Bill Whitmore gleefully took her to court whenever she missed an alimony payment), the IRS was breathing down her neck, she relied on others to pay her bills, and her self-esteem was in the toilet. I don't think she ever quite processed or dealt with the vicious rape in her youth, one of the many dragons that chased her all those years. We all understood this and grieved privately for her.

But June wasn't much for looking at things from our standpoint, and I don't think she understood how much her behavior was hurting our reputation with promoters. Believe it or not, her spotty attendance record after *Ain't Misbehavin'* grew even worse. It seemed as if all she wanted to do was stay in bed all day and smoke crack.

One time when we sent someone to June's house to wake her and bring her to the show, he was robbed at gunpoint by a thug inside the house. June was definitely hanging with a different crowd by this point. We had a private gig in Malibu for an important client, and June didn't show when she was supposed to. After an hour we sent a limo to fetch her—and then wished we hadn't. Accompanying our sister were several members of the Crips, one of L.A.'s most violent street gangs. I was horrified at what I saw from the stage: gang members glugging wine from the bottle, chowing down on the fine cuisine with their hands, and getting down with these elegant white women on the dance floor. The interesting thing was that a lot of those high-society dames seemed to think it was cute and had a ball—at least until they got home and checked their purses and jewelry.

Gang-bangers, druggies, and other hangers-on moved into June's house. So did Bonnie and Jeffrey Bowen. They commandeered the master bedroom for themselves. The house was steadily stripped of everything of value, including beautiful artifacts and antiques, expensive toys, and the contents of June's home recording studio. All her money went into a crack pipe, and there were problems keeping her water and electricity turned on. Neighbors complained about the noise and illegal activity going on in the house 24/7. Cash and sexual favors were traded for drugs, cars pulled up and left at all hours, and low-lifes ran rampant in the neighborhood. A drug lab was set up in the house to supply everyone with the poison that had taken over their lives.

One of the few times June actually made a Pointer Sisters show, a young woman overdosed and died in her basement. A story about that was one of several about June that appeared in the *National Enquirer*. The checkout aisle rag even ran photos taken inside her filthy drug den. Michael Hall, June's drug dealer/boyfriend, tipped off the tabloid about the dead girl in the basement and collected a nice fee. Bonnie also fed the *Enquirer* stories about June in exchange for cash. The irony was Bonnie was just as deep into the crack as June. But the disease doesn't care about anything except where the next hit is coming from. It will use, abuse, and step over anybody to accomplish its one true mission in life: to destroy you.

When Mindy Lymperis, my former assistant and good friend, saw the headlines about June in the *Enquirer* she decided to get involved. Mindy was intelligent, street-smart, and tough as they come (Thomas Hearns taught her how to box in her youth). She started to check in on June on a daily basis. She had a take-no-prisoners attitude that she backed up with the 9 mm Glock automatic pistol she wore on her hip. Her arrival at June's made the occupants scatter like cockroaches. Mindy went way beyond the call of duty as a friend. She cooked for June, made her mortgage and alimony payments for two straight years, and sometimes even paid off a drug dealer or two to get them off June's back. Mindy called the LAPD numerous times, but no matter how many times the house was raided the riff-raff always came swarming back.

Sometimes when June actually made it to one of our bookings, she did more harm than good. When we guested on the *Pop Goes the Fourth* broadcast with the world-famous Boston Pops Orchestra, June showed up hours late for the rehearsal. Maestro Keith Lockhart, the young, charismatic conductor who had just taken over the Pops baton from John Williams, was a big fan of the Pointer Sisters, but he did a slow burn as we all waited on June. When she finally blew in, instead of apologizing for holding everything up June said in a voice loud enough for all to hear, "Okay, let's hurry up and get this shit over with!" That was one tense rehearsal. But that night when the curtain went up everyone brought their A-game and the show was a tremendous success. The broadcast was later nominated for a Cable ACE Award. Needless to say, however, the Pointer Sisters were not invited back to perform with the Boston Pops, and no promoter in the New England region would touch us for several years.

June also blew off an appearance on *Vicki!*, hosted by our longtime friend Vicki Lawrence. We went way back with her to our first time on *The Carol Burnett Show*. Vicki and Carol were not only talented artists, but they were real down-to-earth people. They were genuine, kind, and loyal folks. It was a new talk show for Vicki, and she specifically requested us because it was her birthday. We loved Vicki and we wanted to show our loyalty in return. Anita and I showed up at the studio for the taping, but not June. We grew alarmed and called June repeatedly, but she didn't answer the phone. I'd never seen Vicki upset before, but she sure was now, and our disappointment morphed into anger at June as well. That's when we decided it was time for a full-blown intervention.

Our managers Jason Winters and Erik Sterling contacted Bob Timmins, an addictions specialist and recovery coach who later became well known through his association with Dr. Drew Pinsky on VH-1's *Celebrity Rehab*. Bob gave us the rundown on what to say, how June might react, how to respond, and what we should be prepared to do if June didn't agree to enter rehab.

We all showed up at June's place unannounced. She didn't answer her phone, and when she didn't respond to our loud knocking on her door we grew afraid that she might have overdosed or even be dead. We finally called security to get inside her place. We didn't really know what to expect, but what we found inside June's house blew our minds. Her once beautiful home looked like a ghetto drug den. Dirty clothes, boxes of stuff, and fast-food wrappers (she loved McDonald's) littered the floor, and unwashed dishes were piled in the sink. She was living in squalor.

We found June in her bed, surrounded by all of her pills, powders, and drug paraphernalia. The funny thing was that she didn't even raise an eyebrow when we walked through the door. As Bob had instructed, we each took turns speaking our piece, telling June she had to do something right now about her problem and telling her how much we loved her. Initially she reacted with anger, but then June started to cry and seemed remorseful. But she got her back up when we demanded that she go directly to a rehab facility. June said she would find help on her own, but she wasn't going to enter any facility and we couldn't make her. We hugged her and departed in tears. That was a very hard day.

Coddling June would get her and us nowhere. So Anita and I had to take measures to safeguard ourselves. It had been several years since we had a recording contract, and even though we still collected royalties, live performances were now our main source of income. We had family to feed and support, and The Pointer Sisters could be on the brink of extinction if we didn't do something drastic.

So we had a rider attached to our contracts saying that if only Anita and I showed up we'd get paid our share and June's share as well. Many times we had to perform as a duo, and, as mentioned earlier, we enlisted Wendy Edmead for about a year.

Our boiling point with June came when our management firm, Sterling/Winters Co., was approached by producers of Night of the Proms, the largest annual organized indoor event in Europe. It's a series of concerts in Belgium, The Netherlands, Germany, Luxembourg, Denmark, and Poland. It also tours regularly in France, Spain, Austria, and Sweden. The concerts feature a mixture of pop artists backed by a 76-piece classical orchestra and a 52-voice choir. We're talking about a first-class, high-profile concert series that played in large venues of up to 30,000 seats. It would be a three-month commitment that paid extremely well and afforded a golden opportunity to put the Pointer Sisters front-and-center on the world stage. Yeah, we wanted in on some of that action real bad.

Wanting to meet us in person, the producers flew the Pointer Sisters first-class to Belgium and put us up in a nice hotel. The first sign of trouble came when June insisted that they include Bonnie so she could have a free trip to Europe. They graciously went for it. But Anita and I were biting our fingernails down to the nubs by the time our plane landed.

We had all agreed to meet in the hotel lobby at noon on the day of the meeting. Anita and I showed up on time, dressed to the nines. June wasn't there. We called her room several times, getting no answer. When we'd last seen June the night before she was getting ready to hit the town with Bonnie. Apparently, they had burned the candle at both ends and raised a lot of hell. At one club Bonnie rushed up on stage, grabbed the microphone out of the performer's hand, and slurred her way through several numbers.

With the meeting time fast approaching, Anita and I went up to June's room. She was still in bed, looking like she'd just run the Boston Marathon. We rousted her out, but instead of cleaning herself up and at least looking the part of a Pointer Sister, she accompanied us to the meeting in the clothes she'd partied in and hadn't bothered to take off before she flopped into bed. She reeked of booze.

The gentleman from Night of the Proms looked like a professor in his natty bowtie. I'm surprised it didn't start twirling around like in cartoons when, after introductions were made, June opened the meeting by saying, "What's going on? What'cha got for us?"

It went downhill from there. When the meeting mercifully ended, Anita and I called our managers, Jason Winters and Erik Sterling, and told them we would not honor the commitment with June included. One of her last shows with the Pointer Sisters was on New Year's Eve, the dawn of the new millennium. She partied like it was 1999. We finally had to play our trump card with June and informed her that she would not be allowed to continue performing as a Pointer Sister. She would be welcome to return only if she was enrolled in a certified recovery program.

Like most addicts, June tried to do it her way. She went to seek drug counseling through a questionable character who ran a shady drug treatment center in Los Angeles. This facility was small, unassuming, and not very impressive. The drug counselor and an associate, who passed himself off as a doctor, virtually kidnapped June and stashed her in a small house in Beverly Hills. The only concession they made was to allow June to bring her chocolate lab, Kennedy. The "rehab facility" was a dump. Even though the house had a Beverly Hills address, the roof leaked and it was sparsely furnished inside. The cupboards contained one set of plates. There was no on-site medical staff to monitor June and wean her off her medications. At the time she was taking Xanax, Soma, and Klonopin to treat her anxiety and panic attacks. In addition to her crack addiction she was drinking heavily and smoking marijuana. The drug counselor's solution was for June to quit everything cold turkey. After a few days of that craziness June covered up a bunch of pillows on her bed to make it look like she was sleeping, then hoisted Kennedy and herself through a bathroom window and walked the seven miles to her home barefoot.

While she was gone the parasites had made off with everything that wasn't nailed down: gold records, Grammy awards, Tiffany lamps, personal documents—everything with any possible monetary value. That provided Bonnie another opportunity to cash in with the *National Enquirer*. "My baby sister June has been addicted to crack cocaine and sleeping pills for at least two years," she told the rag. "Our entire family is worried sick that unless she cleans up, she'll die…June let anyone, including drug abusers, stay in her home." Of course, Bonnie neglected to tell the reporter that she herself had a raging crack habit and was one of those drug abusers taking advantage of June.

In May 2000, Mindy paid $22,000 for June to check into Promises West L.A. After a few weeks June asked to see Anita and me. We spent the day with her, met her sponsor, and laughed, hugged, and cried. We were all sisters again. It was such a great feeling. June looked healthy, her spirits were high, and it was one of the best days we'd ever spent together. It was also the very first time we enjoyed each other's company as adults in a totally sober environment. If only it could've lasted.

An addict's path is full of land mines, and avoiding them requires constant vigilance, caution, and self-restraint. June wasn't much for any of that, and when she left Promises she hit the ground running. She relapsed on her first day home. Mindy said barely an hour passed before she heard June's crack pipe flare up.

June's attitude was that she had done her time in rehab, now get off her back because she was going to do as she pleased. Mindy stopped paying her mortgage (the bank eventually took the house back and foreclosed on the property) but took June into her lovely home in Santa Monica near the beach.

Under Mindy's care June was safe and scaled back her drug abuse. For a period of time she experienced relative peace and domesticity. She cooked, made the beds, did laundry, took long Jacuzzi breaks out on the deck, and enjoyed the serenity of the beach. Mindy even bought her a Boston terrier puppy, Betty. According to Mindy, June was making a real effort to get her life in order.

It was when Bonnie showed up that everything changed. She called June with the news that she was homeless because Jeffrey Bowen had thrown her over for a younger woman, another singer for him to oppress and manipulate. (In July 2014 after 10 years of separation, Bonnie finally filed for divorce from Jeffrey after 35 years of marriage. And to that I say good riddance!)

Mindy knew that allowing Bonnie to come into her house was a bad idea, but she did it to please June. They repaid her kindness by trashing the place. In no time June was back to her old ways. One night she went out with a drug dealer. Twenty-four hours later she called Mindy at her work, crying hysterically. Mindy raced home and was horrified to discover the dealer had not only brutally raped June but then demanded $200 from her when he dropped June off at the door. Mindy immediately took June to see her personal physician, Dr. David Kipper, who treated her for several weeks.

Even Mindy's extraordinary patience had its limits, and they were finally reached the night June announced that she and Bonnie were hitting the town and taking June's puppy, Betty, with them. Mindy told June to do whatever she liked but insisted that Betty was staying put. June went ballistic, jumped on top of Mindy, who was lying on the couch, and punched Mindy in the face. The force of June's blow broke Mindy's nose. Mindy could easily have defended herself but instead she calmly set her own nose (I told you she was tough) and then showed June and Bonnie the door for good. From there June went into total free fall, crashing with friends, or sleeping in rundown motels or wherever there was a floor or mattress.

It was around this time when June started singing in public with Bonnie, which confused fans of the Pointer Sisters and infuriated Anita and me. They wreaked havoc just like they did in Belgium, and it was giving us a bad name. We saw it as a form of betrayal and a watering down of the brand. Anita and I quickly moved to trademark the name to protect the Pointer Sisters legacy. The point was punctuated when our attorney, Marty Singer, sent them both a cease and desist letter. While it didn't mean much in regards to Bonnie, it devastated our relationship with June.

It's still painful to talk about June's last years because I often wonder if I might have changed things had I set a better example as the older sister. Part of me thinks yes, but then I realize that ultimately we are all responsible for our own actions and decisions. I had gotten clean. June had the same choice. The disease (also known as the Devil), will do whatever it takes to keep one from making that choice. The only choice an addict has is that they have to want to get help. Even that's questionable.

The heartache of June's addiction was compounded by my mother's steadily failing health. Mom had been suffering with diabetes for several years. Because I lived in Boston the last few years of her life, I didn't get to see her as often as I liked. But we spoke on the phone frequently. As we got older, Mom and I grew closer and became like girlfriends. She was so naïve when it came to things of the world. I took great pleasure in sharing my experiences with her, and she took equal pleasure in listening to them. She wanted to hear all about our exploits on the road, what we wore, the places we'd visit, and the celebrities who came backstage. I even shared with her some things I did as a kid that I probably shouldn't have. She was just a special, special woman. Who loves a child more than their mother?

Mom died on November 15, 2000. Her four eldest children and my oldest daughter, Faun, were at her bedside at Cedars-Sinai Medical Center in Los Angeles. Faun was especially close to my mother, and they enjoyed a very special relationship. She actually watched Mom take her last breath.

"She's gone," Faun said.

Everybody was staying at Anita's, and when I left the hospital, I called my friend Minnie Johnson while in the car. I was so emotionally shaken that I got lost. I was crying my eyes out, cruising around Beverly Hills trying to find the road to my sister's house in Coldwater Canyon. I finally had to go back to the hospital to retrace my route to Anita's. I didn't realize until that moment how deeply her death had affected me.

Anita and I were lucky in that we had strong support systems—I had Mike and the kids and Anita had her daughter Jada and granddaughter Roxie—to help us through our grief. June had nobody, and the loss of the person who loved her the most was the final blow that fetched her, at long last, onto the devil's doorstep.

CHAPTER TWENTY-TWO

Millennial Pointers

....

A MONTH AFTER MY MOTHER'S DEATH I WAS BACK on the road—this time on a trip to Europe for the USO.

My involvement with the USO had started in earnest in the summer of '99 when the organization invited the Pointer Sisters to participate on a tour of bases in Sarajevo, Kosovo, and Bosnia called Operation Allied Entertainment. It was a very hostile war zone and the USO was finding it hard to recruit entertainers to visit the troops there. The government would only cover expenses—no fees—so that and dropping into the middle of a war zone didn't sound very appealing. My sisters elected not to participate, but Mike made the suggestion that I go and perform as a solo act. He said he would go with me and select my backup band for the entire trip. That was a bolt out of the blue. In all my years of performing, I had never gone it alone. I was petrified, but you only live once....

From the moment we jetted off from Boston to Budapest I knew it was going to be a life-altering trip. It was that in spades, as well as a great bonding experience with Mike.

The trip lasted from September 2 to 14, and we spent a lot of time getting to know the outstanding men and women fighting for and protecting this great nation and keeping the peace for others. We flew in Apaches and Blackhawks, sat inside military vehicles equipped with all types of technology and firepower, and were treated with great respect. One of the helicopter pilots asked me to sing "Slow Hand" to him while flying us to our destination. I was happy to comply.

"Oh my god," he said when the song was over, "that's the first time that's ever happened."

Our first stop was Eagle Base near Tuzla. It was from there U.S., Russian, and NATO forces helped stabilize Bosnia and Herzegovina in the mid-'90s. The 401st Expeditionary Air Base Group headquartered there welcomed us with open arms. The base commander graciously allowed us use of his living quarters in the barracks. They were very small, but afforded more privacy than the bathrooms and showers, which were communal. When I needed to use them I posted a sign on the door: "WOMAN IN THE BATHROOM."

The entire base seemed to be outlined in the kind of yellow tape you see at a crime scene on TV. When I asked what that was about, I was warned to never set foot beyond the tape because there were land mines everywhere. *I can't believe these soldiers live like this every day*, I thought.

We mostly played inside the main halls at bases, and an aircraft hangar or two on that tour. The crowds usually ranged from 100 to 500, depending on the size of the base, but the level of appreciation was always the same: rapturous applause.

Our band was really hot and tight and they had my back. Whatever I wanted to perform—"What a Wonderful World," "Slow Hand," "Neutron Dance" and Martha and the Vandellas' "Heatwave"—they were right there with me, even singing background vocals when needed. The lineup included Reggie Royal (piano), Eugene Henderson (lead guitar), Stacy Henry (drums), Jervonny Coller (bass), and Matt Rohde (keyboards). Those guys ended up being friends for life, and the experience of performing solo was not only thrilling but changed my self-confidence forever.

Another life-changing event for me was visiting the war-torn city of Sarajevo. The hotel at which we stayed was half-bombed out; nearby buildings were riddled with bullet holes, and there were homeless children everywhere we went, hungry and raggedy and begging for money and food. The guards accompanying us forewarned us not to pay attention to the kids because they'd end up breaking our hearts. Did they ever.

Sarajevo, where the 1984 Winter Olympics were held, was a shell of its former self. From 1992 to '96 it was the site of the longest siege of a capital city in modern-day warfare. The bloody conflict turned the place into hell on earth. Now makeshift cemeteries surrounded the city, including at the Olympic arena, where we saw markers for thousands of men, women, and children. I heard stories about how entire families were shot while visiting the graves and about kids scavenging for shell casings because they were made of brass and could be sold on the streets for money. I bought a shell casing as a memento, and came away from that tour with a new appreciation for what we have in our country and the freedoms we enjoy.

When Secretary of Defense William S. Cohen heard how popular our expedition was he quickly enlisted us to participate in the Operation Starlife "Handshake Tour" in December 1999. With us was a world-class roster of entertainers: Super

Bowl heroes Terry Bradshaw and Mike Singletary, model Christie Brinkley, comedian Al Franken, country singer Shane Minor, singer-songwriter Mary Chapin Carpenter, MTV's "Downtown" Julie Brown, Supreme Allied Commander Wesley Clark, and a half-dozen Dallas Cowboys cheerleaders. I had befriended one of the cheerleaders, who later sent me a small replica of her uniform for Ali, who was about five or six at the time. It was so cute.

We all gathered at the Ritz-Carlton Hotel in Washington, D.C., and then flew from Andrews Air Force Base in Maryland on Secretary Cohen's personal plane to Europe. We toured bases in Italy, Bosnia, the former Yugoslav Republic of Macedonia, and Kosovo, bringing a touch of home to American comrades in arms.

The shows were amazing, and we did our best to dazzle the troops. Terry Bradshaw zipped footballs into the crowd (on a subsequent tour, one of his passes went astray and knocked John Glenn's wife upside the head!); Al Franken told racy jokes; Christie Brinkley shed a military-style flight-suit to reveal a cherry-red cocktail dress and sparkling spike heels; and the Dallas Cowboy cheerleaders strutted their stuff, shook their pom-poms, and kicked their heels mighty high. Every hand was shaken, every autograph and photo request fulfilled. At one show when I was singing "Fire" I stepped down from the stage to slow dance with a black soldier. It was a spontaneous moment, but the soldiers inspired that in all of us.

The next two years when the USO asked me to play again, I asked just one question: "Where do I sign?"

Speaking of signing, the Pointer Sisters finally inked a deal with the promoters of Night of the Proms for its 2002 tour of Europe, despite our less-than-stellar introduction to them about two years earlier. We sort of pulled a fast one by waiting until the last minute to inform the promoters of a roster change—my daughter Issa in for June—because we didn't want to give them a chance to change their minds. We really needed this one, and by God we weren't about to allow the opportunity to slip through our fingers.

Anita and I had talked for some time about having Issa and her daughter Jada alternate in the third spot in the lineup. They were young, talented, and best of all they were honest-to-God Pointers. It's always been a family affair. Issa was chosen first because she had experience singing solo at a lot of New England–area functions. She is much like her father in that she has great stage presence and self-confidence. But when I told her about the opportunity, she didn't exactly jump for joy. In fact, she protested that she wasn't ready to fill June's shoes.

I explained to Issa that it wasn't possible for June to commit to a three-month tour and that the Pointer Sisters were in a bind and really needed her help. Besides, it was a variety show featuring several other headliners, and our spots were only 15 minutes apiece.

"We'd be on and off before you know it," I said.

I didn't give Issa much time to process the information and started giving orders before she overthought the damn thing.

"Pack your bags and let's go," I said.

It was a first-class affair all the way. That's because the producers, Jan Vereecke and Jan Van Esbroeck, were perfectionists. They staged the show with an orchestra and choir; state-of-the-art lighting and sound system; volunteers to help with every phase of production and wardrobe; five-star hotels; and catered food that was healthy and mouth-watering. People loved hanging around our dressing room because we usually had the boom box cranked up (Motown), and we would dance around, livening up everyone's spirits.

When we got to Belgium, Issa had to be put through her paces. When Anita and I taught her our songs, it dawned on us how natural those harmonies came to us, and how we had taken it for granted all those years. As sisters, we never had to work at it; we instinctively knew what the other was going to sing. Whenever the Pointer Sisters guested on other artist's songs, we'd be handed sheet music for the song before the session. We'd start laughing and politely say, "We don't read music. If you just play the part you want us to sing, we'll sing it." We'd nail it every time, and that always blew everyone away.

I also had to get Issa over her butterflies. This was a huge deal, performing in large indoor arenas. The Elks Club it wasn't. After our first rehearsal, which took place in a small room, I took Issa by the hand, told her to close her eyes, and walked her out to the arena stage. Then I had her open her eyes.

"Whoa, this is big!" she said.

I wanted Issa to see the room before the concert so that she wouldn't be shocked when she stepped out onto the stage. I wanted her to see what the view would be from her perspective, what to focus on, what steps to remember, and where to hit her marks. I assured her she could do this and that everything would be all right. Issa had every right to be afraid, but Anita and I had her back and weren't going to let her fail. We were passing on the baton to a new generation, and we wanted to make sure she knew how to take it and run with it. After standing on the stage for a while, she turned to face me.

"I got this, Mama," Issa said.

If playing to packed houses wasn't intimidating enough, there was the fact that we'd be sharing the spotlight with Foreigner, Michael McDonald, Kiki Dee, Bonnie Tyler, and a beautiful-looking German prodigy named David Garrett. David was a real trip. He took to the stage in a knit skullcap, pierced ears, button-down shirt, baggy blue jeans, and chain wallet—then whipped out his Stradivarius and let 'er rip. All the women went *craaaaazy* over this Juilliard-trained former model. I never saw a violinist get such a strong reaction. In 2013, David starred in the film *The Devil's Violinist*, based on the life of 19th-century Italian violinist/composer Niccolò Paganini. Paganini would've approved of the choice.

The tour reunited Anita and me with Michael McDonald, who'd sung on *Only Sisters Can Do That* nearly a decade before. I love Michael, an unbelievably gifted man. Even when he goofs he's still pretty damned adorable. His set included the No. 1 single "On My Own," which was a duet he'd done with Patti LaBelle in 1986. On the tour I sang Patti's part. One time Michael inadvertently sang the same verse twice, and I just held on to my part. Michael didn't say anything until after we received our applause. We walked offstage arm in arm, laughing our heads off.

"Hey, shit happens," Michael said with a shrug of his shoulders.

In no time at all Issa shrugged her own shoulders and got the hang of things. She was a youthful asset to the Pointer Sisters spirit and fit in perfectly. At each venue the promoters hosted a private bar/nightclub for the performers where Issa socialized with the young adults in the choir. She still maintains some of the friendships forged then. Issa is also fluent in French, and it was handy having her around in Europe.

Issa's medium-range voice and that large orchestra and choir gave our six-song set a huge kick in the ass. Those songs—"Happiness," "Automatic," "Jump (For My Love)," "Slow Hand," "Fire," and "I'm So Excited!"—never sounded so good. I still get goose bumps thinking about it. The promoters used an applause meter to monitor audience response for each artist. At the end of each concert they called us into their office to show us where the meter went off the charts. We broke their applause records every single time out. I will forever be grateful to Issa for coming through at a time when we really needed her.

Our second Proms tour included Joe Cocker, Roger Hodgson (formerly of Supertramp), and the great James Brown. James had slowed down some, but he was still plenty spry and left it all on the stage every night. After our set we didn't have time to change, so we'd throw on our bathrobes over our clothes and run back out and watch James from the side of the stage. We watched James light it up every night and studied his every move. He never cheated an audience. The man just had *it*.

James was also very gracious. I had invited friends Jeanie and Eric Eversley, who were from Boston. They flew to Belgium after we told them how special Night of the Proms was. I had developed a close relationship with Jeannie through the years and Eric was a lieutenant detective with the Boston Police Department. Eric and reggae artist Shaggy happened to celebrate the same birthday. The promoters sectioned off a portion of the backstage to host a celebration for Shaggy, who invited Eric to join him. James happened to be there and joined in the festivities and ate cake with the two men, wishing them a happy birthday.

We also befriended a Belgian couple named Ria and Louisette Von Hooydonk, who owned a great boutique called Bellisimo. Anita and I loved Ria's fashion sense and went crazy in her store. They were sweet and so hospitable, and we developed a much deeper relationship as time went on.

For our second Night of the Proms, producers matched us up with Belgian-born singer Natalia Druyts, a 24-year-old blonde bombshell who was first runner-up on Belgium's version of *American Idol*. After the show she was signed by Sony BMG and tore up the charts with a string of Top 10 singles in her native country. At the end of our set she joined us for our encore of "I'm So Excited!" to enthusiastic applause. We extended our collaboration with her in October 2005 when we released a single and video together, "Sisters Are Doin' It for Themselves." It was our first single in a decade, and it peaked at No. 2 on the Belgian charts. Three months after it was released, we embarked on a 10-date tour billed as "Natalia Meets the Pointer Sisters" in the Sportpaleis in Antwerp. The set list was a mixture of both our catalogs, with us trading songs back and forth. The shows proved to be a big hit and were attended by more than 130,000 people.

The Proms tour went without a hitch until the eve of the last show, when Anita received a transatlantic phone call about her 37-year-old daughter, Jada. After coughing up blood for several days, Jada had entered an L.A.-area hospital for a battery of tests to determine the cause. The results wouldn't be available for several days. After Anita hung up the phone she called my room crying.

"Let's scratch the last show and go home," I said. "Everybody will understand." But my sister, the consummate pro, said she'd get through it and did. Then she jetted back to Los Angeles. I went home to Boston, and a few days later I called Anita to find out what was happening. The news was devastating. Jada had been diagnosed with stage-four pancreatic cancer.

My heart sank, but I tried to stay strong for my sister. I told her this wasn't necessarily a death sentence and that many people were not only living longer with cancer but were even beating it thanks to advanced research and good health care. I promised Anita I would come to L.A. and help her in every way possible. Mike was very supportive and told me to start packing. He would take care of the kids, get them where they needed to be, and run our household in my absence.

Jada was my favorite niece and was just an angel. She was smart, beautiful, kind, and talented. She had the most infectious laugh and beautiful pair of full lips I have ever seen. She made her mother very proud, and they were inseparable. Together they raised and doted on Jada's daughter, Roxie. Jada was an artist with a comb and scissors and was hairstylist for many celebrities, including the singer Usher. She often worked on her mother's hair before shows, and that was an extension of her nurturing personality.

Jada started chemotherapy right away. Everybody jumped in with both feet to help. We got a lot of support from family and friends, including Ria and Louisette Von Hooydonk, who closed their shop and flew from Antwerp to L.A. to be with us in our hour of need. We so deeply appreciated their thoughtfulness and comfort. Everyone rallied around Jada and visited her as often as they could. We also arranged for prayer groups to come in and lay hands on Jada. Friends who had cancer showed up to encourage Jada and show her that they were living full lives while undergoing treatment. One young lady who befriended Jada had been living with cancer for almost a decade and held a big party each year not only to celebrate her birthday but also another precious year of life. Jada attended one of her parties, and she and I danced together and had a ball. I told her, "This is going to be you, Jada. You're going to make it just like this young lady."

I'd have given anything to make it happen. But Jada's cancer was unstoppable, and my beautiful, wonderful niece died on June 10, 2003.

I'd be a flat-out liar if I said the pain of Jada's death has lessened with the passage of time. We live with and try to cope with it every single day. Her loss left a permanent void in all our lives, especially Anita's. When I look at my own five children I can't even begin to imagine the emotional pain Anita endures on a daily basis. Parents are not supposed to survive their children, and how they manage it only God knows. For the life of me I cannot understand why He permits such things to happen. "God's will" seems like such a maddeningly convenient evasion, but they say that all will be revealed and understood on Judgment Day. Wish I didn't have to wait for Judgement Day to understand. I have faith that it will be so, but when I think of what we lost when Jada died, my human emotions take over and I think God will have to be at His persuasive best then.

I'm crying my eyes out right now as I write these words. It still hurts that bad. I'd give anything for the power to bring Jada back. That's how much I loved her, and that's how much I love her mother.

CHAPTER TWENTY-THREE

Baby Sister

DURING ONE OF HER ALL-TOO-BRIEF INTERLUDES OF recovery and self-reflection, June said she didn't want to end up like Billie Holiday, that she wanted her life to have a good ending. We all wanted that for her so badly. June had suffered enough for several lifetimes, and as she entered her fifties, she certainly deserved some peace and serenity in her life. But instead of actively seeking that path she continued to careen down the long, hard, cocaine-dusted road, picking up momentum with every misstep.

Communication with June was sporadic in the wake of Mom's and Jada's deaths. As sisters we had developed a form of telepathy onstage and in the studio. So it only makes sense that when I didn't hear from June for long periods of time, I knew things weren't good. And my worst fears were confirmed every time I saw the tabloids in the supermarket checkout line.

In April 2004, June was partying at Bonnie's apartment in Hollywood on Cherokee Street. Neighbors called police to complain of illegal drug sales, and when narcotics officers arrived they found June and Bonnie inside, along with three others, in possession of crack cocaine and pipes. They slapped the cuffs on June and Bonnie and took them to jail. They were charged with felony drug possession and misdemeanor possession of a smoking device. A few days later they were each released on $10,000 bail. June later pled guilty and was sent to court-ordered rehab. Like all of the other prior attempts, it didn't take.

June was back in the slammer a few months later. By then she was living in an apartment in Hollywood with a loser named Joel Coigney, a French native a dozen years June's senior and the kind of guy she wouldn't have looked twice at when her head was on straight. Coigney had been June's "driver" when she lived in the house near Sunset. Mostly he took her on her rounds with area drug dealers in his dilapidated town car—and then billed her handsomely. June had burned almost every bridge by then, and I'm sure it was circumstances, not love, that drove her to take up with Coigney. Joel's intentions weren't so lofty, either. He did his damndest to get June to marry him in hopes of attaining power of attorney over her and getting a hold of whatever cash and assets he figured she had.

One night Coigney made the mistake of objecting when June invited a dealer over. June pointed out the error of his ways by punching, kicking, and scratching the hell out of him. When the police arrived Joel was a bloody, toothless mess. For that June spent two days in jail on battery and corporal injury charges. After Coigney took out a restraining order on June, he ran to the tabloids with a story painting himself as June's would-be savior from drugs and booze.

June publicly countered with an allegation that Coigney was messing around with her niece, my granddaughter, Onika, who was living with them at the time, and June was simply protecting her. Who knows what the deal really was? Six months later June and Coigney got back together…and then they broke up again. Such was the life of an addict.

When she wasn't in custody, June performed with Bonnie (they were billed as "Bonnie and June") at disco revues, nightclubs, and cabarets, although by then June's voice was completely shot thanks to her drug abuse. One day in late 2005 or early 2006 she called me out of the blue on my cell phone while I was driving around in Boston. I immediately pulled into a parking lot to take the call and at first didn't even recognize June's voice. When I asked what was wrong she said she had laryngitis. We hadn't spoken in a while and it was wonderful to reconnect. I suspect June held some resentment toward Anita and me for booting her from the group on account of her behavior, but now we didn't talk about that. June updated me on her life, performances and future recording plans with Bonnie (with contributions from George Clinton and the Wu-Tang Clan). She asked about Ali and Conor, and I got her all caught up on our lives. It was a nice conversation and I'm so thankful that it happened. Before I hung up I told her that I loved her, then said, "Girl, you'd better take care of your throat."

Mindy Lymperis was back in June's life and was concerned as well. She took June to see an ear, nose ,and throat specialist in Beverly Hills. After doing an upper GI endoscopy on June, the doctor took Mindy aside.

"What kind of drugs does she do?" he asked.

"Crack," Mindy admitted.

"She has paralyzed a vocal chord," the specialist said. "She'll never sing again."

Not long after that I was floored by a video posted online of a December 2005 gig June and Bonnie did at the Wynn Hotel in Vegas. They were scary thin and appeared to this trained eye to be thoroughly wasted. Bonnie was clearly lip-synching to a prerecorded track, and all June did on stage was hold up a sign saying, "I LOVE YOU." I wept when I saw the video, and it still haunts me. June was soon reduced to appearing at raves, where no singing was required and all that was expected of her was that she live up to her reputation as a party girl.

The party came to a screeching halt on February 27, 2006, when June was found unconscious in her bedroom. She and Bonnie were living then with Bonnie's boyfriend, Bruce, a part-time writer and full-time drug dealer who later died of a heart attack after ingesting too many drugs. They lived in a two-story loft in downtown Los Angeles near the arts district and smoked crack nonstop.

Bonnie found June lying on the floor and took her to a nearby physician, who believed she'd had a massive stroke. He immediately called 911 and had June transported to UCLA Medical Center in Westwood.

I was at home in Massachusetts when I received a call from Anita telling me that June had been hospitalized and that I'd better get out there quick. After making the necessary arrangements with Mike, I jumped on the first plane to Los Angeles. I flew to LAX and picked up a rental car and met Anita at the hospital. Mindy was there at June's side.

Seeing June hooked up to several machines in that hospital bed tore us up. But that was just the first blow of a devastating three-punch combination. In addition to a stroke, June had also suffered a heart attack. And further tests disclosed that she also had stage-four lung cancer that had metastasized in her breast, colon, liver, and bones. Anita and I held each other and cried until we could hardly breathe. Then it was time to get to work.

June's Screen Actors Guild insurance, which was one of the best plans available, had lapsed several years before. Mindy asked Mike to help, which he did. He worked hard to get June's insurance reinstated to cover the bills, which of course, would have been astronomical. Mike was a miracle worker and got SAG to cooperate. He came through in a huge way for my baby sister, and it was definitely appreciated by everyone.

Mindy, June's friend Tonji Edwards, Anita, and I sat with June around the clock that first week. Bonnie was mostly a no-show. As best I can recall, she came to the hospital only a couple times. One time she brought Betty, June's Boston terrier, and June's eyes lit up. Bonnie was knee-deep in her own addiction and hard to reach. I'm sure Bonnie deeply regrets this today, but it was probably just as well she wasn't around. Her presence might have been a distraction.

June's stroke left her unable to talk or walk. When she finally woke up she could communicate only by blinking her eyes. Eventually she was able to mouth a few words. Her mind could process information, but her body wouldn't cooperate. She grew impatient and would try to swing her legs over the side of the bed to get up but was incapable of moving by herself. The nurses and therapists would lift her out of bed and hold her up while she took a few halting steps, which always brought tears to my eyes. June's feisty spirit was clearly alive and well. She still had the fight and willpower to live. But damn, it still hurts to remember this picture of my beautiful baby sister this way.

We did our best to lift her spirits and liven up her room, decorating it with toys and figurines purchased from the hospital gift shop. There were plenty of flowers and cards from well-wishers. June loved incense and scented candles, and we lit them when the hospital staff allowed. We also played music every day—the kind that June loved. Of course, the Pointer Sisters got heavy rotation.

Each of us took turns bathing June and massaging her feet and hands. Several times she looked at me and the others and mouthed the words "I love you." That was our baby's sweet and loving nature coming back.

Mindy showed up nightly after putting in 18-hour days at her restaurant. She was an absolute saint, as was Tonji Edwards, who had befriended June several years before and ultimately ended up taking care of Betty.

In spite of all the wear and tear she put it through, we marveled at how beautiful her caramel-colored, long, lean, and flawless body was. She never had kids and so her tummy was flat and toned. Inside, however, it was a different story. The CT scans showed cancer everywhere. The doctors recommended that we move June into UCLA Santa Monica, which had an excellent palliative care unit and hospice and was very high-security. The latter was a necessary consideration because we'd heard that Bonnie had tried to sneak a *National Enquirer* reporter into UCLA to shoot pictures of June. She also called an L.A. radio station to make pronouncements about June's condition. Of course we were angry with Bonnie, but I understood she wasn't herself. The disease will get you to do anything, even turning on your own sister, in order to get high.

We knew hospice meant the end was near, but at the same time we knew June would not have wanted to carry on in her current condition. I can tell you that she was unequivocally at peace in her last days, surrounded by family, friends, and loved ones. She was in a very good place. Besides, I had the feeling June didn't care to live to a ripe old age. She had an all-or-nothing type of personality, and Lord knows she had a few lifetimes of fun under her belt.

Anita and I still had touring commitments that were made months in advance, but we canceled all our remaining dates when Mike called me on the road and said it was time to come and say goodbye to June. When I heard that my stomach sank and I got weak in the knees. I'd known it was coming, of course, but now that June's death was imminent it was like getting the news for the first time all over again.

On April 11, 2006, Aaron, Fritz, Anita, and a couple of June's friends and I were at her side. Bonnie was not, but I give her grace. I'm not sure she could have handled being there at the end. As June's 52-year-old life faded away I climbed into bed and held her, and Anita and I softly sang "Fire" in her ears. That is a memory I will forever hold dear in my heart. June's suffering was over, and now she finally had the peace that for so long had eluded her. I know with every ounce of my being that June is good because every now and then her spirit comes to me and reassures me that she is with God.

Unfortunately, June's death did not bring peace within the family. Bonnie deigned to join the rest of us to discuss burial plans because June did not leave any instructions behind. Bonnie blew up when we voted to have June's remains cremated. She claimed that was not what June wanted and actually likened cremation to consigning June to "burn in hell."

Then, incredibly, Bonnie proclaimed that unless Anita and I agreed right then and there to let her back as a member of the Pointer Sisters, she would not contribute a cent where it concerned June's remains. With that proclamation, our business was finished.

But she wasn't done. On the day of June's memorial service Bonnie asked to have the limousine swing by her place so she could ride with the family. Aaron and Fritz put the brakes on that request—they were more than upset with her behavior at the family meeting and told her to get her own ride. I wished things could have been different with Bonnie at that time so we could have been a united family for June. Again, the devil and his disease working hand in hand together.

Unfortunately, Bonnie retaliated by going to *Entertainment Tonight*, the *National Enquirer*, and *People* magazine with a sob story about how we'd all frozen her out in her time of grief. But my brothers promptly set the record straight and for good measure mentioned Bonnie's tacky attempt to blackmail her way back into the Pointer Sisters. She never tattled again to the tabloids.

Then there was June's ex-husband, Bill Whitmore, who didn't let the fact that he was a whole continent away keep him from trying to horn in on the memorial service at Forest Lawn Cemetery scheduled on April 21 and the celebration of June's life immediately afterward at the Universal Hilton Hotel in Universal City. My former assistant Sue Balmforth and our friend Andrea Williams spent a couple of weeks setting up June's life celebration, and it was a very kind thing for them to do.

Bill sent a barrage of e-mails to Mindy Lymperis from Europe, where he was trying to launch the career of an Irish folk singer he had knocked up, demanding to be included. When the answer was hell no, Bill threatened to show up anyway and shoot up everything in sight. Whitmore was a pathetic blowhard, but just in case we hired two former L.A. cops to provide security. He never did show up.

June's life celebration lifted everyone's spirits. A large screen continually played all of our music videos, and June's photos were everywhere. We even catered the event with Happy Meals: double cheeseburgers, french fries, small toys, and Orange Crush in bottles thanks to a friend of Andrea Williams', who owned a McDonald's franchise. June practically lived on McDonald's and almost always kept a cheeseburger in her purse. She was a nibbler, and would take a bite whenever she felt like it and then put the rest back in her purse.

The service was a reunion of family, friends, former associates, road managers, wardrobe assistants, band members, and fans. We laughed, cried, prayed, reminisced, and told war stories about each other and June; every human emotion was on display.

Most important, we gave June's song the ending it deserved.

About a year later the family gathered at Mt. Tamalpais Cemetery in San Rafael, California, where Mom and Dad rested together. Anita had kept Jada's ashes because she couldn't bring herself to let go. Since Jada and June loved each other so much, we suggested to Anita that their urns be interred together. She liked that idea. When it was done, I looked up to the sky and closed my eyes.

Okay Mom, I said from my heart of hearts, *you've got them back.*

CHAPTER TWENTY-FOUR

Still So Excited!

THOUGH JUNE HADN'T PERFORMED WITH US IN OVER five years, Anita and I always held out hope that she would someday rejoin us on stage. Now that would never happen, at least not in this world. We put our best foot forward and soldiered on. It's simply the Pointer way.

There haven't been many milestones for the Pointer Sisters in the last decade, but that's due in large part to the music industry, or what's left of it. We've weathered the decline of the big record labels, the death of vinyl and CD, the birth of iTunes and Spotify, and done our best to adapt to a sea of change in an ever-evolving industry that most critics say is on life support. In 2008, Anita, Issa (singing many of June's parts), and I rerecorded 10 of our most popular songs on our self-released and distributed *Favorites*. The CD was a big hit with our fans, and we moved a lot of units at our concerts. It's just one of the many new ways of doing business these days.

A year later we added my granddaughter Sadako to the lineup after Issa became pregnant with her first child, Bailan Michael Pointer-King, born on July 31, 2009. Sadako has been a welcome and youthful spark for Anita and me. She makes us feel young again. Sadako possesses a natural class, charm and beauty, and has a great stage presence. It's nice that she's also very respectful. She checks on me before I leave the dressing room and always makes sure Anita and I enter doors before her. Sadako is a big hit with the men when we perform: she's half Japanese and very exotic looking, and has a smile that lights up a room. And she does things with her hips that sometimes make Nana Ruthie blush and look the other way.

Over the years, Issa and Sadako have built up their own fan base, and depending on what type of engagement it is, we alternate them. Sometimes promoters will specifically request one or the other, and we always try to accommodate them as best we can. Some nights there are three generations of Pointers on stage, which is surreal. The two girls were born at the peak of our career and knew every song growing up. They also know the Pointers have a simple business philosophy: get up on that stage and make the customers forget about their problems for a while.

We show up ready for work and sing the songs our fans want to hear. We don't want anyone sitting in their seats looking like they're watching TV. We want people to get up and boogie. Only then do we know we've done our job properly. We are realistic and know our fans aren't clamoring for any new Pointer Sisters material. As Anita likes to say, we are headed for the finish line, and if it ain't broke, don't fix it. And it ain't broke.

According to a March 2015 *Billboard* magazine article, the Pointer Sisters are the fourth most successful female group of all time, behind the Supremes, TLC, and Destiny's Child. We registered 15 Top 40 singles—many of them considered modern-day classics—and sold approximately 40 million records. We brought light and love to countless people and have several generations of fans. Not bad for a bunch of ghetto kids from Oakland.

Health-wise, the Pointer Express has hit some bumps in recent years. My granddaughter Onika suffered a life threatening car-pedestrian accident in September 2005. I happened to be in Los Angeles at the time and getting my nails done when I received the call. I bolted out of my chair and drove straight to Cedars-Sinai to be by her side along with Anita. She stayed in a coma and was on life support for eight days. Her arm almost had to be amputated, her spleen was removed, and her colon was severely damaged. It was a miracle she survived. Onika still bears the tire marks across her chest where she was run over. Asshole never stopped.

In 2011, Anita was diagnosed with ovarian cancer and successfully underwent chemotherapy. Today she is cancer-free. Hallelujah!

A year later we were preparing for a trip to Amsterdam when I felt a twinge in my back. It didn't go away, so I got it checked out and discovered I had a blood clot in my left lung. The doctor said it was a result of sitting on airplanes for extended periods of time. I started taking blood-thinning medication immediately and was green-lighted for the trip to Amsterdam, where we filmed a holiday TV special. Then I flew back and swung by Ali's college in Connecticut to bring her home for Christmas. As we were about to get in the car I doubled over in pain. At first I thought it was just a stomach cramp, but as the pain steadily increased Ali pulled the car over and called Mike. He told her to get me to the hospital as soon as we arrived in Massachusetts. My "Warrior Princess" put the pedal to the metal, and we got to the emergency room in record time. But I was writhing in pain the whole way.

Tests showed I had an abdominal hematoma the size of a tuna. The doctor said it would take about a year for it to heal and gave me some really strong meds for the pain. But the pain didn't go away, and I ended up in the hospital three more times. When the doctor said I might have a cancerous cyst on my ovary and that the only way to find out for certain was to operate, I told Mike to call Anita and Bonnie in case things didn't go well. They both came immediately to be at my side.

It was my first quality visit with Bonnie in several years, and I was so grateful to her for coming. That counted for a lot and helped some old wounds to heal. I love my sister. As I've made clear in this book, we had our differences and problems, but what siblings don't? The fact that Bonnie came all the way cross-country to be with me when I needed her at my side says all that needs to be said about our relationship.

Coming out of the ether after the surgery, the first thing I heard was the beeping heart rate monitor. Then Ali was telling me to wake up. I opened my eyes, looked around the room, and saw all my loved ones. Ali spoke first.

"Mom, there's no cancer," she said. "Yaaaaayyyeee!"

That little scare made me so grateful to be alive—and I finally felt God's grace. He had blessed me with something that I didn't feel worthy of, but He gave it to me anyway. Yes, I considered myself a Christian, but in truth I was, like many, just a nominal one. I called on God for help when I needed it or it was convenient but was not truly invested in Him, heart and soul.

That finally changed one day not long after my cancer scare when I was driving in my car and listening to Kirk Franklin's praise station on satellite radio. The funny thing was, I had been listening to that station for several years because it took me back to when I was a kid getting ready for church. Gospel music has always been my inspiration, and often I'd go out into the car on Sunday mornings and sit in the driveway and listen. But now on this particular drive, as I was on my way back home from running errands and grocery shopping, something about the music just hit me in the heart and in the gut. I started bawling my eyes out and praising God for not only sparing me but also for His protection over me and my loved ones for so long.

I don't know why it happened when it did; I only know that I finally allowed God inside my heart, and He has resided and ruled there ever since. It brought full circle a lifetime of searching.

I am happy and do things on a daily basis to reassure myself that I have Christ's love in my life. I roll out of bed literally onto my knees and pray for my family. I pray for my girlfriends. I pray for all the soldiers in battle. I pray for our president Barack Obama and his family, Michelle, Sasha, and Malia, and the people in government offices who are running our country. I don't care what political views they have. They all need the guidance of God's steady hand.

Prayer is one of the most precious things in my life today. Every morning I read and study my Bible, along with a daily passage from *Sparkling Gems from the Greek*, by Rick Renner. Mindy Lymperis turned me on to the book, and it has enriched and redefined my life. The prayer on the day I put this book to bed beseeches: *Lord, help me overcome the hurts and disappointments I've experienced because of people who proved to be unfaithful. When I am tempted to judge those who have wronged me, help me to remember those whom I myself have wronged in the past. Just as I never intended to hurt some-one, help me realize that my offenders probably didn't intend to hurt me either. As I was forgiven then, I am asking You now to help me forgive—and not just to forgive, but to stick my neck out again and begin to rebuild my life with other people in the Body of Christ. I pray this in Jesus' name!*

I don't have to understand every element of my salvation in order to fully embrace it. No one has to explain it to me or should even try. I doubt they could. I just know that I believe in the bountiful love and mercy of our Creator, and I love it and don't ever want to lose it.

In a way it all goes back to all those restrictions and conditions people put on us as requirements for being born again and truly saved. In my lifetime I've seen that those restrictions—a lot of them conceived in the mind of man, not God—cause more harm than good. They're not pathways to redemption, but roadblocks. Nowhere in the Bible does it say that you can't wear red lipstick and six-inch heels or that you can't sing rock 'n' roll music. I choose to believe my salvation is free. It was paid for on the cross, and I don't need other people's opinions about my salvation or my relationship with my Savior. That's personal for me. I know that I'm loved and that I'm going to Heaven one day.

I've taken a different approach to salvation, and no longer believe we all have to march to the same drum. I know God is so much bigger than people make Him out to be. It's not that narrow. It's about freedom, peace, joy, mercy, grace, fellowship, wisdom, caring, sharing, and love. It's more love than you and I could ever imagine. It's interesting that the very first verse I ever learned has remained my favorite: "God is love."

Having Christ in my life doesn't mean that all my problems have gone away. Our family still struggles with drug and alcohol addiction, jealousy, depression, mistrust, and that root of all evil itself—money. But I pray for everybody, and as long as there is prayer there is hope. I pray for them now just like my mother prayed for me all those years when my behavior, choices, and problems must've caused her so much personal despair but never diminished her faith in the ultimate power of God's love and benevolence one iota.

As I've confessed to God and now to you, I was a mess. And if there's hope for someone like me, there's hope for everyone.

My life is filled with both blessings and heartaches...but the blessings far outweigh the other. Life is far from perfect—I don't know anyone whose is—but it's still pretty damn good.

I'm still so excited...and I just can't hide it....

Preachers, Players, Pointers: Who Knew We Had So Much in Common?

Dear Mom,

Let's see, where do we start and how should I address my best friend and running buddy? Let's get high and now it's let's go to a meeting, go dancing, and talk about clothes, hair, and music and the places I've gone because of you. I wouldn't change a thing...okay, maybe four things: 1. Sarah 2. June 3. Jada 4. Time—I wish I had more of it.

I love the good and the older I get, I'm loving the bad. I'm every bit of both and I like it that way. I'm such a cry-baby finger-pointing little bitch but when I think of the hand you were dealt and what you've done with your life, it's the most inspiring part of my life.

You're a badass and your life says no matter where you come from, you can do and become anything you want...and that's what my mom Ruth Pointer's life is all about. I got lucky.

—Malik Pointer

Discography

THIS DISCOGRAPHY IS A CHRONOLOGICAL GUIDE TO the Pointer Sisters' musical output as a group and as solo artists. For the records that charted in the United States, the *Billboard* chart categories and peak positions are indicated.

SINGLES

Pointer Sisters (Bonnie Pointer, June Pointer, and Anita Pointer)
"Don't Try to Take the Fifth," Atlantic, 1971
"Destination No More Heartaches," Atlantic, 1972

The Pointer Sisters (Bonnie Pointer, June Pointer, Anita Pointer, and Ruth Pointer)
"Yes We Can Can," Blue Thumb Records, 1973 (Pop #11; R & B #12)
"Wang Dang Doodle," Blue Thumb Records, 1973 (Pop #61; R & B #24)
"Steam Heat," Blue Thumb Records, 1974 (Pop #108)
"Fairytale," Blue Thumb Records, 1974 (Pop #13; Country #37)
"Live Your Life Before You Die," Blue Thumb Records, 1974 (Pop #89)
"How Long (Betcha' Got a Chick on the Side)," Blue Thumb Records, 1975 (Pop #20; R & B #1)
"Going Down Slowly," Blue Thumb Records, 1975 (Pop #61; R & B #16)
"You Gotta Believe," MCA Records, 1976 (Pop #103; R & B 14)
"Having a Party," Blue Thumb Records, 1977 (R & B #62)
"I Need a Man," Blue Thumb Records, 1977

Pointer Sisters (Anita Pointer, Ruth Pointer, and June Pointer)
"Fire," Planet Records, 1978 (Pop #2; R & B #14)
"Everybody Is a Star," Planet Records, 1978

"Happiness," Planet Records, 1979 (Pop #30, R & B #20)

"Blind Faith," Planet Records, 1979 (Pop #107)

"Who Do You Love," Planet Records, 1979 (Pop #106)

"He's So Shy," Planet Records, 1980 (Pop #3; R & B #10)

"Could I Be Dreaming," Planet Records, 1980 (Pop #52; R & B #22)

"Where Did the Time Go," Planet Records, 1980

"Slow Hand," Planet Records, 1981 (Pop #2; R & B #7)

"What a Surprise," Planet Records, 1981 (R & B #52)

"Sweet Lover Man," Planet Records, 1981

"Should I Do It," Planet Records, 1982 (Pop #13)

"American Music," Planet Records, 1972 (Pop #16; R & B #23)

"I'm So Excited," Planet Records, 1982 (Pop #30; R & B #46)

"If You Wanna Get Back Your Lady," Planet Records, 1983 (Pop #67; R & B #44)

"I Need You," Planet Records, 1983 (Pop #48; R & B #13)

"Automatic," Planet Records, 1984 (Pop #5; R & B #2)

"Jump (For My Love)," Planet Records, 1984 (Pop #3; R & B #3)

"I'm So Excited" (rerelease), Planet Records, 1984 (Pop #9)

"Neutron Dance," Planet Records, 1984 (Pop #6; R & B #13)

"Baby Come and Get It," Planet Records, 1985 (Pop #44; R & B #24)

"We Are the World" (as part of USA for Africa), Columbia, 1985 (Pop #1)

"Dare Me," RCA, 1985 (Pop #11; R & B #6)

"Freedom," RCA, 1985 (Pop #59; R & B #25)

"Twist My Arm," RCA, 1986 (Pop #83; R & B #61)

"Back in My Arms," RCA, 1986

"Goldmine," RCA, 1986 (Pop #33; R & B #17)

"All I Know Is the Way I Feel," RCA, 1987 (Pop #93; R & B #69)

"Mercury Rising," RCA, 1987 (R & B #49)

"Be There," MCA Records, 1987 (Pop #42)

"He Turned Me Out," RCA, 1988 (R & B #39)

"I'm In Love," RCA, 1988 (R & B #67)

"Power of Persuasion," Columbia, 1988

"Friends' Advice (Don't Take It)," Motown, 1990 (R & B #36)

"After You," Motown, 1990

"Insanity," Motown, 1990 (R & B #62)

"Voices That Care" (with various artists), Giant Records, 1991 (Pop #11)

"Don't Walk Away," SBK, 1993

"Christmas in New York," YMC Records, 2005 (with Issa Pointer)

Pointer Sisters with Natalia

"Sisters Are Doing It For Themselves," Sony BMG, 2005 (with Issa Pointer)

ALBUMS

The Pointer Sisters (Bonnie Pointer, June Pointer, Anita Pointer, and Ruth Pointer)

>*The Pointer Sisters*, Blue Thumb Records, 1973 (Pop #13; R & B #3)
>
>*That's a Plenty*, Blue Thumb Records, 1974 (Pop #82; R & B #33)
>
>*Live at the Opera House*, Blue Thumb Records, 1974 (Pop #96; R & B #29)
>
>*Steppin'*, Blue Thumb Records, 1975 (Pop #22; R & B #3)
>
>*Having a Party*, Blue Thumb Records, 1977 (Pop #76; R & B #51)

Pointer Sisters (Anita Pointer, Ruth Pointer, and June Pointer)

>*Energy*, Planet Records, 1978 (Pop #13; R & B #9)
>
>*Priority*, Planet Records, 1979 (Pop #72; R & B #44)
>
>*Special Things*, Planet Records, 1980 (Pop #34; R & B #19)
>
>*Black & White*, Planet Records, 1981 (Pop #12; R & B #9)
>
>*So Excited!*, Planet Records, 1982 (Pop #59; R & B #24)
>
>*Break Out*, Planet Records, 1983 (Pop #8; R & B #6)
>
>*Contact*, RCA, 1985 (Pop #25; R & B #11)
>
>*Hot Together*, RCA, 1986 (Pop #48; R & B #39)
>
>*Serious Slammin'*, RCA, 1988 (Pop #152)
>
>*The Right Rhythm*, Motown, 1990
>
>*Only Sisters Can Do That*, SBK, 1993
>
>*Highlights from Ain't Misbehavin': The New Cast Recording*, RCA Victor, 1996

Pointer Sisters (Anita Pointer, Ruth Pointer, and Issa Pointer)

>*The Pointer Sisters Live in Billings*, Madacy, 2004
>
>*Natalia Meets the Pointer Sisters*, Sony BMG, 2005
>
>*Favorites*, Nathan East, 2008

COMPILATION ALBUMS

>*The Best of The Pointer Sisters*, Blue Thumb Records, 1976 (Pop #164; R & B #33)
>
>*Retrospect*, MCA, 1981
>
>*Pointer Sisters Greatest Hits*, Planet Records, 1982 (Pop #178)
>
>*Jump: The Best of the Pointer Sisters*, RCA, 1989
>
>*Greatest Hits*, RCA, 1995
>
>*Yes We Can Can: The Best of the Blue Thumb Recordings*, Hip-O, 1997
>
>*The Best of the Pointer Sisters*, RCA, 2002
>
>*Platinum & Gold Collection*, RCA, 2004
>
>*The Millennium Collection: The Best of the Pointer Sisters*, Hip-O, 2004
>
>*Playlist: The Very Best of the Pointer Sisters*, Legacy, 2009
>
>*Goldmine: The Best of the Pointer Sisters*, Sony Legacy, 2010

RECORDING SESSIONS FOR OTHER ARTISTS

"Friends," Fillmore Corporation, Sun Bear, 1970; (Bonnie, June, and Anita Pointer)*

Sisyphus, Cold Blood, San Francisco Records, 1970; "Your Good Thing" (Bonnie, June, and Anita Pointer)

"Hallelujah (I Feel Like Shouting)," Gideon and the Power, Bell, 1971 (Bonnie, June, and Anita Pointer)*

Feel It!, The Elvin Bishop Group, Fillmore Records, 1970; "I Just Can't Go On," "So Good," and "Be With Me" (Bonnie, Anita, and June Pointer)

Lights Out: San Francisco, Various Artists, Blue Thumb Records, 1972; "Why Was I Born" (Sylvester & The Hot Band)

Recycling The Blues & Other Related Stuff, Taj Mahal, Columbia Records, 1972; "Texas Woman Blues"

Baron Von Tollbooth & The Chrome Nun, Paul Kantner, Grace Slick, and David Freiberg, Grunt/RCA, 1973; "Fat"

Betty Davis, Betty Davis, Just Sunshine Records, 1973; "Steppin' In Her I. Miller Shoes" (Bonnie, June, and Anita Pointer)

Ooh So Good 'n The Blues, Taj Mahal, Columbia Records, 1973; "Little Red Hen"

Muscle of Love, Alice Cooper, Warner Bros., 1973; "Teenage Lament" and "Working Up a Sweat"

Thriller!, Cold Blood, Reprise Records, 1973; "Live Your Dream"

Skinny Boy, Robert Lamm, Columbia, 1974; "Skinny Boy"

Tarzana Kid, John Sebastian, Reprise Records, 1974; "Friends Again"

Survival of the Fittest, The Headhunters, 1975; "God Make Me Funky"

Safety Zone, Bobby Womack, United Artists Records, 1975; "Daylight"

Struttin' My Stuff, Elvin Bishop, Capricorn Records, 1975; "Fooled Around and Fell in Love" and "Hold On" (June Pointer)

Stone Alone, Bill Wyman, Rolling Stones Records, 1976; "A Quarter to Three," "Soul Satisfying," "Apache Woman," "Every Sixty Seconds," "Feet," "Peanut Butter Time," "Wine and Wimmen," and "What's the Point" (Bonnie and Ruth Pointer)

Rick James Presents The Stone City Band In 'n' Out, Motown, 1980; "Little Runaway" (Ruth and Anita Pointer)

Super Jammin', Earl Scruggs, Columbia, 1984; "Third Rate Romance"

Vox Humana, Kenny Loggins, Columbia, 1985; "Vox Humana" (Anita and June Pointer)

The Return of Bruno, Bruce Willis, Motown, 1987; "Respect Yourself"

Unison, Celine Dion, Sony Music, 1990; "Love By Another Name" (Ruth Pointer)

Leap of Faith, Kenny Loggins, Columbia, 1991; "If You Believe" (Ruth Pointer)

*Denotes single

ANTHOLOGIES

We Are the World, Columbia/CBS Records, 1985; "Just a Little Closer"

A Very Special Christmas, A&M Records, 1987; "Santa Claus is Coming to Town."

Garfield: Am I Cool or What?, GRP Records, 1991; "Nine Lives"

Pulp Fusion, Harmless Recordings, 1997; "Don't It Drive You Crazy?"

Rhythm, Country and Blues, MCA, 1994; "Chain of Fools" with Clint Black

Sweet Soul Music 1973, Bear Family, 2014; "Yes We Can Can"

Sweet Soul Music 1975, 2014; "How Long (Betcha' Got a Chick On the Side)"

SOUNDTRACKS

Taps, 1981; "Slow Hand"

Summer Lovers, 1982; "I'm So Excited"

Night Shift, 1982; "The Love Too Good to Last"

National Lampoon's Vacation, 1983; "I'm So Excited"

Bagets, 1984; "Jump (For My Love)"

Grandview, USA, 1984; "I Want to Do It With You"

Beverly Hills Cop, 1984; "Neutron Dance"

Protocol, 1984; "I'm So Excited"

Perfect, 1985; "All Systems Go"

Children of a Lesser God, 1986; "Jump (For My Love)"

Playing for Keeps, 1986; "I'm So Excited"

Jumpin' Jack Flash, 1986; "Set Me Free"

Beverly Hills Cop II, 1987; "Be There"

Spaceballs, 1987; "Hot Together"

Stake Out, 1987; "Hot Together"

He's My Girl, 1987; "Neutron Dance"

Action Jackson, 1988; "He Turned Me Out"

Caddyshack II, 1988; "Power of Persuasion"

Working Girl, 1988; "I'm So Excited"

The Karate Kid Part III, 1989; "Summer in the City"

Riff-Raff, 1991; "I'm So Excited"

Richochet, 1991; "Automatic"

American Heart, 1992; "Slow Hand"

Hot Shots Part Deux, 1993; "I'm So Excited"

Two If By Sea, 1996; "You Got Me Hummin'"

The Nutty Professor, 1996; "I'm So Excited"
The Associate, 1996; "Yes We Can Can"
Donnie Brasco, 1997; "Happiness"
Rudolph The Red-Nosed Reindeer: The Movie, 1998; "Christmas Town"
The Story of Us, 1999; "I'm So Excited"
Big Momma's House, 2000; "Yes We Can Can"
Ali, 2001; "Yes We Can Can"
The Trip, 2002; "Jump (For My Love)"
Maid in Manhattan, 2002; "Yes We Can Can"
Love Actually, 2003; "Jump (For My Love)"
Sunday Driver, 2005; "Yes We Can Can"
Welcome Home, Roscoe Jenkins, 2008; "Jump (For My Love)" and
    "Neutron Dance"
Transformers: Revenge of the Fallen, 2009; "I'm So Excited"
I'm So Excited!, 2013; "I'm So Excited"
Last Vegas, 2013; "Neutron Dance"

SOLO WORK
Ruth Pointer
Oliver & Company (soundtrack), 1989; "Streets of Gold"
Iron Eagle II (soundtrack) 1988; "Enemies Like You and Me" (duet with
    Billy Vera)

Anita Pointer
Love For What It Is, RCA, 1987

Bonnie Pointer
Bonnie Pointer (Red Album), Motown, 1978
Bonnie Pointer (Purple Album), Motown, 1979
If The Price is Right, Private Records, 1984
Like a Picasso, Platinum Trini Records, 2011

June Pointer
Baby Sister, Planet Records, 1983
June Pointer, Columbia Records, 1989